Early Acclamation for
TERROR IN YPSILANTI

"Though less widely known than criminal contemporaries Ted Bundy and John Wayne Gacy, John Norman Collins was unquestionably one of the most terrifying sex-killers of his time. Gregory A. Fournier's thoroughly researched and highly readable account is certain to stand as the definitive work on this all-American monster."

—Harold Schechter, author of THE SERIAL KILLER FILES

"Gregory A. Fournier has crafted an insightful and engrossing account of Michigan's worst sexually sadistic serial killer. He details the relentless 'boots on the ground' investigation by Michigan law enforcement agencies and the complexity of the forensic expert testimony with authentic and intense detail. With every chapter, the reader learns something new about John Norman Collins, and why he is behind bars where he belongs."

—Mark Safarik, Director of Forensic Behavioral Services International and FBI Profiler (Ret.)

"*TERROR IN YPSILANTI* is the riveting true crime story of a serial killer on the loose. As his need to murder escalates, law enforcement searches frantically to apprehend him before he kills again. The portrayal of John Norman Collins is well-delineated, and the details are gruesome but fascinating."

—Peter Leonard, national bestselling author of crime novels

"In the late sixties, a serial killer held the community of Ypsilanti hostage to its fears. *TERROR IN YPSILANTI* tells the probing tale of one of America's most unknown and heinous murderers, John Norman Collins. This fact-based story is told with the precision of an investigative report. Through years of painstaking research, Gregory A. Fournier has captured the raw emotions of the community and the complexity of the killer."

—Detective First Lieutenant David Minzey (Ret.), Michigan State Police, Violent Crimes Unit

"Master storyteller Gregory A. Fournier reveals the last moments of John Norman Collins' victims and ensures that memories of the girls are not lost to time. This series of fifty-year-old murders and the ensuing trial were all but forgotten. *TERROR IN YPSILANTI: John Norman Collins Unmasked* pays a long overdue debt to history."

—Frank Castronova, president of the *Book Club of Detroit*

"I see this book as more than a thriller and more than a good read. It is an epic righting of a wrong and the lancing of an abscess inside the collective mind of those who remember living through this nightmare."

—Kristin Bronson, Ann Arbor resident

Terror in Ypsilanti

John Norman Collins Unmasked

GREGORY A. FOURNIER

Terror in Ypsilanti: John Norman Collins Unmasked

Cover photo by Anthony Cornish
Original cover design by Kathleen Wise
Original map by Eureka Cartography
Photo restoration by Hartworks Graphic Arts
Author photo by Lisa K Photography

Published by Wheatmark®
2030 East Speedway Boulevard, Suite 106
Tucson, Arizona 85719
www.wheatmark.com

ISBN: 978-1-62787-403-8 (paperback)
ISBN: 978-1-62787-404-5 (ebook)
LCCN: 2016936356

GregoryaFournier.com

rev201601

Contents

Part Three

Acknowledgments

FIRST AND FOREMOST, I want to thank Ryan M. Place for his tireless work researching and compiling the documentation that made the writing of *Terror in Ypsilanti* possible over the five-year span of this project. Also key to the writing of this book are George Ridenour and Deirdre Fortino from the Ypsilanti Historical Society and Cathy Banish, who arranged some important interviews for us. Many thanks to my beta readers Carleen Hemric, Victoria Campbell, Phillip Murphy, John Philip Chapman, Cris Bronson, Sally Foster, and Professor Paul McGlynn who helped me fine-tune the material and see errors my eyes were blind to.

Thanks to the members of law enforcement who agreed to speak with us: Michigan State Police detective David Minzey, retired Washtenaw County deputy Basil Baysinger, retired Washtenaw County deputy Frank C. Niehaus, Eastern Michigan University patrolman Larry Mathewson, Undersheriff Harold Owings, Michigan State Police FOIA coordinator Brittany Goodwin, and former FBI serial killer profiler Mark Safarik. I want to especially thank former

Washtenaw County Sheriff Douglas Harvey for his candor, perspective, and enthusiasm for this project.

To help Ryan and me sort out the autopsy and medical reports, a personal thank you goes to Marc Hulet, senior investigator for the Wayne County Medical Examiner's Office, and Michelle Waters, forensic technician for the Macomb County Medical Examiner's Office.

The members of the media whose reporting kept this story alive deserve honorable mention, notably William Treml of the *Ann Arbor News*, Walker Lundy of the *Detroit Free Press*, Marianne Rzepka of the *Detroit Free Press*, Robert A. Popa of the *Detroit News*, John Cobb of the *Ypsilanti Press*, and Cindy Cygan of the *Macomb Daily*. Also noteworthy are Jack Kelly and Marilynn Turner of *Kelly & Company* and anchorman Bill Bonds—all from WXYZ Channel 7 in Detroit.

Ryan and I cannot thank enough the many people who allowed us to speak with them: John Philip Chapman, Wendy Beringer, Adam Galvan, Harold Britton, Sandra Morgan, Robert Francis, John C. Louisell, Marge Delhey, Diane Delhey, Dale Leslie, Karen Naylor, Alan Metzger, Robert Purvey, Stephanie Hurkos, Jan Kaulins, Laima Starwas, Rebecca Hamlin Mikkola, Cheryl Jordan, Tony Hale Dees, Connie Tandy Mills, Dianne McKinney Delcourt, Karen Stapleton, Mark S. Grow, Ron Kardynski, Mark Kennedy, Tom Zarski, Mark Pilarski, Pamela A. Vincent, Toni Carlbom, Allen Rentschler, Dr. Vonda Pelto, Christie Collins Lypka, John Clark, Pat Wehrman, Ron Swartz, Dr. Phillip D. Schertzing, Ben Cologie, Kim Maki, Jeff Odegaard, Dr. John Hulsing, James Zellen, Pearlene Sullivan, Dr. Joseph C. Fisher, Nick Marsh, Jack H. Miller, Marge Divine, Dr. Rex Julian Beaber, Russ Marian, Sandy Traskos, Lonny Head,

Alan J. Wakenhut, Lois D'Oranzio, Robert Kroeger, Christa Morletti McIntyre, Professor Emeritus Paul D. McGlynn, Professor Emeritus Franklin Case, Elizabeth Kay (Mann) Wawrzasek, Tom Henry Stefina, Bonnie L. Penet, Eddie Phelps, Pam Sherock, the Fleszar family, and the many people we spoke with who wished to remain anonymous.

It would be the height of ingratitude if I failed to thank Rene Greff of the Corner Brewery, Linda French of the Sidetrack Bar and Grill, and Sandee French of Aubree's Pizzaria & Grill in Ypsilanti's historic Depot Town for the use of their taverns as my branch offices. A special thank you goes to Jim and Roberta Orme for providing me with a home away from home on my many visits to Ypsilanti. And last, my loving gratitude to my wife Sue, whose husband wandered off into a deep and dark cavern leaving her to wonder if he would ever return.

Introduction

NOTICE OF A PSYCHOTIC killer in their midst did not resonate with the Ypsilanti, Michigan community in the summer of 1967. On July 9, a nineteen-year-old Eastern Michigan University coed did not return to her apartment after an early-evening walk. Thirty days later, her remains were found outside the Ypsilanti city limits near the ruins of a timber-framed barn on the abandoned Scotney farm in Superior Township. Local residents paid little attention to the gruesome murder. Riots had broken out in Detroit two weeks before and dominated media coverage pushing other news aside. After the initial Michigan State Police investigation, the murder was listed as unsolved. A year passed before the murder of another Eastern Michigan coed. Subsequently, a rapacious killer lured five more young women to their deaths within a two-year period.

Then on July 31, 1969, the Michigan State Police arrested John Norman Collins, a clean-cut, square-jawed athlete, and charged the twenty-two-year-old Eastern Michigan senior with the sex slaying of yet another Eastern Michigan coed.

Like so many people in Ypsilanti, I recognized the suspect when his photograph ran in the local papers. In fact, he was someone who lived a block down the street from me. The Ypsilanti and university communities were relieved and grateful an arrest had been made, but some police investigators feared the prime suspect had accomplices or accessories still at large.

After the arrest, the rash of mutilation murders ended. Certainly, other young women were killed before and after that period in Washtenaw County, but none with the same contempt for womanhood and other signature characteristics these murders bore. After becoming better acquainted with the facts and circumstances of the Washtenaw County murders, readers may draw their own conclusions about the guilt or innocence of John Norman Collins.

PART ONE

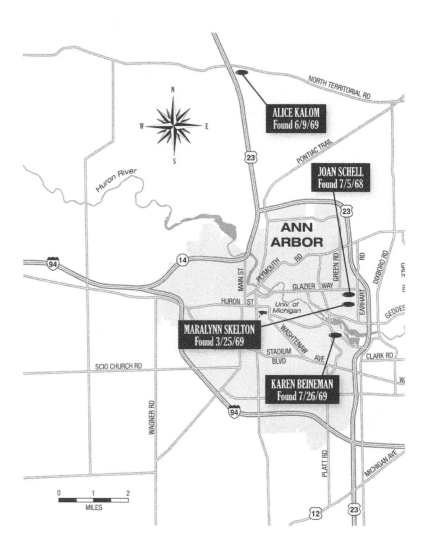

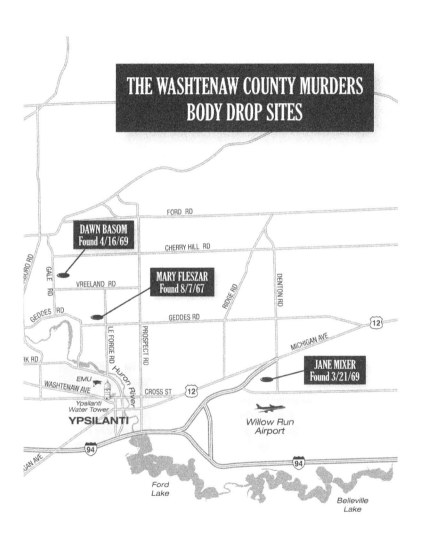

THE WASHTENAW COUNTY MURDERS
BODY DROP SITES

DAWN BASOM
Found 4/16/69

MARY FLESZAR
Found 8/7/67

JANE MIXER
Found 3/21/69

FORD RD

CHERRY HILL RD

VREELAND RD

GEDDES RD

GEDDES RD

MICHIGAN AVE

WASHTENAW AVE

CROSS ST

EMU

Ypsilanti
Water Tower

YPSILANTI

Willow Run
Airport

Ford
Lake

Belleville
Lake

GALE RD

GEDDES RD

LE FORGE RD

PROSPECT RD

RIDGE RD

DENTON RD

Huron River

12

12

12

94

94

— 1 —

An Isolated Incident

ON THE AFTERNOON OF August 7, 1967, fifteen-year-old Russell E. Crisovan Jr. and his friend Mark Lucas were about to plow a cornfield on some farmland Russell's father leased near Geddes and LeForge Roads in Superior Township, just north of the Ypsilanti, Michigan, city limits. The teens were gassing up the tractor when they heard the unexpected slam of a car door and voices down the road. This secluded area was known as a lovers' lane used by college students from the nearby Eastern Michigan University campus. The boys made their way quietly to the source of the sounds—the ruins of a deserted barn.

According to the statement they gave the Michigan State Police, another car door slammed, but the car pulled away before they saw it or its passengers. The boys immediately noticed twenty-five feet of fresh tire tracks in the weeds leading from the horseshoe-shaped driveway that rounded behind the barn and led back to Geddes Road. As the teens followed the tracks, they noticed a foul odor. Then they saw what they took to be a decomposing deer carcass—not a rare sight in Michigan farm country. There was a head but no discernible face. Both boys noticed at the same time what looked like a human ear. Panicked, they drove to the Ypsilanti state police post on Michigan Avenue and reported what they had seen to Corporal Harold Rowe. He sent out detectives to investigate the site.

When Dr. Henry J. Scovill—assistant Washtenaw County medical examiner—arrived, he officially identified the remains as human. The body was a nude female lying facedown on the damp ground. Due to decay found at several locations, state police investigators deduced that the deceased was moved at least twice from her original position—perhaps by feral animals or by the murderer(s). The first location appeared to be on top a pile of rusted cans and broken bottles dumped in the area. The next position was five to six feet away to the southeast. Discoloration of the grass indicated that the body may have lain there for some time. The body was moved again about three feet to the northeast from the second position. Dr. Scovill estimated the victim had been dead approximately one month. As it turned out, he was correct.

A six-man team searched the area surrounding where the body had been dropped and found numerous items of clothing unrelated to this case. Several paths in the two-foot-tall grass leading to the body indicated that someone—possibly multiple individuals—had been there numerous times. This suggested to investigators that more than one person may have been involved with or had knowledge of the murder. The boys who found the body mentioned they heard two voices before the car took off.

Twenty minutes after investigators began their search, Detective R. J. Johnston dug through a pile of soggy cardboard rubble thrown over another large piece of cardboard stapled to a section of packing crate. When Johnston lifted the packing crate, he discovered clothes stacked beneath it.

On top of the stack was an orange-and-white polka-dot dress cut down the front from the top almost to the bottom; the short zipper was still fastened at the back. Under the dress was a piece of white cloth whose size and shape suggested a diaper. On the bottom of the stack was a pair of white underpants torn at the seam, and a white brassiere with ripped shoulder straps. Part of one strap was later found on the trail about ten feet from the wet and moldy clothing crawling with insects. A single, right-footed tan sandal—size 6½ B—was also found.

Investigators determined the victim was killed elsewhere and transported to the Scotney brothers' deserted farm. After a month of exposure to nature and the elements, her blackened remains were the worst sight these state police investigators had ever seen.

Dental records identified the corpse as Mary Terese Fleszar—the missing Eastern Michigan coed. Her dentist, Dr. T. J. Smeckert, provided Mary's x-rays, which Dr. Edward Haenick from University of Michigan Hospital used to make a positive identification. The nineteen-year-old sophomore was majoring in accounting and working at Eastern Michigan University's Field Services Office as a secretary. Mary was from Willis, Michigan, a rural community south of Ypsilanti in Washtenaw County.

State police detectives arrived at the Fleszar home around 6:30 p.m. When they showed the Fleszars the tan sandal found at the scene, Chester and Theresa said in unison, "That's Mary's shoe!" Theresa Fleszar told police Mary had purchased those shoes at Baker's in Arborland just before going to Expo 67 in Canada sometime last spring. The other sandal was never found.

On August 8, pathologist Dr. B. Naylor began the autopsy completed by the head pathologist Dr. Robert M. Hendrix on August 9. Chester Fleszar requested permission to be present for his daughter's autopsy but was refused. The autopsy report indicated the victim suffered approximately thirty stab and puncture wounds in the chest and abdomen, at least twenty of which were inflicted by a knife or similar sharp object. The rest were irregular in shape and attributed to ravaging insects and feral animals. Small teeth imprints could be seen on the flesh and exposed bones. One forearm and hand were missing, and the fingers of the other hand had been removed. Both feet were severed at the ankles—definitely not caused by animals, as there was no evidence of sawing or clean cutting of the ankle bones. The pathologists believed bones were smashed. There was also a long slash across the victim's back. Severe putrefaction had damaged the internal organs and mummification was pronounced. The pathologists could not determine if Mary Fleszar had been sexually violated.

———

Upon completion of the autopsy, Mary's remains were placed in a black body bag and taken to Moore Funeral Home at 101 South Washington Street in Ypsilanti. Harold Britton, an employee of the funeral home, called the state police the next day saying a person had come into the funeral home just before closing and requested permission to take a photograph of the body. Britton told the young man that because of the family's wishes, the casket would remain closed.

Britton asked the young man if he was a friend of the family. He said he was. Britton told him it would be impossible to view the body, but he could sign the funeral book. The young man said he would at the funeral service and left. It was then that Britton noticed the young man was not carrying a camera.

Britton told police investigators the unidentified male left the funeral home in a silver-blue car. Because the driver had parked off to the side rather than in front of the building, Britton could not see the license plate number or identify the make or model as the vehicle disappeared up South Washington Street.

Britton described the person as a white male, eighteen to twenty years old, five feet ten inches tall, with a medium build and light complexion. He was wearing a long-sleeved white shirt with no tie. Some papers were sticking out of his shirt pocket. His black trousers had no cuffs, and he was wearing loafer-style shoes. When the parents of Mary Fleszar were contacted by Michigan State Police about the young man, they said they had no knowledge of him.

———

State police were able to find out from their subsequent investigation that Mary had lived with Nancy DeMasellis at 413 Washtenaw Avenue, apartment fourteen, since the first of June. This was Mary's first time living away from home. She had sublet an off-campus apartment for the summer, so she could be close to her job in McKenny Hall. Mary discovered she felt more comfortable living at home and planned to move back for the fall semester.

When Mary left the apartment at 8:30 p.m. on Sunday night, she told her roommate she needed "to get some fresh air." The July heat and humidity were oppressive, so she dressed lightly in a summer dress. She was wearing a pair of woven tan sandals. Mary was not someone who particularly liked walking, but she headed down the street alone that night.

About thirty minutes later, a campus policeman who recognized Mary spotted her walking alone. A short time after that, a young man driving a bluish-gray two-toned car pulled up beside Mary on Ballard Street and offered her a ride. Neighbors Gerald and Nancy Durand—who knew Mary—witnessed this from their front porch.

Gerald Durand reported to police that Mary shook her head no and continued walking. The driver then sped around the block and pulled up aggressively into a driveway, blocking her way on the sidewalk. Mary once again shook off his advances and walked around the car. Frustrated, the unidentified driver backed out onto the street and sped away screeching his tires. The witnesses lost sight of Mary as she drew closer to her apartment building. Her neighbors were the last known people to see Mary alive.

Mary's purse was not missing from her apartment, but her car keys were gone. Her mother, Theresa, noticed Mary's light-blue Mercury Comet was across from where she usually parked it. She felt this was odd leading the Fleszars to believe Mary was overpowered and abducted in the parking lot of her apartment building.

Police investigators reconstructing Mary's last day discovered the following:

- At 6:30 a.m., she attended Mass at St. John's Catholic Church on Cross Street in Ypsilanti.
- At 7:30 a.m., she left for work in McKenny Hall at

the Eastern Michigan University Building Services office. She was working over the weekend handling registration for an upcoming cheerleading conference on campus.

- Mary left work at 4:30 p.m. to return to her apartment. She changed her clothes and went to go swimming. She was supposed to meet up with her sister and two cousins, but Mary never found them at Silver Lake.
- At 5:45 p.m., a lifeguard friend named Mike saw Mary at Half Moon Lake. She was also seen at 6:30 p.m. by a coworker named Husey.
- At 8:20 p.m., Mary went back to her apartment, changed into her summer polka-dot dress, and told her roommate Nancy DeMasellis it was too hot in the apartment so she was going for a walk.
- At 9:00 a.m. the next morning, Nancy called Mary's younger sister Sandra, and told her Mary did not return home from her evening walk.

———

By all accounts from people who knew Mary, she was a sweet, lovely person—a devout Catholic who sang and played the organ regularly at church services. Mary's close friends say she was reserved and naïve about men and by no means a party girl. In fact, she was essentially a quiet, private person.

Tom Henry Stefina, who knew Mary in high school, saw her at a wedding for a mutual friend in Willis the night before she disappeared. Mary played the organ for the service and did not appear worried. She was in good spirits.

Tom recalled that when he left the wedding reception to go home, Mary gave him a big smile and a friendly wave from across the room. Tom never saw her again.

———

When Mary Fleszar was still missing, Michigan State Police interviewed everyone they could find who had recent contact with her. Kathy Jones had met Mary through a mutual friend, Ellen Rose, when they took a women's self-defense class together. Police hoped Mary had confided in her friend where she had gone. The police asked Jones if she had any idea where Mary might have run off. She had been missing for several days by then. Jones admitted she had known Mary for only a year.

State police detective Sergeant Ronald Schoonmaker asked Jones if Mary was seeing anyone special, but there was no one she knew about. According to Jones, Mary was inexperienced about relationships for a girl her age. She described Mary as a conservative Catholic who was just starting to feel comfortable with her femininity. Jones believed Mary never would have gotten into a car with a stranger. When asked if she knew of anyone who might want to harm Mary, she answered, "No one. Mary was a lovely person—sweet and good—one of life's innocents."

After interviewing Jones, Detective Schoonmaker called upon the Fleszar family in Willis to ask about Mary's Canadian trip. Her parents explained Mary had taken a trip to the Canadian Expo 67 in Montreal with her sister and two friends. Mary convinced her parents to let her use the family car—a 1965 Mercury station wagon. She worked out the route, the mileage, where they would stop, how much gas they would need, and how much the trip would cost. This

trip was a rite of passage for Mary. She was asserting her
independence to herself as much as anyone. The four girls
set out on Thursday, June 1, 1967. The trip was uneventful
but for a souvenir she bought—a Canadian Expo 67 medallion necklace.

———

In the course of their original investigation, Michigan
State Police investigators Sergeant Earl James and Sergeant
Bert Maxwell consulted with Dr. Marx, director of clinical
services at Ypsilanti State Mental Hospital. Dr. Marx
reviewed the facts from Mary's murder with the hope he
might be able to advise police about the type of individual who would commit such a heinous crime. In his report
dated August 18, Dr. Marx surmised the person likely:

…has had a traumatic experience with a female,
be it his mother, girlfriend, or wife. He could very
easily be a person who is outwardly very religious. His religion is a defense mechanism against
emotions he has built up. The victim would be a
symbol of someone whom the perpetrator wanted
to get back at. For example, he could be a person
who is very dependent upon his wife or mother.
He would not be a person who is outgoing when it
comes to sex. The perpetrator would be more likely
to attack someone he does not know. This behavior
frequently results from an irresistible impulse at the
time. The fact that the victim's body was placed on
a trash pile would be symbolic of the perpetrator
thinking that the female was trash—something to
get rid of. This type of individual would tend to

keep to himself and probably not get along well with neighbors.

Dr. Marx's rudimentary attempt at psychological profiling demonstrates that criminal profiling was still in its infancy. But it was a start. What state police detective Sergeant Ronald Schoonmaker told the Fleszar family turned out to be more accurate: "If we don't catch this person within thirty days, he will kill again with increasing frequency within the next year or so." Sadly, his prediction would come to pass.

— 2 —

The First Link

A FULL YEAR AFTER the remains of Mary Terese Fleszar were found just north of Ypsilanti, the image of her mutilated, decomposed body and the terror of what she had to endure were the only lasting impressions investigators had of her. As if on cue, another EMU coed went missing. Joan Elspeth Schell was last seen getting into a red car with a black convertible top which conflicting eyewitnesses described as either a Pontiac or a Ford. Joan Schell was waiting with her roommate, Susan Carol Kolbe, in front of McKenny Hall sometime after 10:30 p.m. to catch the last transit bus to Ann Arbor.

Joan had just spent the weekend with her parents in Plymouth, Michigan—a pleasant, middle-class community between Detroit and Ypsilanti. Before they returned Joan to her apartment at 703 Emmet Street, the Schell family ate dinner at Haab's restaurant in Ypsilanti. Her parents did not know that Joan planned to rendezvous with her boyfriend, Dale Schultz—recently Absent Without Official Leave (AWOL) from Fort Gordon, Georgia. Private Schultz managed to get a job in Ann Arbor working under the false name of Jason Cord. He was hiding out with friends in town.

After dinner with her parents, Joan arrived at her apartment anxious to see Dale. Her roommate told her Dale had called. Joan immediately called Dale back at the Mental Health Research Center of the University of Michigan where he worked. Joan was very much in love with Schultz and secretly engaged to him. Despite the late hour, she agreed to catch the last bus to Ann Arbor to meet with him.

Susan Kolbe decided to keep Joan company while she waited for the bus. The girls watched it speed past them with a full load of passengers at 11:15 p.m. Frustrated but undeterred, Joan was determined to get to Ann Arbor. She stuck out her thumb and began hitchhiking. Shortly after, a red and black car with three young men inside pulled up. The young man sitting in the front passenger seat hollered out, "Do you want a ride?"

Joan walked up to the car while Susan stayed on the sidewalk. "Are you going all the way to Ann Arbor?" Joan asked.

Susan heard one of the other guys in the car answer, "Yeah, all the way!"

Joan turned to Susan and said, "I'll call you when I get to Ann Arbor."

Susan tried to dissuade Joan from getting in the car, but Joan ignored the risk. Her need for a ride overruled her judgment. The person in the front passenger seat of the two-door coupe got out and pulled the seat forward so Joan could climb into the back seat. The male in the rear seat was vaguely described by Susan as "young with blonde hair."

She gave no description of the driver because she could not see him from where she was standing.

Susan Kolbe had a bad feeling about Joan getting into that car, especially when the driver did not go down Washtenaw Avenue toward Ann Arbor. The red and black car unexpectedly turned right onto the street that ran alongside McKenny Union and turned right again heading east down Forest Street in the opposite direction. Susan went back to their apartment to wait for Joan's call.

Joan never arrived in Ann Arbor. Dale Schultz called Susan at 12:35 a.m. She told him Joan got into a car with three guys over an hour ago. Schultz asked Susan to call the Ypsilanti and Ann Arbor police. With some friends, he went searching for a red and black car without success. Susan's call was received by the Ypsilanti police at 12:43 a.m. They sent out a squad car so police could take a missing person report. Susan described Joan as twenty years old, five feet four inches tall, and ninety-eight pounds with medium-length, reddish-brown hair.

After telling her story to police, Susan described the person who got out of the passenger seat to let Joan into the two-door vehicle. He was a white male, five feet eight inches tall, with a slender but muscular build. He had midlength dark-brown hair and a medium suntan with a clear complexion. Ypsilanti police sergeant William Stenning drew the original composite drawing of the suspect using an Identi-Kit—a book with pages of horizontal strips for various facial features. Eyewitnesses would flip through pages until they found a match for their descriptions. Chosen types of eyes, noses, mouths, and chins guided the police artist—some of whom are more gifted than others—to create a likeness of a suspect. The first two pencil drawings of Joan Schell's abductor were for police use only. Detectives felt the drawings were too sketchy. A third version showing more detail was released to the media and distributed on Eastern Michigan University's campus.

Kolbe identified the make of the car as a Pontiac with three square taillights on each side. Two days later, McKenny Union custodian Johnson Propps was interviewed by police. He said three white males were in the building after-hours earlier that evening making a phone call from the pay phones. Another custodian told them to leave and escorted them outside. The custodians checked all the ground-floor doors for signs of forced entry but found none. They thought one of the intruders might have had a building key. From the second-floor stairwell, Propps looked out the window and saw the three young men get into a car he described as a Pontiac Bonneville. Propps said the trio sat there for several minutes before pulling away.

The Ypsilanti police found and interviewed two other eyewitnesses who saw the two women standing at the bus stop that evening. Helen Haines was sitting on her porch across the street from McKenny Hall when she witnessed Joan Schell get into a red and black car. She described the car as a Ford with taillights stacked on each other. From another vantage point just west of McKenny Union, service station attendant James Overheul of K & H Marathon witnessed the same scene and believed the car was a Ford Fairlane with rectangular or square taillights—either a 1966 or 1967 model. The police needed to find the red car with the black top and then prove Joan Schell had been in it. But now they had conflicting information on the make. Was the car a Ford or a Pontiac?

Five days later in rural Ann Arbor—about 350 yards west of Earhart Road—two construction workers smelled the foul odor of decomposing flesh and happened upon a nude female body. Their foreman, Lynn H. Bailey, called Ann Arbor police saying his workmen had discovered a body tucked under some scrub brush twelve feet off Glacier Way Road next to a wire farm fence. When police arrived, they found a naked torso partially covered with tufts of grass. Little serious effort was made to conceal the body. The field investigation was postponed twice due to heavy rain. Superior Ambulance Service arrived and took the body to the University of Michigan hospital morgue.

That evening, Dr. Robert Hendrix—who had co-performed the autopsy on Mary Fleszar the previous summer—conducted this autopsy. Dental records and fingerprints identified the missing Eastern Michigan University coed as Joan Elspeth Schell. An examination of the contents of Schell's stomach indicated she died—or was in mortal fear for her life—at about 1:00 a.m. on July 1. That is when her digestion ceased.

Joan Schell's body had at least twenty-five stab wounds—clear evidence of overkill. Three of the stab wounds were on her back indicating a failed attempt to flee. Her left carotid artery was severed, and the spinal bone at the back of her neck was cut by the force of the blow. A stab wound at the base of her left ear traveled upward into her brain and fractured her skull. Her liver was punctured as was her right lung. Joan's miniskirt was found twisted around her neck. It was used to choke her. She was sexually molested before she died.

From these wounds, Dr. Hendrix believed the murder weapon was a knife with a four-inch-long, one-inch-wide blade—possibly a hunting knife. When her carotid artery was severed, there would have been an extreme amount of blood loss—about four pints. No blood pool was found at the scene, and the grass beneath the body showed no signs of discoloration or bleaching indicating the body had been relocated there recently. Dr. Hendrix deduced the victim was at this location for less than a day. He noted that Joan's body was remarkably clean considering the carnage her body sustained. It was as though she had been bathed.

Ann Arbor police investigators needed to find the murder site and the place where the killer had stored Joan's body for four days. The upper portion of her torso and head were black and leathery as if subjected to extreme heat, but most of her torso and legs were well preserved, as if they were covered and in contact with cool ground or a spring-fed stream.

At the jurisdictional request of the Ann Arbor police, the Michigan State Police crime lab was called in to make a further search and examination of the drop site. All of Schell's clothing was accounted for: her blue Crazy Horse miniskirt, a slip, panties, and a bra. However, one item was missing—the victim's red burlap shoulder bag, approximately eighteen inches wide at its open top. Susan Kolbe thought the shoulder bag contained a change of underwear, a purple beaded purse, cosmetics, and Joan's identification.

The crime lab reported finding a powdery grade of sediment embedded in the fabric of Joan's blue skirt. This led investigators to collect water, sand, and silt samples along the Huron River at secluded lovers' lanes and near abandoned buildings like the Peninsular Paper factory. The area around the Superior Road Bridge was checked. Of all the microscopic tests done on sand and silt samples from around the area, none were similar except a white porous material obtained from the Whittaker-Gooding Gravel Company on Cherry Hill Road. The secluded sand and gravel pit was thoroughly searched, but nothing incriminating turned up—another dead end for police.

———

Dale Schultz came under immediate suspicion. Joan's parents did not approve of his involvement with their daughter. He had a minor police record and was presently AWOL from the army. When polygraphed and interrogated on August 5, Dale volunteered everything he knew. The polygraph examiner indicated Schultz was being truthful, and investigators noted that his benumbed grief appeared genuine. The young deserter was released to military police and dropped from suspicion.

The Eastern Michigan campus police took on the task of interviewing every male summer-school student and employee who fit the general description of the suspects. Over 150 red cars with black tops were checked out statewide with no luck locating the suspected car. Many of the cars' owners were polygraphed but none had incriminating results.

Several police investigators felt the Schell murder resembled the horrific murder of Mary Fleszar. The day after Joan's body was found, state police detective Ronald Schoonmaker, Ypsilanti police detective Sergeant Bertrand C. Maxwell, and Ann Arbor police detective Lieutenant Eugene Standenmier met to discuss the similarities between the Fleszar and Schell murders. Both girls worked part-time in McKenny Hall, both lived in off-campus apartments two blocks from each other, and both girls were petite and posed no apparent threat to anyone. When their bodies were discovered, both showed signs of overkill, neither girl was slain where her body was found, and both were dumped in the countryside not far from each other. For now, the Fleszar and Schell murders were officially considered isolated incidents. The Ann Arbor and Ypsilanti police agreed there was no sense creating panic within their communities.

The Ypsilanti police received numerous phone tips stating that Susan Kolbe knew the boys in the car that picked Joan up. Callers claimed she dated one or more of them. The tips seemed orchestrated to discredit Susan Kolbe, so Detective Bert Maxwell requested the state police give her a polygraph test. She willingly took the test and denied the allegations. The polygraph examiner believed she was being truthful. It appeared to police someone was trying to sidetrack their investigation.

A more promising lead came to the notice of the Eastern Michigan University campus police a week later. A supervisor from the Alumni Relations Office in McKenny Hall phoned in a tip that one of his student employees was tormenting a coworker with graphic details about Joan Schell's mutilated body. The employee's name was John Collins.

When Collins was questioned by campus police, he told police he had spent the weekend at his mother's house in Center Line, Michigan fifty miles away. When asked about his inside information about the condition of Schell's body, he credited his uncle—Michigan State trooper Daniel Leik—with telling him. When Corporal Leik was asked to corroborate his nephew's statement, he said he had not discussed the case with his nephew beyond saying he had not worked on that case.

EMU campus police asked Corporal Leik about his nephew. He said John was a police buff who was known to fraternize with off-duty officers at the Bomber restaurant on Michigan Avenue across from the state police post. John often sat with local police for breakfast. The restaurant owners had a large, round table tucked in the corner for them to congregate between shifts. Off-duty Washtenaw County sheriffs, Ypsilanti police, and Michigan state troopers routinely went there to unwind and discuss their tough cases. The restaurant was unofficially a clearinghouse for local police to informally share information. Perhaps Collins had picked up some inside information there.

For now, investigators decided John Collins did not fit their profile. They did not follow up on Collins's alibi that he was at his mother's house over the weekend Joan Schell was killed. Perhaps out of professional courtesy for a fellow cop, this lead was never pursued. Because police were cautious to act and had no solid evidence, Collins was virtually eliminated as a suspect. The searchlight of suspicion would not fall upon him for another year until four more Michigan young women—and one in California—would die horrible deaths.

—— 3 ——

The Wrinkle

JANE MIXER—A LAW STUDENT at the University of Michigan—needed a ride to her hometown of Muskegon two hundred miles west of Ann Arbor. Like many students before and since at the University of Michigan, Jane posted a notice on the campus ride board located in the basement of the student union building. The ride board consisted of two large maps stapled to a bulletin board—one of Michigan and the other of the United States. Students posted notices on a Ride Wanted section or a Riders Needed section. The system worked well most of the time.

According to Jane's boyfriend, her notice read, "Ride wanted to Muskegon, Thursday. Call Janie," and then she gave her phone number at the law quad and her room number. Jane probably did not think twice about writing her address in her notice. That may seem reckless today, but people were generally more trusting and less fearful back then. Jane came from the western side of the state where many people still left their doors unlocked at night. People who knew Jane said she was trusting and compassionate.

Her need for a ride home superseded her caution. She had some unwelcome news for her parents.

A person giving the name David Johnson quickly responded to her message, saying he was headed for Muskegon on March 20 at about 6:30 p.m. Pleased that her notice got such a speedy reply, she agreed to meet Johnson at the law quad. At 7:00 p.m., Jane's boyfriend called her to check if she had left. Jane was still waiting for her ride. When he phoned back an hour later, no one answered.

When Jane did not arrive home within a reasonable amount of time, her father Dr. Daniel Mixer called the Michigan State Police post in Grand Haven on Michigan's western coastline. Dr. Mixer had a personal connection with Muskegon County sheriff Marion Calkins—and contrary to standard operating procedure in most missing person cases—a report was immediately entered into the Michigan Law Enforcement Information Network. All state troopers in Washtenaw County were alerted of Jane's disappearance.

Nationally, police policy customarily requires a delay of twenty-four to forty-eight hours before any action is taken on a missing person report because of the many calls police get daily. Most of the missing individuals turn up unharmed. Without this policy, police would do little else but chase down teenaged runaways, deadbeat parents, and truant spouses. But when someone's daughter goes missing, the logic of a cooling-off period seems like nothing more than a head start for predators and child molesters. The waiting period was waived in this case. The Muskegon County sheriff took immediate action.

The next day was a cold March morning: cloudy and windy with occasional blowing snow. Thirteen-year-old junior high school student Mark Steven Grow was walking along Denton Road, which runs beside the Denton Township cemetery. He was heading to his school bus stop when he spotted a shopping bag set off by itself on the road's edge. The bag was across the street from the cemetery. Mark looked inside and saw a blue wrapped present, a birthday card, some college notebooks, and some typed reports. The contents looked like they might be important, so he returned home with the bag and gave it to his mother Nancy Ann Grow. Mrs. Grow told him she would take care of it and rushed her son off to catch his school bus. Mark hurried past the cemetery a second time and waited on a neighbor's front porch for the bus to arrive.

Meanwhile, upon closer examination of the shopping bag, Mrs. Grow noticed what appeared to be two brown spots on the bottom. She removed the contents of the bag and discovered a dark, gooey substance on the bag. It was blood. Sensing something was terribly wrong she got into her car, drove to the cemetery, and turned in.

Nancy Grow saw the body of a woman laid out on the ground about one hundred feet inside the fenced grounds. A yellow raincoat covered most of the body, a nylon stocking was tied around the victim's neck, and one arm was positioned over the dead woman's head. Panicked, Mrs. Grow got behind the wheel and drove to her sister's house several blocks away. She ran crying to the front door and started knocking frantically until her sister opened it. When she was able to tell her sister what she had seen, her sister called the Ypsilanti state police post and reported the incident. Nancy was in shock. The state police post in Ypsilanti was the nearest despite being in the next county. They sent some officers anyway which would cause jurisdictional problems later.

For the rest of the school day, Mark did not think about what he found that morning, but on the way home on the bus, the driver asked if anyone lived by the cemetery. That is when Mark found out a woman's body was discovered across the street from where he lived. Walking up the gravel road just after 3:00 p.m., he saw heel drag marks going across the road he had not noticed that morning.

Mark remembers his father coming home from work early because he was so shaken by the news. Jack Grow told police that late the previous night, he was doing some auto body work in his garage. He saw a cream-colored station wagon cruise by, enter the cemetery, and loop back onto Denton Road at midnight. He remembered the time because the household clock struck twelve. He was busy and did not make a whole lot of it. He finished working and closed everything up before going to bed.

———

State police troopers, detectives, crime lab personnel, and members of the Wayne County Sheriff's Department were involved in the investigation. The body drop site was in Wayne County—less than five miles east of Ypsilanti in Washtenaw County. The specter of a serial killer haunted everyone. This was the third murder of a coed in the area. Once the press took up the drumbeat, the Ypsilanti community was worried that a maniacal killer was on the loose slaughtering university women.

Detectives most familiar with the previous cases had their doubts. This victim was not raped or mutilated with a knife. She was shot in the head. The body was neatly laid out with a yellow raincoat covering her upper body and clothes still on their hangers covering her lower body. The previous victims were left nude with their clothing torn or cut with a sharp knife indicating murder frenzy. This victim was fully clothed, albeit with her skirt hiked up to her shoulders and her panty hose pulled down to her ankles. A sanitary napkin was in place undisturbed, indicating to investigators that she had not been sexually violated. Found with the body was a paperback copy of *Catch-22* by Joseph Heller. Investigators wondered what significance that might have. Was the killer making a statement?

The press had their story. Articles about a possible multiple murderer in the area appeared. Locals felt a sustained mixture of outrage, panic, and fear. When would he strike again? Was he local? Did he work alone? Police were unable to answer these questions.

The Wayne County medical examiner, Dr. J. C. Shaday, arrived on the scene and pronounced the victim dead at 1:05 p.m. Investigators used a photograph to tentatively identify the victim as missing University of Michigan law student Jane Louise Mixer. It was not until the next afternoon that Daniel and Marian Mixer were able to make a positive identification of their daughter at the university hospital morgue in Ann Arbor.

The autopsy began at 4:00 p.m. after Jane's parents had viewed her body. Washtenaw County medical examiner Dr. Robert Hendrix determined the cause of death to be a .22-caliber gunshot wound to the head. He estimated the shooting took place between midnight and 3:00 a.m. at a site undiscovered. Police surmised Jane was held for approximately four hours in a laundry room in a home or apartment building, because of soap granules found on her coat. In addition to the gunshot wounds, Jane was strangled with a single cinnamon-colored nylon stocking wrapped twice around her neck and tightly tied with a granny knot to make sure she was dead.

A handgun was used as a murder weapon rather than a knife for the first time. Jane's fully clothed body indicated to investigators that there was no sexual attack. The autopsy confirmed that observation. Her attacker covered Jane's body with her yellow raincoat to shield the sight of her. Only the murderer knew why.

The two previous murders were marked by their savage brutality and frenzied mutilation. Jane Mixer's murder did not display the same level of carnage and overkill. Nonetheless, fear and suspicion gripped the public. A homicidal maniac was on the loose preying on university women in the area. That's all Ypsilanti residents knew or cared about.

———

Phillip Marshall Weitzman—Jane's boyfriend—was located at his apartment and taken to Ann Arbor police headquarters on the afternoon of March 21. His name was written inside the cover of the novel found with Jane's body. Weitzman was advised of his constitutional rights and gave investigators a taped interview. He told police he was presently working on a doctoral degree in economics and had been a student and teaching fellow at the University of Michigan since 1964.

Weitzman told investigators he met Jane Mixer about eighteen months earlier when she attended one of his classes. They had dated for the last year and planned to marry. Jane came over to his apartment at 2:30 a.m. on March 20 and spent the night. In the morning, he drove her to the law quad and taught his scheduled classes. After his last class, Weitzman went to Jane's dorm room until about 6:00 p.m.

when he drove home. He phoned her at six fifteen. Jane said her ride had not shown up yet. When he called back at seven, nobody answered. Weitzman assumed she and her ride-share driver had left for Muskegon.

Phillip Weitzman settled in for the evening to prepare for his classes the next day. At midnight, Jane's father called him saying Jane had not arrived in Muskegon, and he and Jane's mother were worried. Phillip told Dr. Mixer that Jane left from her dorm room sometime before 7:00 p.m. He did not witness her leave nor did he see whom she left with. Weitzman received a second call from Dr. Mixer at four o'clock Friday morning. He told Jane's father he would drive over to the law quad and see if she had returned home for some reason. He drove by and saw that the lights were out in her room.

At 8:00 a.m., Weitzman received a third call from Dr. Mixer saying he had called in a missing person report. After the third call, Phillip rushed over to the law quad, identified himself as Jane's boyfriend, and signed for a key to Jane's dorm room. He checked her room and found nothing unusual.

When detectives asked Weitzman about Jane, he admitted they were intimate on numerous occasions and planned to marry soon. Phillip said she was a good student who was reliable and able to take care of herself. Jane had no enemies or ex-boyfriends as far as he knew. She was in the process of transferring to Columbia or New York University Law School to be with him because he had accepted a professor's post at a university in the East.

At this point of the interview, Weitzman was told a body found at Denton Cemetery that morning was Jane Mixer. Phillip was visibly shaken by the stark news. Hoping against hope, he asked to call Jane's number. No one was there to answer. Shock set in. Ann Arbor police believed Phillip Weitzman was profoundly disturbed over his fiancé's murder. He was allowed to go home but advised not to leave the area.

———

The name David Johnson was used by the person responding to Jane's ride board message. Investigators began checking all of the Dave or David Johnsons in Washtenaw County—then the call went statewide. Countless man-hours were consumed in checking each and every person. Because a handgun was used in the commission of this murder, every small-caliber gun the police came across was test fired and compared with the recovered bullet fragments. The police investigators' painstaking work led nowhere.

———

On April 1, the police interviewed Phillip Weitzman again after Dr. Mixer expressed a suspicion Weitzman could be the killer of his daughter. Jane's parents did not approve of Weitzman. Jane knew this of course. Despite their disapproval, Jane accepted his marriage proposal and decided to move to New York with him. She knew her parents would have trouble accepting the marriage. Weitzman was Jewish and the Mixers were Lutherans. Moreover, Dr. Mixer was a Barry Goldwater conservative while Jane and Phil were Eugene McCarthy liberals. The sixties were politically and culturally divisive times for many families, and the Mixers were no exception.

The police interview took place in Phillip Weitzman's apartment. In his initial statement, it appeared he was the last known person to see Jane alive. Weitzman told investigators Jane said someone named Dave Johnson was going to drive her to Muskegon on Thursday. In fact, she had written his name down on an index card and left it next to the phone. He gave the police the index card. Weitzman said he heard Jane mention the name to her parents when she told them she was coming home Thursday. Her parents insisted Jane never mentioned the name of the ride-share driver to them.

Phil Weitzman admitted the paperback book found with Jane's body—*Catch-22*—was one he loaned her. Weitzman mentioned Jane had a zippered beige clutch purse where she carried her driver's license, student ID card, and her makeup. Weitzman thought Jane had about ten dollars in the purse. The purse was nowhere to be found.

Weitzman signed a release for investigators to search his car and his apartment—especially his shoes. He also agreed to take a polygraph test. The polygraph examiner determined Weitzman was being truthful when he denied any knowledge of Jane's death.

———

A report came from the Muskegon County sheriff to the Grand Haven state police post that Dr. Dan Mixer was unhappy about his daughter's murder investigation. Dr. Mixer called Captain Arnold Van Dam of the Muskegon police complaining. It had been forty days since Jane's body was found in Denton Cemetery. No one from the police had contacted the Mixer family to update them on the status of the investigation or to question them about whom they thought could be responsible for their daughter's murder. Jane's older married sister, Barbara Jo Nelson, had not been contacted, nor had Jane's younger brother Dan. Jane's father did not want to accuse anyone outright, but he felt his daughter was killed by someone who knew her.

———

On Thursday, May 1, Sheriff Marion Calkins of Muskegon County contacted the Grand Haven state police post and advised them he was a friend of Dr. Dan Mixer. The distraught father's original theory was someone who knew Jane had killed her. Now he believed someone had paid another person to kill his daughter. Still, there was no motive or evidence to go with this theory.

Dr. Mixer further mentioned Jane's boyfriend Phillip Weitzman had a girlfriend before his daughter started going with him. This girlfriend could have been jealous and angry enough to arrange this murder. Dr. Mixer additionally threw out the name of Professor Bob Harris, who was running for Ann Arbor mayor. Jane did some volunteer work typing for him. Jane also volunteered for a legal-aid group and was a strong believer in the civil rights movement. Perhaps she made some enemies through her work. Police investigators pursued Dr. Mixer's theories but neither area of inquiry contributed any useful information.

———

Jane Mixer was believed to be the third victim of an elusive killer primarily because her murder was unsolved, she was a coed, and her body was found in a rural area outside of Ypsilanti. Jane seemed to fit the basic victim profile of the other two murdered university women. The press ran with the story as fear tightened its grip on parents statewide with daughters going to Eastern Michigan University or the University of Michigan.

— 4 —

Another Hitchhiker

ONLY TWO DAYS AFTER the body of Jane Mixer was found, State Trooper Herbert Kruipers received a missing person call at the Michigan State Police post in Ypsilanti. Sharon Santucci reported she received a phone call from her friend—sixteen-year-old Maralynn Skelton—to meet her at McKenny Student Union on the Eastern Michigan University campus. Maralynn never arrived nor did she call back. This sent up a warning flag for Santucci, who was keenly aware that three young women had been killed in the area within the last twenty months.

Santucci explained to the Michigan state trooper how she tried to enlist the aid of the Ypsilanti Police Department in filing a missing person report, but they refused to take the report because Maralynn Skelton went missing outside their jurisdiction. Santucci indicated Maralynn phoned her at about 4:00 p.m. saying her father had dropped her off at a gas station at the intersection of Carpenter Road and Washtenaw Avenue, the main road leading east to Ypsilanti. Maralynn asked Santucci if she or her husband John could pick her up. Sharon answered she had no transportation but would meet Maralynn at McKenny Student Union. Maralynn planned to hitchhike the three miles into Ypsilanti.

The Michigan State Police refused to take a formal missing person report because it was not coming from a proper source—a relative or a parent. Sharon Santucci was thwarted twice trying to report the disappearance of her friend.

The next day, Santucci returned with Michael Millage to the Ypsilanti state police post to inquire about Maralynn. She was missing for over twenty-four hours by then. Corporal Luckey told them he did not have any information but asked them to come back that evening. By then, he would have a chance to look into the matter. Corporal Luckey noted in his report that Mrs. Santucci "appeared to be about fourteen years old." In fact, Sharon was seventeen and recently married to nineteen-year-old John Santucci, Jr.

Michael Millage pressed Corporal Luckey to take a missing person report, but Luckey told him Maralynn's parents should be the ones making the report—even if they had to phone it in. Millage insisted he had talked to Maralynn's parents twice by phone, but they were unconcerned whether Maralynn had run away or not. The Skeltons were in the process of moving to Flint, about seventy-five miles north of Detroit.

Corporal Luckey explained he could not broadcast a missing person report, but he would note the information and pass it on to the road patrols. Millage was not happy with the response and pressed the issue. He and Sharon Santucci left the state police post angry and convinced nothing would happen.

Early Monday morning, Trooper Luckey discovered that the Wayne County sheriff's office had taken a missing person report on Maralynn Skelton from Michael Millage on Sunday. Despite Maralynn being last heard from in Washtenaw County, a report was filed on the pretext she had lived in Romulus, located in rural Wayne County. Wayne County sheriffs were on the lookout for a white female by the name of Maralynn Skelton—no middle name—sixteen years old, five feet five inches tall, 115 pounds, with shoulder-length medium-brown hair and brown eyes.

On Monday morning, Maralynn's mother came to the Ypsilanti state police post of her own accord. Helen Skelton told Corporal Ciochetto she and her family were in the process of moving from Romulus to Flint after learning Maralynn had taken drugs since age thirteen and was an addict. Maralynn refused to move to Flint and preferred to live with her hippie friends. At that time, the officer noted Mrs. Skelton did not appear overly concerned about her daughter's disappearance.

Mrs. Skelton came to discuss Maralynn's problem with narcotics and other difficulties she was having with her daughter. She told Corporal Ciochetto she could not understand what Michael Millage was trying to pull by reporting Maralynn missing. Mrs. Skelton said Maralynn told her she was going to Ypsilanti because she owed some hippies money. It seemed odd to Corporal Ciochetto that Maralynn's mother downplayed her daughter's disappearance, but he learned Maralynn had run away from home on numerous occasions and always returned.

Mrs. Skelton wanted information on how to contact the Women's Division of the Wayne County Sheriff's Department. Officer Beverly Scannell was familiar with Maralynn's problems. Mrs. Skelton tried to contact her without success. At that time, Corporal Ciochetto suggested Skelton phone in a missing person report in Wayne County. She did half-heartedly.

———

Tuesday morning, March 25, was cold and dreary. The overnight precipitation left a light dusting of blowing snow. At 11:06 a.m., Allen Rentschler, an employee of Washtenaw Engineering Company, phoned the Ann Arbor Police Department and reported that his surveying crew had found a nude female body in the area of Earhart and Waldenwood Roads, north of Geddes Road in the rural outskirts of Ann Arbor.

The body was discovered at 11:00 a.m., and Ann Arbor Police Department detectives arrived on the scene minutes later. They requested the Michigan State Police crime lab and their Latent Print Unit be sent to the location. The victim's nude body was found lying on her back in a newly developed subdivision on the west side of Pemberton Lane. The head was facing north and lying on its cheek. A piece of blue cloth was stuffed into the victim's mouth with the rest partially covering her face. A garter belt was found knotted tightly around the girl's throat. Her left arm was extended above her head while her right arm was at her side and slightly away from the body. Both hands were partially closed but not tightly clenched. The left leg was drawn up toward the body with the thigh extended away from the body at a forty-five-degree angle in what police refer to as rape position. The right leg was extended in the normal anatomical position. An eleven-and-a-half-inch branch protruded seven inches from the girl's vagina.

The victim's ears were pierced but only the right ear had an earring. She had suffered injury to the right side of her face with massive bruising and lacerations. There were also numerous welts and bruises over her breasts, abdomen, and thighs. These bruises showed the distinct outline of a belt buckle and violent strapping.

Her clothes were near her body. A white bra was draped over her head with one of the straps. A blue windbreaker jacket was lying on the ground beneath the teen's buttocks. A few feet north of the victim's left leg were a pair of brown loafers, a torn pair of light-blue underpants, a used Tampax, a torn portion of a blue T-shirt, and a pair of jeans. At 1:15 p.m., Washtenaw County Coroner Dr. Robert Hendrix arrived and officially pronounced the victim dead. An ambulance took the young Jane Doe to the University of Michigan hospital morgue.

A foot search of the surrounding area found shoe prints in the mud some forty-five feet northwest of the victim leading up to a muddy embankment toward the spot where the body was found. Because of the rainy weather, the prints were lacking detail. After pictures and measurements were made of the crime scene, Ann Arbor police chief Walter E. Krasny held an impromptu press conference at the scene. He told reporters, "This is the worst thing I've seen in thirty years of police work. We can't say this has no connection with the other three murders. There almost has to be some link." The Ann Arbor police felt a profile of the murderer was forming, but how many more young women would die before the murderer's identity would be known?

When Allen Rentschler was further interviewed, he told Ann Arbor police his road crew was surveying when they saw what looked like a body south of Pemberton Lane. Two carpenters were working inside a house under construction. Rentschler asked them to check if the body in the back area of the yard was an actual person.

Ben Romans and Joseph Lobbestael—both from Ypsilanti—left from the rear of the house and approached the body. When Romans was interviewed by police, he said he got within two feet and knew it was a corpse. Romans told police the surveyors did not approach the body but reported it to police. The carpenter also noted that the owner of the house under construction was on the roof the day before and would have been able to see the body. He had said nothing. The police surmised this Jane Doe was killed at another location and probably dumped there in the middle of the night.

Sergeant William Canada of the Ann Arbor Police Department was placed in charge of the investigation. He checked recent missing person reports and found three possible matches. One report from neighboring Wayne County looked likely. Wayne County police officer Beverly Scannell was listed as the contact person. Sergeant Canada called and requested that Scannell come to the university hospital to identify a body. Officer Scannell made a positive identification of Maralynn Skelton.

The Wayne County sheriff's narcotics officer briefed Ann Arbor police about Maralynn. "She tried it all—marijuana, speed, heroin, and LSD. Miss Skelton was all over Wayne County buying and selling drugs to support her habit. After being picked up in Westland on a drug charge, Maralynn became a police informant to mitigate her situation." Officer Scannell said she met Maralynn at the request of Romulus High School officials. The narcotics officer said she notified the Skeltons what their daughter was involved with, but they were in denial and did not want to accept it.

Then, Detective Canada asked Officer Scannell if she would notify the victim's father who was already at the hospital. She agreed and advised Archie Skelton of his daughter's death. There was nothing Mr. Skelton could do there, so she suggested he go to the Ann Arbor Police Department with his wife and make a statement.

Dr. Paul Gikas and Dr. Robert Hendrix began the autopsy at 3:45 p.m. with nine investigating police officers present. Scaled photos of the victim's injuries were taken in color and black and white. In addition to the injuries previously mentioned, the doctors believed it likely Maralynn Skelton was sexually assaulted. They noted that her right eye socket was crushed and the surrounding tissue was bruised. The cause of death was determined to be severe brain damage from a crushing blow to the face.

Also visible were traces of blood in her hairline and in the area of her right ear where a white-gold earring was affixed. On her right inner forearm was a large bruised area. The victim was found on her back with numerous welts across her breasts, her stomach area, and both thighs. The bruises showed the outline of a belt-buckle design. It was Dr. Robert Hendrix's opinion that Maralynn Skelton's body was at the location all night until it was found the next morning.

Officer Vesalles from the state police crime lab had done a visual inspection of the mud on Skelton's shoes. It compared favorably with the mud in the area where her body was found, leading him to believe she had walked into the area.

This fourth unsolved murder of a young woman in Washtenaw County had many of the same trademarks as the others with two fundamental differences. Maralynn Skelton was younger—a teenager barely sixteen years old—and she was not a university student. Had the murderer cast a wider net for his prey? The press ruminated while the Ypsilanti community panicked.

———

Four days after Maralynn's body was identified, investigators interviewed her older brother Thomas Wayne Skelton at his home. In his statement, he said he last saw Maralynn on Saturday afternoon, March 22 before noon. She helped their father load a U-Haul truck in Romulus for the family's move to Flint. With her father driving, Maralynn reluctantly returned to Flint. Her mother had spent the previous night in their new home preparing the house for the family's possessions.

Thomas and his friend Larry Glinski drove to Flint in Larry's car and helped Mr. Skelton unload the U-Haul and return the truck to the rental agency in Flint. They visited for a short while, ate lunch, and returned to Romulus at about 5:30 p.m. Thomas said Maralynn left Flint shortly after arriving there. Maralynn told her mother she needed to return to Ypsilanti and would take the city bus to the Greyhound station and catch the next bus for Ypsilanti.

The Ann Arbor police received a tip from someone named Eddie Phelps that Thomas Skelton and a man known only as Larry returned Maralynn to Ann Arbor on Saturday afternoon. Confronted by police with this conflicting information, Thomas Skelton denied returning from Flint with Maralynn or knowing anyone named Eddie Phelps.

Two days after Thomas was interviewed, the state police interviewed Larry Glinski. His version of what happened corroborated the account given by Thomas Skelton. He denied giving Maralynn a ride back to Ypsilanti and stated he never associated with her or any of her friends. He knew Thomas and Archie Skelton for many years and had no further information about the case. Glinski told police he drove Mr. and Mrs. Skelton to Ann Arbor after they learned Maralynn's body had been found. It was the opinion of the investigators at the time that Glinski and Thomas Skelton were truthful and innocent of any involvement in this case.

———

Maralynn's parents were interviewed on Monday, March 31. It was learned that in addition to an adult son, they had a married daughter named Barbara. Investigators discovered that Maralynn often spent weekends with her friends John and Sharon Santucci in Ypsilanti.

Mrs. Skelton confirmed that Maralynn left the house wearing the same clothing found near her body. In addition, Maralynn carried a brown leather, pouch-style purse with brass eyelets and a long drawstring. A black wallet with her identification and approximately thirty dollars should have been in the purse. Maralynn was wearing a diamond engagement ring her boyfriend Michael Millage gave her on her sixteenth birthday, March 4. None of these items was found with the body.

Helen Skelton told police Mike Millage called her in Flint Sunday night to say Maralynn was missing. He urged the Skeltons to file a missing person report, but Mrs. Skelton refused. Millage lost control and said, "What are you going to do? Wait until she is found with three bullet holes in her head?" Mrs. Skelton told police Millage called her a number of names and hung up. Millage regained his composure and called back ten minutes later, again urging them to file a missing person report.

Disturbed by Millage's phone calls, Archie and Helen Skelton drove to the Ypsilanti state police post shortly after midnight on Monday, March 24. They learned that John Santucci Sr. had already called to report Maralynn missing. Only then did the Skeltons file their own report before returning to Flint. Early Wednesday morning, they were informed by Ann Arbor police that Maralynn's body was found.

When asked for a list of suspects, the Skeltons were unable to name anyone at first. They said the family lived in Romulus for twenty-six years and never had trouble with anyone. They did provide police with the names of Maralynn's friends.

During another interview two days later at the Ypsilanti state police post, Archie and Helen Skelton were asked when they first noticed they had a problem with Maralynn. Her mother said the problems started on Thanksgiving Day in 1968 when Maralynn claimed she was going to a banquet with some people at Romulus High School where she was a freshman. A car brought her home at 8:30 p.m. Mrs. Skelton questioned Maralynn about where the banquet was and who she was with. Maralynn dropped the names of several people connected with the high school—including the principal and the assistant principal.

From prior experience, Mrs. Skelton doubted her story. Thanksgiving is a family holiday. Why would the school host a Thanksgiving banquet taking students away from their families? Mrs. Skelton called around asking Maralynn's school friends if they knew anything about a school banquet or Maralynn's whereabouts. She came up empty. Confronted with this information, Maralynn changed her story and told her mother she was at the home of Wayne County sheriff detective Beverly Scannell—someone with whom she had been working. This excuse was less credible than the first, but Maralynn was home, so her mother let it pass.

Shortly after that incident, Maralynn started bringing Sharon Sanders—who was soon to become Mrs. Sharon Santucci—home for the weekends. Maralynn spent several weekends with Sharon at her parents' home in Ypsilanti. Mrs. Skelton met Mrs. Sanders and thought she was a nice person, so Mrs. Skelton did not worry about her daughter when she visited the Sanders's home.

Maralynn's behavior grew increasingly rebellious. In December 1968, two friends wanted to take her to a party. Maralynn was not allowed to go. Consequently, a rift developed between mother and daughter. It was then that Maralynn started running away and spending time at a Woodland Hills apartment in Ann Arbor police described as a hippie crash pad. There she met Mike Millage, and they started going together. Maralynn was fifteen years old and Mike was nineteen.

On January 28, 1969, Maralynn was admitted to Belleville Hospital. Mrs. Skelton insisted her daughter was given too many flu shots. That is what she told people when they asked about Maralynn. She met John Santucci at this time, and he announced he was King of the Hippies and popped two pills into his mouth. Mrs. Skelton said his eyes started to roll almost immediately.

Mrs. Skelton said someone named Jim Cooney also came

to the hospital frequently to visit Maralynn. He would sit in the lobby and stare like he was in a trance. Mike Millage spent lots of time visiting Maralynn, too. Skelton thought Millage was afraid of the hippies—like they had some kind of power over him and Maralynn.

Mrs. Skelton told Maralynn the family was moving to Flint, so her father could be closer to his new job and get her away from her hippie friends. Maralynn objected. This was when she told her mother she would not be living with them after March 21. Maralynn announced she was engaged and going to marry Michael Millage that weekend. Maralynn's parents were livid.

On Sunday evening, March 16, Maralynn did not come home. She returned to Flint three days later telling her mother she was in Ypsilanti at the Santucci apartment helping Sharon sell cosmetics. While Maralynn was in Flint, she received a phone call from Mike Millage and Bobby Wren saying she "had better be there with the money." Maralynn was desperate. She sold her typewriter to her mother for twenty-four dollars and her bicycle to her brother for ten dollars.

Then on Friday afternoon, Archie Skelton rented a U-Haul truck in Flint and drove with Maralynn to Romulus to load up the last of their belongings. While Mr. Skelton made a call to his wife at 6:30 p.m., Maralynn ducked out of the house and arranged a ride to Ann Arbor. She went to the Woodland Hills apartment to see Mike Millage, but he was not there. Maralynn returned to Romulus around midnight. The next morning was moving day. She was expected to help her father load the U-Haul.

At nine o'clock the next morning, she and her father left Romulus and arrived in Flint at noon. Maralynn told her parents she needed another ten dollars badly. Her mother said Maralynn seemed scared and sat there staring into space. Mrs. Skelton reported to police Maralynn left home between 1:30 and 2:00 p.m. Mr. Skelton told police Maralynn left before he got home from returning the U-Haul truck. Archie Skelton furthermore stated his son and his friend were with him.

On April 3, Helen Skelton with her eldest daughter Barbara called Lieutenant Simmons and told him she was in Romulus. This was the first opportunity Mrs. Skelton had to talk with police without her husband present. Helen Skelton said her husband threatened her, saying, "If you tell how she [Maralynn] left the house on Saturday, I will kill you." She said her husband also threatened their son and his friend. They were all told to say nothing about how Maralynn got to Ann Arbor.

The Ann Arbor police had conflicting accounts that Mrs. Skelton soon resolved. She said Thomas and Larry took Maralynn to the Standard Oil service station across from Arborland Shopping Center on Saturday afternoon. She admitted her husband was at home when her son and his friend took Maralynn. Of special interest to investigators was Mrs. Skelton's revelation of a violent quarrel between Maralynn and her father. They screamed about how much they hated each other, and threats were thrown back and forth just before Maralynn left for Ypsilanti.

Detective Simmons thanked Mrs. Skelton for coming to the station and was told polygraph tests would be arranged for her and her husband. He stressed she should not say anything to her husband. That was not a problem since Helen Skelton was deathly afraid of him. It was now clear to police that the Skeltons were a dysfunctional family.

To corroborate Mrs. Skelton's account, Lieutenant Simmons and Roy Tanner—Washtenaw County prosecutor's investigator—approached Larry Glinski at his home and read him his Miranda rights. Glinski was warned he could be an accessory before the fact in the death of Maralynn Skelton. The investigators asked if he brought Maralynn back to Ann Arbor from Flint on Saturday afternoon. He clung to the original story as dictated by Archie Skelton.

Lieutenant Simmons told Larry Glinski, "I don't have time to listen to your lies. I know what the truth is, and it's up to you to come clean. You're writing your own ticket." He then turned his back and walked over to where Glinski's father was standing. Roy Tanner took a turn and managed to get Glinski to admit he and Thomas Skelton returned to Ann Arbor with Maralynn and dropped her off at the Standard station on Washtenaw Avenue. Larry Glinski agreed to take a polygraph test at any time, but he worked the afternoon shift at the Ford plant. Suspicion now shifted to Archie Skelton. When Sharon Santucci first spoke to police, she mentioned Maralynn said her father dropped her off.

The Ann Arbor Police Department requested that both Archie and Helen Skelton take polygraph tests. Archie Skelton was unaware his wife had spoken with police. The Skeltons were tested separately by different examiners. Archie Skelton was tested as a suspect, while Helen Skelton was questioned about whom Maralynn left Flint with Saturday afternoon.

Archie Skelton showed himself to be deceptive with some of his test results. During the posttest interview, he was given another chance to tell the truth but continued to lie about how Maralynn got to Ann Arbor. He told police she took the bus. When confronted with his lies, Archie Skelton finally admitted that Thomas and Larry drove Maralynn to Ann Arbor. On the question of whether he had killed his daughter, Mr. Skelton answered no and was found to be truthful. Mrs. Skelton's polygraph test results indicated she was being truthful in all of her responses.

When their polygraph tests were completed, Mrs. Skelton wanted to help police as much as she could to get the truth about her daughter's violent murder. Mr. Skelton appeared sullen and disoriented after the polygraph test. He was proven to be a liar and a bully.

Three days later, a plastic bag arrived at the Ann Arbor Police Department from Helen Skelton with some items she thought investigators should have. It contained an application for an apartment lease in the names of Michael D. Millage and Maralynn Millage, a Michigan Bell long-distance billing statement with phone numbers of people Maralynn called, a postcard of Detroit's Grande Ballroom with nothing written on it, a piece of music written on musical notation paper for Maralynn by Jim Cooney, a drawing of Maralynn signed by Chuck Clinton, a number of business cards for Detroit rock bands and head shops in the Plum Street area of Detroit, and seven back issues of the *Fifth Estate*—a Detroit-based underground newspaper.

Thomas Skelton was finally contacted on April 14 at his home in Taylor, Michigan. He corroborated what his mother, Larry Glinski, and his father finally admitted to. Thomas added he dropped her off at the gas station driveway and said, "We offered to take Maralynn wherever she needed to go, but she said she was going to call her friend to pick her up."

Thomas told police he was older than Maralynn and admitted they were never close, so he did not quibble with her. He said good-bye and left her standing in the parking lot. When Thomas got home, he showered and went over to the Ponderosa Bar with a friend. His alibi checked out.

————

The day after Maralynn's body was found Officer Taylor of the Romulus Police Department received a phone call from a Mrs. Baker in Livonia. She worked at Romulus High School and volunteered information saying she had known the Skelton family for a long time. Baker told Officer Taylor the Skeltons' oldest boy Tom was a heavy drinker. That's all she knew about him.

A transcribed phone conversation taken from police records shows Baker was asked if Archie Skelton was prone to violence if his daughters got out of line.

"Yeah, he beat them."

"How bad?"

"Well, I guess it was quite bad. That's the reason why the oldest girl ran away from home. That's what she said anyway."

"That would be Barbara?"

"Uh-huh. And listening to one of the conversations at school today, I found out that Maralynn had been on dope for about a year."

"That's right. She was a known user."

"Mrs. Kinkner—a counselor at Romulus High School—said she talked with Maralynn at the beginning of March. Maralynn told her she was going to run away from home and get married. The boy's name was Mike—from Belleville."

"Did Maralynn ever talk about how her parents treated her?"

"No. Mrs. Kinkner could never get anything out of her. The girl was silent about everything."

"Mrs. Baker, we want to find out what kind of father this guy was and whether he would be prone to really laying her up with a belt or not."

"Ah, I think that he would use discipline. I don't think he would break any bones. He has been using a paddle a lot. I think he could be hard on it."

"Well, this is pretty severe, I can tell you that."

———

On March 31, Sergeants Lyons and Olmstead canvassed the street where the Skelton family had lived in Romulus to find out more about the family. Mr. Hahn told police he had known Archie Skelton for quite some time. Mr. Skelton was on workers' compensation because of a construction job injury. Hahn said he knew the family was moving to Flint because Archie found a new job there.

Mr. and Mrs. Victor Taliman lived on the same side of the street as the Skeltons. Mr. Taliman said he observed a green pickup truck at the Skelton house all day Saturday and a blue Corvair on Sunday he thought belonged to the Skeltons' oldest daughter. On Wednesday, Taliman observed Archie Skelton burning furniture in their backyard at 7:00 a.m. Taliman commented he had seen Mr. Skelton on different occasions when he was drunk. "Sometimes, he would damage furniture and burn it."

Mr. Taliman also stated he knew Mr. and Mrs. Skelton were both heavy drinkers. Mrs. Skelton was once active in the church but became involved in drinking as much as her husband. He further stated the Skeltons slept in separate bedrooms. What that had to do with Maralynn's murder case was unclear to investigators, but it did speak to the relationship between her parents.

Floyd Luck lived across the street from the Skeltons. He corroborated Taliman's story about the early-morning furniture burning and confirmed that the blue Corvair belonged to the Skeltons' oldest daughter Barbara.

Delores Ryan seemed better informed about Maralynn than any of her neighbors because Maralynn babysat for her. She wanted to help the investigation in any way she could. Ryan told police Maralynn was selling drugs for a girl named Nora from Highland Park. Maralynn said she passed some forged prescriptions for Nora at a downtown drugstore.

Ryan revealed she had visited Maralynn in Belleville Hospital and was told Maralynn was being examined for a borderline case of leukemia. When she spoke to Maralynn alone, Ryan learned Maralynn had taken an overdose of heroin. Maralynn also confided to Ryan that she was afraid she could not get off the speed (crystal meth).

When Ryan was asked about Mike Millage, she said Maralynn always spoke fondly of him—almost worshipped him. Maralynn said she and Mike wanted to get married, but her parents were against it. They were afraid Maralynn would get pregnant. They wanted their daughter away from the bad crowd in Romulus and Ypsilanti.

Mrs. Bledsoe, who lived on Wayne Road, knew the Skelton family well. She said that on numerous occasions, Archie Skelton beat Maralynn. At one time, Bledsoe was going to intervene and adopt Maralynn but nothing came of it. She offered to help police in any way to find Maralynn's killer.

Early in the investigation, Archie Skelton was the prime suspect. But both he and his wife argued that Maralynn was murdered because of drugs and a debt she owed. Mr. Skelton's polygraph indicated he was guilty of lying but innocent of his daughter's murder. Police were able to corroborate Archie's alibi that he was in Flint at the time of his daughter's death, so they dropped him as a suspect.

———

In mid-April, the Michigan Department of Public Health released the results of their lab findings. Chemical tests were made on what was believed to be the murder weapon—a branch two feet long and two and three-quarters inches thick. An indentation in the branch approximately four inches from one end indicated the presence of type O blood—Maralynn's blood type. One single human hair found on the branch had the properties of an eyelash of light to medium brown color matching her hair coloration. It was noted that extensive comparisons between head hair, pubic hair, and eyelash hair cannot be made. Because the eyelash found on the suspected murder weapon was similar in color to other hair samples, it might have come from the same source as the other samples. All other hairs found on the branch were either too small for conclusive determination or were of animal origin.

Chemical tests were also performed on the soiled tampon, the branch found sticking seven inches out of the victim's vagina, and a bloody cotton swab used to swab the vagina. Much to the surprise of the investigators, the tests failed to reveal the presence of semen. The chemical analysis of Maralynn Skelton's blood also failed to show the presence of drugs in her bloodstream. Maralynn tested clean. A thorough examination of the victim's clothing failed to reveal anything of any evidential value. The police were once again baffled.

———

At the request of the Ann Arbor police, the Romulus police began to interview people who knew Maralynn. A sixteen-year-old high school friend said Maralynn was selling orange tablets of methadrine for fifty cents apiece and nickel bags of marijuana at school last January. Maralynn told this friend she got the stuff from Mike, but the friend didn't know his last name. Police already knew Mike's last name.

Police learned Mike purchased an engagement ring, a housecoat, and slippers for Maralynn while she was in Belleville Hospital withdrawing from drugs. The rumor at school was Maralynn was in the hospital for hepatitis. Maralynn's school friend said Maralynn was hooked on drugs and wanted to get off them.

Another friend of Maralynn told investigators she had been good friends with Maralynn since the seventh grade. She described Maralynn as active in school, a musician who played clarinet in the school band, and an A/B student. She remarked, "There wasn't anything that Marilynn couldn't do. But last summer, she started to fade away and became involved in smoking marijuana, and she became a speed freak."

Maralynn's friend said she once had gone with Maralynn to Nora's place next to a motorcycle clubhouse in Detroit. Heroin, speed, and LSD were available there. The friend believed Nora was paying the Detroit police not to bust her. "The place was wide open and anything could be obtained there," the teen said. Maralynn's friend also revealed that Maralynn and her friend Sharon Santucci took karate lessons together, but she did not know where.

———

While Romulus police interviewed Maralynn's friends and neighbors, Ann Arbor police detective Sergeant Raymond Winters and Michigan State Police detective Kenneth Taylor questioned Michael Millage in an unmarked police vehicle parked in front of his parents' house. Millage told police he worked delivering cosmetics for his father but expected to be officially hired by the Holiday Magic Cosmetic Company soon. He was laid off from St. Regis Paper Company a week before Maralynn was murdered.

The last time Millage heard from Maralynn was a phone call Saturday morning. She was in Romulus with her father and brother about to move their belongings to Flint. She asked if Millage could help, but he was already committed to assisting his friend Jerry move. He worked with Jerry until about 5:00 p.m. when he went home, showered, and returned to eat pizza and watch basketball with Jerry and his family—including Jerry's in-laws.

He returned to his parents' home at 10:00 p.m. and briefly talked with his father until he gave Maralynn a call in Flint. Her mother answered, "Is this Mike?" Then Mrs. Skelton told him Maralynn was staying with Sharon Santucci in Ypsilanti and hung up. Millage said that was news to him. Monday evening—together with the Santuccis and their friend Bobby Wren—Mike Millage drove to Detroit looking for Maralynn. They hung out at a friend's place for a couple of hours asking if anyone had seen her. They returned to Ypsilanti just before midnight.

"Does your friend have a name?"

"Nora," he answered.

Sergeant Winters told Millage he was familiar with Nora's place and wanted to know what they were doing there.

Surprised and cornered, Millage answered, "I bought a hundred caps of Seco-Synatan for ten dollars." When asked what he did with the capsules, he claimed he flushed them down the toilet when he heard about Maralynn's murder.

The detective asked Millage how long he had known Maralynn.

"I met her last November. Maralynn was selling Seco at Romulus High School. The caps cost us ten cents apiece, and we were getting fifty cents for them."

The detectives advised Millage he would be contacted again, so he should stay in the area. They asked if he would be willing to take a polygraph test, and he readily agreed. With that, they left him standing on the sidewalk in front of his parents' house.

Michigan State Police detective William Canada interviewed Sharon Santucci by phone.

Santucci stated that at around 3:00 p.m. on Saturday, Maralynn called her from a pay phone but did not mention her location. She said her father dropped her off at US-23 and the Washtenaw Avenue exit. Maralynn asked Sharon if her husband could pick her up near Arborland Shopping Center. Since John Santucci needed the car to deliver some beauty supplies and Sharon had no transportation, Maralynn decided she would hitchhike to McKenny Union on Eastern's campus. Sharon agreed to meet her near the pay phones. When Sharon's husband came at 5:00 p.m. to pick them up, Maralynn still had not arrived.

Officer Canada discontinued the phone interview and arranged to interview Sharon Santucci at her home the next day. In addition to Sharon and John Santucci, Michael Millage was there. Once again, Sharon told Canada the identical story she had the previous evening, except this time she added that Maralynn told her she had "a nickel bag of grass and something to run on." Somewhere, Maralynn obtained some speed. Sharon said she warned Maralynn not to use the stuff.

When it was apparent Maralynn was not going to show up, the Santuccis went looking for her. They drove to the Woodland Hills apartment where Maralynn sometimes stayed and knocked on the door, but nobody answered. They continued on Packard Road looking for Maralynn on their way home to their apartment.

Sharon Santucci told Detective Canada something she thought police should know. "Maralynn was a third-degree, red-belt karate expert, and she was pretty good. Mike charged her with a knife once as a test, and she threw him on the ground almost breaking his wrist. I imagine whoever attacked her was pretty big or had a weapon of some kind."

Santucci went on to describe Maralynn's purse. "Maralynn carried a brownish suede purse with different colored brown patches on it, some light and some dark. The purse had fringe on the bottom and draw strings on the top. She kept an address book in the purse, a driver's license that wasn't hers, and a wallet with many photos of her friends."

Detective Canada asked if Maralynn ever wore just one earring. Sharon said Maralynn would never wear just one earring. "The pair she has been wearing had a mate, but it would fall off her ear."

Now, it was Michael Millage's turn to speak with the investigator. Millage was there because he wanted to be interviewed someplace other than his parents' house. He told Detective Canada that Maralynn had a large black and blue bruise on her right forearm. This happened approximately two weeks before when she was trying to inject methadrine. She punctured a vein in her forearm. He admitted Maralynn used heroin before but was not an addict like the newspapers were saying.

"Most of Maralynn's drug contacts are in Detroit," he said. "I introduced her to the group at the Sunny Good House on South University Avenue in Ann Arbor. I know that last summer she spent a lot of time at John Sinclair's place in Ann Arbor. She frequented the White Panther house on Hill Street."

The Ann Arbor police and the Washtenaw County Sheriff's Department were familiar with the White Panthers and John Sinclair, the self-appointed guru of Ann Arbor's counterculture scene in the late 1960s. He was a white male, six feet three inches tall, with a wild shoulder-length mane and mustache.

The White Panthers had been under police surveillance for quite some time. Their commune, known as Trans-Love Energies, had recently migrated from Detroit to Ann Arbor, where they mistakenly thought they might get less police harassment. The city of Ann Arbor was liberal, but the rest of Washtenaw County was conservative. The group morphed into the White Panther Party and attracted even more police attention from the Washtenaw County sheriff.

When Mike Millage was asked if Maralynn owed anyone money, he answered the only debt he knew about was twenty-four dollars she owed a girl named Nora. When asked if he knew how to get in contact with Nora, Millage pleaded ignorance.

Detective Canada asked Millage if he and Maralynn were supposed to be married last weekend. Millage quietly answered. He bought her a diamond engagement ring that was missing from her things, but he still had the matching wedding band. Canada asked if police could use the band for evidence if they ever found the engagement ring. Millage agreed and brought it to Ann Arbor police headquarters the next day.

On April 1, Millage was taken to the Redford state police post and given a polygraph test. The examiner stated Millage passed it "unqualifyingly [*sic*]." He appeared to be telling the truth.

———

The Michigan State Police were following another lead that Maralynn Skelton was last seen getting into a light-blue Ford Econoline van with flowers painted on the sides and a Playboy bunny and STP stickers on the back window. A number of calls came in from locations around the state saying such a van was seen in their town. Information was received that a blue van was in for repairs at Arborland Dodge on Washtenaw Avenue. Michigan State Police investigators Winters and Taylor contacted the service manager, Bill McDaniels, and learned the vehicle was repaired on March 11 and returned to its owner on March 17. The vehicle was registered to the Bob Seger System in Southfield, Michigan.

Detective Taylor checked out the vehicle and gave it a clean bill of health. State police ran down every vehicle lead statewide, but they all led nowhere. Even if Maralynn was picked up hitchhiking by a van, she could have been dropped off and picked up again by someone else. Police were no closer to solving this murder than they were the previous three.

Area police ran down every lead in this case from Ann Arbor to Detroit, but they could not find enough evidence to make an arrest. Investigators theorized that Maralynn's murder was related to her drug use and the company she kept. This was the direction Archie and Helen Skelton initially pointed the investigation. After her murder, Maralynn was revealed to be a police informant for the Westland police and the Wayne County Sheriff's Department. Law enforcement could not rule out a drug-related killing. Her murder may have been an example to others who were talking to police.

But some investigators thought it unlikely Maralynn owed some drug dealer twenty-four dollars and paid with her life. The level of emotion and brutality pointed elsewhere. The carnage was too personal and extreme. Furthermore, this was not an isolated message murder but rather one of a series of such murders that pointed to one sinister conclusion: a serial killer was in their midst.

— 5 —

Panic in Small-Town America

AFTER THEIR EXHAUSTIVE INVESTIGATION failed to turn up a prime suspect in the Skelton case, law enforcement was discouraged, especially after another young girl was found murdered twenty-two days later. The latest victim was thirteen-year-old Ypsilanti native Dawn Louise Basom. News of her abduction and murder spread quickly throughout town, sending the city into shock.

Dawn Basom was an eighth grader at West Junior High School in the University Heights area of Ypsilanti—a more affluent residential area than those where Dawn and many of her friends lived. University Heights was adjacent to the western edge of Eastern Michigan University's sprawling campus and was considered the nice part of town. Dawn rode the school bus with her friends, many of whom came from blue-collar families like hers. They migrated to Ypsilanti in search of jobs at the Willow Run Liberator Bomber plant during World War II. When the war ended and the plant closed, many workers made a life for themselves in Ypsilanti. Some found work at the Ford plant in town while others found low-paying jobs at the university. This was the Ypsilanti into which Dawn was born two months premature at Beyer Hospital on November 28, 1955.

The Basom family lived at 1312 LeForge Road in a two-story house with a large, screened front porch overlooking wooded terrain. Their home on the north side of the Huron River was less than a quarter mile away from Eastern's campus. Dawn's father—Louis Junior Basom—died of cancer in 1964 when Dawn was nine years old. She was the youngest of four Basom children and was raised by her mother in a single-parent household. Dawn's older sisters were married with families of their own. Dawn was closest to her brother Louis, who was one year older than she was. She got along well with her family and had no trouble making and keeping friends.

One of Dawn's school friends remembers, "Dawn had many friends and was popular at school. She had a unique bedroom decorated unlike any I had ever seen. The walls had huge decals of guitars and record album covers stapled everywhere. She had a large poster of a guy who resembled Elvis.

"Dawn's mom let kids come over to their house to listen to music. Dawn had lots of slumber parties. Dawn loved to dance, and Mrs. Basom let us have chaperoned mixed parties of boys and girls. Dawn was a sweet, thirteen-year-old girl who looked older than she was."

The Ypsilanti Press reported that Dawn's school records indicated she had a high IQ of 133, but her grades were only slightly above average. Her homeroom teacher Gerald Schielke said, "Dawn was a wholesome girl who associated with a nice group of kids." West Junior High principal

Harold Goodsman described Dawn as "an average-to-good student with a happy disposition."

Although Dawn's hair was naturally light brown, she dyed it reddish blonde the weekend before her death. She was petite at five feet two inches and 120 pounds, with bright blue eyes and a kid's grin. Dawn was athletic and energetic, strong enough to compete with boys her age. Dawn's friends considered her a tomboy, but like other thirteen-year-old girls, Dawn's interests were maturing. She was beginning to outgrow the awkward stage between childhood and womanhood.

A seventeen-year-old neighbor friend of Dawn's, Karen Stapleton, remembered picking up Dawn hitchhiking on West Cross Street a couple of days before her murder. After Dawn settled into the car, Karen asked her what the hell she thought she was doing.

Dawn replied she was meeting friends at Arborland mall where just two weeks before, Maralynn Skelton was last seen hitchhiking before she was murdered.

"Are you stupid, Dawn?"

Without hesitation, Dawn answered, "You and your friends hitchhiked before you could drive. So what's the big deal?"

"The difference now is there is a killer on the loose."

"Yeah, but he's only killing brunettes. I'm a blonde now."

Exasperated, Karen let Dawn out at the mall. Karen saw Dawn for the last time when Dawn was wrestling with her brother on their front lawn. The next day, Dawn went missing.

These are the facts of Dawn's disappearance as they are known. During the early evening on April 15, 1969, Dawn Basom was dropped off in Depot Town by her brother-in-law Robert Hess at the intersection of East Cross and River streets during the early evening. By the 1960s, Depot Town had been neglected for decades. The train no longer stopped to deliver freight or drop off passengers. Parents would warn their children to avoid that part of Ypsilanti.

Before Dawn left home, her mother asked who she was meeting in Depot Town. "A guy named Earl," was her vague reply. When Mrs. Basom asked if Earl had a last name, Dawn dismissed the question, "Yes, but I don't remember it."

Not happy with the answer but not wanting to make an issue of it, Mrs. Basom told Dawn to be careful and get home before dark.

Dawn hurried down the front porch steps at about five o'clock in the afternoon wearing a white plastic jacket, a white cotton blouse, an orange wool sweater, and some blue nylon stretch pants. She was dropped off at Depot Town and met seventeen-year-old Earl K. Kidd. Dawn hung out with him and some other people she knew for about an hour before Earl started walking her home.

Dawn and Earl went through the back parking lot of Depot Town and made their way to the Forest Avenue railroad tracks near the Michigan Ladder factory. Earl says he offered to walk Dawn home, but she told him he did not have to. Dawn may have been concerned her mother would not approve of her hanging out with a male four years older than she was. They waited for a train to pass and they parted. Dawn went west on the tracks toward her home while Earl went east toward where he lived. Dusk was approaching.

On a small footbridge over the Huron River, two of Dawn's friends were fishing. She spoke with them for about five minutes and asked if they would mind walking her home. It was getting dark. The boys declined. When questioned afterward by police, the boys reported Dawn did not act afraid, so they did not think anything about saying no until they learned she had disappeared.

Dawn was last seen at the brief, forty-foot shortcut that leads from the Penn Central tracks to Railroad Street running parallel on the north side of the tracks. A thirty-one-year-old railroad buff who lived on Railroad Street with his maiden aunt was waiting to time the train's arrival, something he did nightly. While standing on a knoll alongside the tracks, he saw Dawn rush past him like she was in a hurry. The train buff told police he last saw her approaching the old Riverside building, used by Ypsilanti City Schools as a storage warehouse and motor pool for district buses and maintenance vehicles.

At that moment, the *Wolverine*—one of the last running passenger trains on the Penn Central line—arrived on schedule at 7:25 p.m. The passenger train stopped on this stretch of track waiting for the track line to be switched before pulling out again in ten minutes. On this evening while the train idled in place, the cook handed the train buff a dinner menu as a souvenir. When interviewed, the cook told police he glimpsed the young girl walking down Railroad Street. Now, investigators could set the last time Dawn Basom was seen at no later than 7:35 p.m. when the train pulled out on schedule.

Dawn was less than a 150 yards from her front porch. Within a brief span of time and distance, she disappeared. The weather service indicated the sun set at 7:15 p.m. that evening, so it was past dusk by the time she rushed home. Either Dawn took a ride from someone because she was late—which is unlikely because she was so close to home—or she was quickly abducted by one or more people and driven to an unknown location. Nobody saw or heard anything. Dawn vanished with the light of day.

When Dawn did not return home by eight o'clock, Cleo Basom began calling her daughter's friends to learn if any of them knew where she might be. None of her friends had seen her. Mrs. Basom's anxiety grew until she called the Ypsilanti police after midnight telling them Dawn had been missing for over five hours.

———

After daybreak, a truck driver going to work saw the body of a young girl lying on the side of Gale Road just north of Vreeland Road. The Michigan State Police Investigative Services was dispatched from Plymouth, Michigan, and arrived on the scene at 7:40 a.m. Washtenaw County sheriff Douglas Harvey was there waiting for them. The body was officially identified on the scene by Sheriff's Deputy Lieutenant William Mulholland. Dawn was one of his daughter's school friends. Late Tuesday night, Mrs. Basom called their home looking for Dawn. Early Wednesday morning, Mulholland was standing over her dead body.

The Michigan State Police complaint report from that morning read:

- The scene was located in Washtenaw County, Superior Township—section 9.
- The victim was on the east side of Gale Road between Vreeland Road and Cherry Hill Road.
- A white female was clothed in a ripped, white

long-sleeved blouse and white brassiere. The above clothing was pulled or pushed upward toward the shoulders and neck. The body was exposed from the breasts down. Her blouse was open in the front. The blouse covered the shoulders and part of the upper back and the full length of the arms. Both sleeves were still buttoned at the wrists.

- There was one piece of insulated electrical wire twisted around the victim's neck.
- The victim was laying on her back with her head to the east. Her legs were spread apart and extended toward the west with the right knee slightly bent.
- The left hand was facing palm up. Both hands of the victim had more than the normal amount of dirt on them.
- The bottoms of both feet had dirt on them. It appeared the victim had walked or had her feet on the ground with no shoes on.
- There was dirt found on the top of the left foot above the big toe.
- There was also more than the normal amount of dirt on her knees.
- There were visible lacerations and puncture wounds to the left breast and lacerations to the chest, stomach, and left thigh.
- A balled-up piece of white cloth was found in the victim's mouth.
- A woman's dark-blue shoe was found on the embankment on the west side of Gale Road across the road from the body.

An hour after police found the first shoe, they located

the second one on the opposite side of Gale Road farther south toward Geddes Road. Police investigators theorized the killer threw one of the shoes out of the driver's side window on the way to the drop site. Then after he deposited the body, he threw the other shoe out the driver's side window returning the same way he had come.

Sheriff's deputies were dispatched to check out every abandoned farm building in the area between the drop site and the victim's home. Three hours into the search, a deputy sheriff found Dawn's orange mohair sweater behind a deserted farm building at 1888 LeForge Road. The site was less than a mile from the victim's home and a scant third of a mile from where Mary Fleszar's body was found on Geddes Road almost two years earlier. The investigation shifted its attention to the barn shell and the dilapidated farmhouse.

When crime scene investigators arrived at the barn, Sheriff Harvey and his men quickly discovered a coil of insulated electrical wire in the barn, the cut edge of which matched the forty inches removed from around the victim's neck. After four unsolved murders of young women in the area, the police felt for the first time they had discovered a murder site.

The state police forensic investigators turned their attention to the abandoned farmhouse facing Geddes Road. They first checked the house for latent palm or fingerprints. The rear outside door on the north side of the building returned negative results. The door frame leading from the south side of the kitchen to the basement had partial latent prints. The door and door frame leading to the basement also had a partial latent finger and palm print. The team processed the entire stairwell leading to the basement and obtained one partial palm print made up of dirt and heavy moisture from the wall. Dawn Basom's finger and palm prints were taken during her autopsy at the University of Michigan Hospital morgue. Forensic investigators were unable to match the latent prints found on the scene with Dawn's inked impressions.

Items removed from the stone floor of the basement were cataloged as evidence. They consisted of two large boards with footwear prints on them, a piece of white cloth, a pair of size 42 blue underpants—not Dawn's—various fabric fibers, one gray button, four white buttons, and numerous pieces of broken glass with evidence of blood spots on them. Recovered near the back of the house was a wad of eight, two-ply tissues containing a crusty, yellowish-white substance and what appeared to be a pubic hair.

University of Michigan forensic pathologists Dr. Robert Hendrix and Dr. Paul Gikas were not able to set the time of death because the victim's body temperature was so low when her body was found. Dawn had not eaten any supper which would have been useful for gauging her time of death. The doctors were certain this victim was not having her menstrual period.

———

On April 17, the Michigan Department of Public Health released its lab report on the chemical and serological analysis of Dawn's blood. It showed no evidence of alcohol or drugs. Dawn had type O blood.

- Three stained cotton vaginal swabs showed the possible presence of seminal fluid, but microscopic examinations of the extracted substance did not reveal spermatozoa.

- An eleven-by-sixteen-inch piece of white fabric with red-brown stains was taken from the mouth of the victim. Chemical and serological analyses indicated type O bloodstains on the cloth but no presence of seminal fluid. The white fabric was crudely slashed and ripped from the tail portion of the victim's blouse.

- An eight-by-fifteen-inch piece of white cotton fabric, the lower left front portion from the blouse, had at least three buttons ripped from it when torn open. The fabric was crudely slashed and cut along the top portion. Tearing was the means of separation along the left side. Type O bloodstains were present on the garment remnant. Chemical analysis did not indicate the presence of seminal fluid.

- Eight two-ply facial tissues, each measuring eight inches by eight inches, found near the back door of the farmhouse had crusty yellowish-white stains and one pubic hair approximately sixty millimeters long. Chemical analysis indicated the stains were seminal fluid. Microscopic examination of the extracted material showed the presence of spermatozoa from a blood type O secretor.

- Microscopic examination and comparison of the pubic hair found in the wad of tissue revealed that it was not similar to pubic hair taken from the victim.

- Four pieces of broken mirror glass with red-brown stains also had type O human blood on them.

The state police laboratory released its report on Tuesday, April 29, 1969. It said:

- The piece of white cloth removed from the mouth

of the victim and the piece of cloth recovered from the farmhouse basement floor were identified as having been at one time part of the victim's blouse.

- Four long blue fibers were recovered from the outside of the victim's blouse. These fibers are dissimilar to fibers that the blouse and bra are made of and dissimilar to known fibers from the blanket used by ambulance attendants. In our opinion, these fibers were not from these sources.

- Fibers recovered from a leaf under the victim's body are red and blue wool fibers and are dissimilar to the fibers in the victim's clothing and known fibers from the two blankets. In our opinion, these fibers did not come from any of these sources.

- Examination of the victim's blouse revealed four missing buttons. The four buttons from the farmhouse basement floor exhibit a size, pattern, and molding similar to the buttons remaining on the blouse, and are sewn with similar cotton thread in the same commercial pattern. In our opinion, they came from the same source.

- The gray button recovered from the farmhouse basement floor is dissimilar to all the buttons on the victim's clothing.

- Fibers adhering to a piece of glass recovered from the farmhouse basement floor include wool, rayon, and nylon and are microscopically similar to fibers the victim's sweater is made from. They could have come from the same source.

- Footwear prints on the two boards recovered from the farmhouse basement were photographed and preserved in the event they have evidential value.

- The dark-blue leather loafers had glass pieces embedded in the soles similar to glass pieces found in the basement of the farmhouse.
- The thirty-seven-inch piece of insulated electrical wire removed from the victim's neck was identified as having been at one time joined together with the end of the electrical wire found in the barn at the crime scene.
- Fibers recovered from the wire around the victim's neck are microscopically similar to known fibers from the victim's sweater and likely came from the same source.

—————

Once the area was cleared of evidence, regular patrols and checks were made of the farmhouse and barn. On May 6, three weeks after Dawn's murder, Michigan State Police investigators George Smith and Ronald Schoonmaker were making a routine check of the crime scene. Schoonmaker saw something on the basement floor he was certain was not there the previous day. He located a simulated-pearl post-type earring with a missing clip that fit the description of the one missing from the victim. They also found a remnant of white cloth that was not there before. It matched Dawn's torn blouse.

Schoonmaker called Sergeant Kennard Christensen, commander of the state police crime lab, and told him what they had found. Christensen was asked if it was possible the lab guys missed something on the basement floor in the farmhouse. Christensen said they had searched it with a fine-tooth comb and taken every scrap of fabric out of the basement. The crime lab commander wanted to compare the found earring with the earring in evidence. The new evidence was turned over to the state police crime lab. The microscopic comparison of the pearl earring taken from the basement floor with the one found attached to Dawn's left ear was similar in all respects. The remnant of white cotton fabric also matched the blouse pieces in evidence. Police were left with one inescapable conclusion: the killer had returned to the scene of the crime and was taunting them.

———

At 3:17 a.m., twenty-nine days after Dawn was murdered, the barn at the crime scene was burning. The timber-framed barn was thirty feet by forty feet and built over a basement. It was only one hundred feet from the abandoned farmhouse and stood next to an adjoining garage where county police had found Dawn's orange sweater.

The Superior Township Fire Department allowed the fully engulfed structure to burn. The smoldering embers were doused so the arson squad could get in and perform their duties. County sheriff officers with two Washtenaw County jail inmates removed the corrugated metal roofing and other debris from the basement floor and searched through them with shovels and rakes. Police feared they might find a body in the rubble, but they made no such discovery. Nothing was found to indicate what started the blaze. Since the arson squad found no evidence of an accidental cause, the fire was deemed arson.

Because arsonists often show up at fires to admire their work, firefighters wrote down the license plate numbers of a couple of suspicious vehicles that came to view the fire at that early hour of the morning. The following day, the state police arrested an Eastern Michigan University student at his apartment at 1431 LeForge Road. He was twenty-one-year-old Ralph R. Krass from Harper Woods. He lived near the Basom home on the same street. State police hoped they had finally captured their killer and expected to make more arrests. But investigators were unable to confirm the arson had anything to do with the murder investigation. Ralph Krass was arraigned and stood mute when District Judge Rodney E. Hutchinson set his bail at $5,000. Unable to post bond, he was taken to the Washtenaw County Jail.

Three days after the arrest of Ralph Krass, his nineteen-year-old roommate Clyde Surrell stood mute as he was charged with aiding and abetting. Surrell was released on a $2,000 bond pending a hearing on the matter. The name of the third suspect was never publicly revealed—perhaps he was a minor and his records were sealed.

Police say Krass admitted walking to the farm with two friends after they had been drinking all night. He went to the barn loft and set some dry hay on fire. The three men ran away but returned by car while the fire department allowed the barn to burn. Firefighters stood by to prevent the farmhouse from catching fire.

When the blaze was extinguished, Ypsilanti press reporter John Cobb looked over the smoldering ruins. He discovered five freshly cut, purple lilac blossoms lying next to each other near the driveway leading to the property. Cobb theorized to police that some person left one for each of the five murdered girls. Police never discovered who left the flowers, but they were more than a little suspicious of John Cobb. He was new to the area and always seemed to turn up at the murder drop sites before other reporters did—sometimes even before the police. When it was discovered his car was equipped with a high-gain antenna and a police-band radio, Cobb produced a permit and showed it to Sheriff Douglas Harvey. Everything checked out to the sheriff's satisfaction except finding who left the lilac blossoms. Was this another police taunt?

After a thorough investigation of the barn burners, authorities charged both men with arson and cleared them of any involvement in the Basom murder. Ralph Krass gave no reason for burning down the barn except he had been drinking. Both men served out their jail sentences.

———

News of Dawn's murder hit Ypsilanti hard. Until recently, the murdered girls came from other parts of the state and were part of the greater university community—except sixteen-year-old Maralynn Skelton, who hung out in the college area of Ypsilanti. Less than three weeks later, Dawn Basom—a hometown girl—was wantonly slaughtered in their midst. Public confidence in local law enforcement plummeted. The police had difficulty finding anyone who would talk to them about Dawn's murder. The citizenry was withdrawn and in shock.

The day after Dawn's body was found, her grief-stricken mother was overwhelmed by the constant parade of police and press looking for clues or tips that might reveal the elusive serial killer. The *Macomb Daily* reported on the Huron Hills apartment complex across from the Basom home on LeForge Road. Reporters Dan Trainor and Cathie Misch wrote, "The road has become a symbol of hatred and animosity for the homeowners toward the riotous apartment complex filled with students from EMU."

They interviewed a neighbor who lived three houses up

from the Basom home. Leon Blackmer reminisced about Dawn playing with his poodles in his front yard. "It's weird, the goings-on over there (Huron Hills)...They (the students) race up and down the road. There are all kinds of weird noises coming from over there. I don't venture out at night."

Another neighbor, twelve-year-old Terri Goddard, did not know Dawn well because Terri's family had just moved into the neighborhood. "I don't like living around here because of the college kids," she said. "Two of them tried to pick me up a couple of weeks ago." The Goddard family had a For Sale sign in their front yard. Mr. Goddard was quoted as saying, "We're getting out of here as quickly as we can." Terri Goddard and her brother last saw Dawn around 5:00 p.m. on Tuesday when she turned and waved to them before going to Depot Town. They learned of Dawn's death Wednesday when the dreadful announcement was made over the public address system at West Junior High School. "There was complete silence," Terri Goddard said.

Dawn's mother Cleo—overwhelmed with grief—could barely rouse herself to attend her daughter's burial on Monday, April 21. She fell apart at the sight as six of Dawn's young classmates bore Dawn's white coffin to her grave.

The day of Dawn's funeral, Sandra Fleszar, a twenty-one-year-old Eastern Michigan University student and sister of Mary Fleszar, the first victim, wrote an open letter to the people of Ypsilanti which ran on the front page of the *Ypsilanti Press*. It was an appeal for the public to stand up and cooperate with police.

To the Public

Have you ever walked from class to class on campus without looking over your shoulder for fear of someone watching you? I haven't!

Have you been able to sleep without awaking in the middle of the night from an endless nightmare? I haven't!

Have you ever had a stranger smile at you and want to smile back, but have been afraid to? I have!

Have you ever driven down Geddes Road without shedding a tear? I haven't!

I am the sister of one of the five victims of the brutal, perverted murders that have taken place in this community within the last two years. My sister was the first—whose sister will be the last?

Many of you will read this letter and pass it off by consoling yourselves with "it could never happen to me." But I believe that after five of these slayings, it should be obvious that the murderer(s) have no respect of persons and that any one of you could be next.

I think it is time for the people of this community to exercise their rights as citizens and do their part to see that justice is brought about.

I am, therefore, making a personal appeal, not only for myself but for all young girls who are forced to live in this constant fear for our very lives. This appeal being that you—the public—come forth with any information you may have, which in some way may be relevant to these murders.

Sincerely, Sandra Fleszar

The appeal worked; tips and clues started coming in. Anyone even remotely suspected or accused in this case was polygraphed. Police checked latent finger and palm prints of at least two hundred potential suspects. Leads came in from wives accusing husbands, anonymous callers trying to implicate others to settle old scores, employers suspecting their employees, and the usual prank and nuisance calls. The underbelly of Ypsilanti was being examined one bit at a time, and it was not pretty.

Investigators began to think the killer might be a policeman or a priest because of his apparent ease in luring his victims to slaughter. One Washtenaw County policeman was suspected and placed under surveillance for a short time. He and another officer were sent out of state to check on some leads while the crime lab searched his personal vehicle and his residence. The county cop came up clean, much to the relief of his fellow officers. Local law enforcement was receiving pointed criticism from the press. The specter of a psychotic rogue cop was the last thing police needed. The unsolved murders were enough of a public relations disaster for the five law enforcement agencies involved with investigating these cases.

— 6 —

The Phantom Killer
Strikes Again

THE GRIM CALCULUS OF serial killers is that as the body count increases, the time between their murderous attacks decreases. Although not an absolute, the period between these murders was shortening. Between the Mary Fleszar and Joan Schell murders almost a full year passed. Eight months later, Jane Mixer was found dead in Denton Cemetery. Five days later, Maralynn Skelton's body was slaughtered and dumped at a construction site. Three weeks after that, thirteen-year-old Dawn Basom was found strangled to death along a country road. The population of Ypsilanti was beside itself. One of their own was a victim of an elusive killer or killers.

After a brief lull, a sixth victim was found two months later on Monday, July 9, 1969. Three teenagers driving along a dirt lane on an abandoned farm saw a nude female body lying in the weeds. Brothers Dale (15) and Dave Christie (17) with their friend Bill Parrish (16) were on their way to cut some lilacs for a local florist. Dale Christie told police, "We couldn't miss her. She was practically in the lane."

This was the sixth murder in the last twenty-two months and the fourth one in the last eighty days. This victim was discovered within a clearly defined fifteen-mile triangular area where all of the bodies were found. Some of the murders may have taken place within this drop zone as well. Other than establishing the body drop area, the Washtenaw County authorities were no closer to solving this string of murders than they were two years before.

The body was lying in two feet of grass-covered ground just off a trail that ran through an abandoned farmyard off North Territorial Road. There was a timber-framed barn skeleton sitting on the property. The victim was 21½ feet from the barn. Investigators noted the body was a white female estimated to be about twenty years old. There was no blood pool under the body, indicating she was killed someplace else.

Some of the victim's clothing was lying about the area. She was still wearing her multicolored, striped raincoat which bore an inside store label from Ruby's of Kalamazoo. Her long-sleeved, purple blouse was partially on her body and buttoned at the sleeves, and her bra was cut up the middle. State police investigators were dispatched to Ruby's. They asked the store manager Mrs. Jones if the store carried any multicolored raincoats like the one described to her, "Three-quarter inch, horizontal striped in purple, red, white, black, pink, and green."

Jones said she carried them for a short time about a year ago and sold out the stock. The store had no record of who bought the coats. Coincidentally, a reporter from the *Kalam-*

azoo Gazette came into Ruby's while the state police were there. The enterprising reporter showed a photograph of the dead girl to all the store's employees. Nobody recognized her.

———

The body was removed from the field at 5:30 p.m. and taken to the University of Michigan hospital morgue. The autopsy was performed by Dr. Robert Hendrix, the only person who had examined each of the murdered girls. There was ample evidence of overkill on the body. Hendrix indicated the cause of death was either a gunshot wound to the top of the head angling back to the spinal column or two deep slashing wounds in the neck area. One stab wound was deep enough to cut a jugular vein and could have caused death at a later time. There were also two chest stab wounds to the heart, one of which could also have been fatal.

There was another bullet wound at the right forehead with entry and exit wounds. It tunneled under the skin but did not penetrate the skull. The victim's right thumb showed signs of a defensive gunshot wound as she tried to shield her face with her hand. The murder weapons were a .22-caliber handgun and a sharp knife with a five-inch-long blade.

———

The morning after this latest Jane Doe was found, Washtenaw County prosecutor William Delhey called a meeting in the county supervisor's office to brief officers from the five police agencies working on the six unsolved murder cases. The prosecutor's summary points were:

- The authorities have no idea who the victim might be. She is a white female with greenish-blue eyes who was wearing contact lenses at the time she was found. She is five feet five inches tall, 135 pounds, and estimated to be anywhere from seventeen to twenty-two years of age.

- Her body was found on Monday by three young men driving across an abandoned farmyard on a deserted lane near Territorial Road in section twenty of Northfield Township. The farmyard is on the south side of the road.

- Autopsy findings are still inconclusive, but the victim was shot two or three times in the head and slashed severely on the neck and stabbed in the left chest. The stab wounds went into her heart, but both neck slashes and the head wounds were also of a fatal nature.

- The victim was raped as sperm cells were present in the victim. She was partially disrobed and her clothing appeared to be expensive. She had a bandana in her hair affixed with a large hairpin with an *A* on it. She also had a ring on each hand. The left hand had a plain, expandable ring, and the right hand had a large ornate ring.

- The victim was wearing a velour raincoat—gaudily striped with an oil-cloth liner. Two velour covered buttons were missing from the raincoat.

- The victim was wearing a purple blouse that was torn open and small pieces were cut out of it. Some of these pieces were lying by her, but others were missing. One pearl-type button was missing.

- The victim had been wearing large, ornamental, dangling earrings that were three and a half inches long. One was still attached and the other was found under her head.

- She was wearing a black brassiere cut in front and dangling loose on either side of her body.
- She had a black lace slip that had been cut at the waistband. The slip was tucked under her buttocks, as she was lying on her back with her legs outstretched and together.
- She had been wearing a white miniskirt which was lying beside her that had been used to do some wiping. An outline of a boot print in blood was visible against the skirt's white fabric.
- The victim was wearing panty hose that were cut in the thigh and crotch area.
- Present near the body was a pair of minibrief panties cut up into separate pieces and stuck between two toes on the right foot.
- Of less consequence, small pin-prick-type punctures were found on the left thigh near the groin area. No shoes were present at the scene. No personal effects were found—with the exception of eight cents in the right hand pocket of her raincoat.
- The gun used is believed to be a .22-caliber revolver, and the victim appears to have a defensive bullet wound on one of her thumbs.

Prosecutor Delhey told the assembled police officers many avenues were being pursued, and he would brief them the next morning with the latest information.

———

The next day, Joseph Kalom of Kalamazoo contacted the Paw Paw state police post and said he believed his daughter might be the murdered girl in Ann Arbor. Then he called the Washtenaw County Sheriff's Department and was notified a positive identification of his daughter had been made. The victim's roommate Elizabeth Rogers was taken to the morgue and identified the body as twenty-one-year-old Alice Elizabeth Kalom from Kalamazoo, Michigan. She resided at 311 Thompson Street in the heart of the University of Michigan campus.

Washtenaw County authorities wanted Mr. and Mrs. Kalom to drive the one hundred miles from Kalamazoo to Ann Arbor so the police could question them about Alice and make arrangements to claim her body. But Mr. Kalom said he could not drive because of a heart condition, and he would not allow his wife to drive because of her state of mind after hearing the devastating news. A shuttle relay was quickly arranged by the county police to take the Kaloms to the Calhoun-Jackson County line, then another squad car drove them to the Washtenaw County line, and finally, Mr. and Mrs. Kalom were taken to university hospital in Ann Arbor. The trip took two hours and fifteen minutes.

Alice's father confirmed the identification of his daughter at 9:30 p.m. On the way out of the hospital basement morgue, Mr. and Mrs. Kalom were met by a throng of waiting reporters. Joseph Kalom vented his grief by lashing out at the University of Michigan.

"I don't want her body. I want her alive. I didn't come here for her body. I'm not going to claim her body. I'm going to tell them (the public) not to go to this university. It's too big. They don't give a damn about anything but money and politics. I'm not going to bury her. Let them bury her on the president's lawn. I've worked too damn hard to raise her, to send her here. I don't want her dead." The following day, arrangements were made by the family to have Alice's body retrieved and laid to rest at Mount Ever Rest Memorial Park in Kalamazoo.

———

On the same day the Kaloms learned of Alice's murder, Lieutenant Stanton Bordine of the Washtenaw County Sheriff's Department asked the Michigan State Police crime lab to process the possible death site of Alice Kalom. Investigators gathered at the entrance of the Washtenaw Sand and Gravel Company driveway on Earhart Road between Joy and Warren Roads in Ann Arbor Township—not far from where Alice's body was found.

Evidence discovered at the scene was measured using a steel post on the south side of the driveway and a tree twenty-two feet south of the post as reference points. All of the items discovered were east of Earhart Road. They included:

- One button from the raincoat, sixteen feet three inches from the tree and seventeen feet four inches from the post.
- A second raincoat button found two inches north of the right shoe.
- One brown, left-footed loafer, size 7, found thirteen feet ten inches from the tree and fifteen feet ten inches from the post.
- One brown, right-footed loafer, size 7, found seventeen feet one inch from the tree and twenty-two feet from the post.
- Blood evidence discovered one-quarter inch below the surface of the gravel thirteen feet two inches from the tree and nineteen feet nine inches from the post. The blood was confined to an area four inches

deep and a circle four inches in diameter. Gravel was taken from a circle four feet in diameter and four inches deep.

- A shoe print found ten feet ten inches southeast of the tree measured 1¾ inches long and 4½ inches wide at the ball of the foot with a heel length of 4 by 3¾ inches wide.

The loafers were taken to the morgue and fit the victim. It was subsequently confirmed they were Alice's shoes. Photographs taken of the evidence were turned over to Staff Sergeant Kennard Christensen of the Michigan State Police crime lab the following morning.

Investigators discovered Alice Kalom was last seen late Saturday, June 7, or early Sunday morning, leaving a party of over two hundred people held at the Depot House at 416 South Ashley Street in Ann Arbor. The Depot House was a converted railroad passenger-freight station that rented out as a rehearsal hall for local bands or for private parties. There was a birthday party for a local musician that night. Some witnesses at the party claimed they saw Alice dancing with a longhaired hippie while others who knew Alice said a woman who looked like her was there. These people thought she never made it to the party, but they were not sure. The ambiguity did not give the police any useful information.

Percy Lee Claiborne was at the Depot House that night and was questioned by police. He was given a polygraph test as were many of the people who were there that night. Claiborne admitted dating Alice and being intimate with her on occasion. He stated he did not see her at the Depot House. On his polygraph, he was asked: "Did you know her? Did you see her at the Depot House that night? Did you leave with her that night? Did you kill her?" The polygraph examiner believed Claiborne told the truth on all counts.

The Ann Arbor Police Department received information by telephone that two young women—the Patterson sisters—were at the Depot House the night Alice Kalom disappeared and had seen her. Despite being two weeks slow with the information, they were willing to talk to someone in authority about the matter. Assistant Prosecutor Booker T. Williams, Chief John Hayes of the Eastern Michigan University police, and Sergeant Fred Carpenter of the Michigan State Police questioned the girls. Their mother was also present for the interview.

Gloria Patterson and her sister Beverly were at the Depot House dancing. While there, Gloria saw a girl she thought looked like the murdered girl in the newspaper photograph. Gloria insisted she knew for sure this was the same girl at the dance party that night.

Gloria said that while cooling off outside the Depot House, she saw this girl making out with a guy who had his hand under her skirt. Gloria was close enough to overhear him ask her to go with him and she said no. Gloria and her friends went back into the Depot House and danced some more. At about 3:30 a.m., she went out again to get some fresh air and saw this same girl and guy get into a red Volkswagen. Gloria was about ten feet from the girl and said she got a good look at her.

When Prosecutor Williams asked Patterson for more information about the vehicle, Gloria said the guy drove and the girl sat in the front passenger seat. There was another person sitting in the back seat. She was unable to describe that person. There was nothing unusual about the red Volkswagen except there was something wrong with one of the headlights. The car left the Depot House and turned right on Ashley Street.

When asked to describe the young woman, Gloria said she was wearing a purple silk blouse with buttons, a white hip-hugger miniskirt, and nylons. She had no coat or jacket on or with her. She appeared to have shoulder-length brown hair and no pony tail. Gloria remembered the girl may have had a headband worn close to the top of her head. She had no memory what kind of shoes the girl was wearing.

The person she described as the girl's boyfriend looked to be about twenty-three years old and six feet tall, with a slim build and long brown hair with a beard and mustache. He was wearing black motorcycle boots about sixteen inches high with tight green corduroy pants, a plaid button-up shirt, and no coat or jacket. The shirt appeared to be multicolored, lightweight cotton. Patterson stated she was at the dance with her boyfriend, James Roberts, and he might be able to give more information about the couple.

James Roberts of Ypsilanti was located and agreed to be questioned at the Ypsilanti post on June 24 by Chief John Hayes of the Eastern Michigan campus police and Sergeant Frederick M. Carpenter of the Michigan State Police. Roberts said he worked the afternoon shift at the Ford plant and arrived at the Depot House close to midnight. He stated he went to the party with four friends from Ypsilanti. He did not go with Gloria Patterson but caught up with her later in the evening. He did dance with her and was with her outside the Depot House near the parking lot. He said he saw a few white girls were there but none who resembled Alice Kalom. If he knew anything more, he would tell them.

When Roberts was told what Gloria Patterson had seen, he said he did not remember seeing the girl or any heavy petting going on between her and another person. Roberts did not see anyone drive away in a Volkswagen either. He gave police the names of the Ypsilanti friends he went with to the party: Otis Gregory, Walter Gripps, Eddie Addie, and John Walker. All of their stories checked out.

———

- Investigators believed this sex slaying could be the work of more than one male because of the inordinate amount of semen found in her body. Police were sickened and baffled. The official lab report on the physical evidence obtained from the scene indicated:

- The cotton suede coat exhibited heavy bloodstaining on the inside back with very light staining on the outer back. The top two buttons were missing and two round cloth-covered buttons remained on the coat. The third button fastening loop was pulled out at the seam on one end. The two buttons recovered on Earhart Road were similar in all respects to the buttons remaining on the coat and could have come from the same source.

- The white cotton skirt was cut the entire length of the front two inches left of center at the top to three and a half inches right of center at the bottom. The skirt had numerous bloodstains both front and back. At least one of these stains was put on the skirt after it was cut. The skirt had black smudges both inside and out that appeared to be partial shoe imprints. The imprint had a wavy pattern and appeared to be caused by a greasy material.

- The pair of panties was cut from the top portion of each leg through the waistband.
- The black panty slip was cut from the waistband through each leg of the garment.
- The black brassiere was still hooked in the back but was cut in the middle approximately two inches left of center.
- The lavender blouse was heavily bloodstained at the collar area but exhibited no bloodstaining on the back. There were five imitation pearl buttons remaining on the blouse, with the top two buttons missing. The buttons had been forcibly removed. The button found under the victim's head was similar in all respects to the remaining buttons on the blouse. The piece of lavender cloth found near the victim's left leg was identified as having come from this blouse. The blouse was cut near the button line from the bottom up about nine inches.
- The nylon panty hose were cut on the left waistband and badly torn in the crotch area.
- The section of skin tissue from the right thumb exhibited a hole, characteristic of a bullet entrance wound. Microscopic examination revealed small lead deposits; however, no gun powder residue was found.
- The section of scalp tissue exhibited no gun powder residue; however, small lead deposits were discovered. From an examination of the fired bullet, the thumb tissue, the scalp tissue, and the skull of the

victim, it was apparent the bullet passed through the thumb before entering the head.

- The brown loafer shoes from the scene were size 7, similar to those worn by the victim. The soil deposits on the left shoe appeared extremely wet. The right loafer had a pad of toilet tissue placed inside over the heel area. It had the same pink pattern design as toilet tissue found in the Kalom apartment.
- The bullet removed from the head of the victim was from a .22 caliber long rifle with six lands and grooves that spun the bullet clockwise.

The bullet exhibited the same rifling specifications as the bullet removed from the head of earlier victim Jane Mixer, thought by many to be the third victim. Due to the extreme damage to the Mixer bullet and the differences in the ammunition used, it was impossible to render an opinion whether the same weapon fired both bullets.

———

In a search of Kalom's three-room flat, Alice's bedroom was tidy—none of her belongings was missing. Cash and identification were found inside her wallet and her purse was undisturbed. Robbery was ruled out as a motive. Police wondered why she would leave the house without her purse and driver's license. An empty Jacobson's shoe box found on the floor with a receipt in it revealed Kalom purchased a pair of purple dress shoes Saturday afternoon before she left for the Depot House.

University of Michigan student Ben Cologie and Alice Kalom were good friends who took a photography class together over the summer session. They were shooting a photo essay about decaying farmhouses and barn skeletons in the countryside surrounding Ann Arbor. On Friday night, they developed the film at Alice's apartment in a closet converted into a darkroom. They made some prints with a photo enlarger he brought over, and then he went home. When Alice did not return home over the weekend to finish their project, he called the Ann Arbor police reporting her missing. That Monday afternoon, Alice's body was discovered.

The police asked Cologie to come to Ann Arbor police headquarters on East Huron Street, so they could take a more detailed report. Once there, Cologie was taken to the university hospital basement morgue and asked to identify Alice's body. Her roommate, Elizabeth Rodgers, had already made a tentative identification. Police could not be positive because Rodgers looked away in horror and only said, "I think so."

"They pulled out the slab," Cologie remembers. "She [Alice] had been outside for a couple of days. Her eyes were wide open, her skin discolored, a bullet wound in her forehead. That vision of Alice dead on the slab is something I will never forget. I identified her and the cop said to the morgue tech, 'Go tag her' and coldly walked away. The police held me overnight and different police departments took turns interrogating me in teams."

While Cologie was being questioned, investigators searched Alice's Thompson Street flat and came upon a photo of Alice's head in a noose. When investigators returned and showed him the photo, Cologie shuddered. "We were taking photos at an abandoned farmhouse off Pontiac Trail for a project Alice and I were working on. Hanging from the ceiling was a length of electrical cord looped at one end like a noose. Alice placed her head inside and asked me to take the photo. She thought it would make a great gag shot." Police investigators were not amused. Alice's body was found not far from that farmhouse.

"The police had no decency or politeness and asked overly personal questions about our sexual relationship," Cologie said. "I had to repeat things over and over. Four departments were working on the case and didn't seem to be sharing information. I was harassed so badly I wished I had never known Alice." After he established his alibi, police released him. "Someone leaked my name to the press. I lost a lot of friends over the media mess," he remembers.

The police and forensic investigators were amassing a growing body of evidence. They discovered their second murder site where they recovered blood and tissue evidence. They found a pair of loafers and raincoat buttons that linked Kalom to the site. But without a viable suspect, what good were they?

— 7 —

The Psychic

SOME PEOPLE THOUGHT IT was supernatural how each girl disappeared without a trace until her body was found at a drop site in farm country outside Ypsilanti. The investigators had little physical evidence to work with. A task force was formed and a headquarters set up at the vacated Holy Ghost Fathers' Catholic Seminary on Washtenaw Avenue, halfway between Ypsilanti and Ann Arbor. This site had easy access to both university towns. The vacated seminary was transformed into a crime center called the Washtenaw County Citizens Service Center. Michigan State Police chief of detectives Captain Dan Myre was appointed leader of the task force comprised of fifty detectives from five area police agencies.

The purpose of the task force was to share and coordinate information to make better use of manpower. Investigators from the Michigan State Police, the Washtenaw County Sheriff's Department, the Ypsilanti police, the Ann Arbor police, and the Eastern Michigan University campus police were now housed under the same roof. There had been too much duplication of effort and fragmented information sharing. Seeing the authorities getting organized made the public feel like progress was being made. However, law enforcement was no closer to apprehending this killer who had been eluding them since the Fleszar murder.

Washtenaw County had a stealthy psychopath on the loose. This series of six savage murders hit Ypsilanti hard. Four of the six victims were from the EMU campus area. All of the bodies were found within a ten-mile radius of one another, with the exception of Jane Mixer whose body was found five miles east of Ypsilanti. A modus operandi was forming, but could the police capture the killer before he struck again? This was the question preying on everyone's mind. Arresting this homicidal maniac became the personal quest of every law enforcement officer in Washtenaw County, but none more than the county sheriff, Douglas Harvey.

———

The last thing the police needed was a media circus, but Trans-Love Energies—a counterculture group led by local hippie guru John Sinclair—had other ideas. The large Victorian residence Sinclair leased at 1520 Hill Street housed the Trans-Love Energies commune and was the headquarters of their counterculture political wing called the White Panther Party. During the week of June 16 to 20, 1969, what started as a routine protest for rent control soon grew into a mass protest of generalized grievances. It was not long before the civil disobedience degenerated into a street riot. The *Ann Arbor News* dubbed the ruckus the Battle of Ann Arbor. The disruptions lasted for three days. Most of the people arrested were members of Trans-Love Energies and the White Panther Party. They were identified collectively as "outside agitators."

The Washtenaw County sheriffs were commanded by their no-nonsense leader, Douglas Harvey. Simply known by the counterculture as Harvey, he was elected to two terms as Washtenaw County sheriff (1964–1972) and was an act-now-question-later, law-and-order sheriff. He gained his police experience through on-the-job training as a patrolman with the Ypsilanti Police Department.

Earlier in his life, Doug Harvey was a popular stock-car driver on the local racing circuit. He would find a sponsor with a fast car and make a deal with its owner. He would hand over the prize money but keep the trophies. *Ann Arbor News* correspondent William B. Treml reported on May 27, 1967 that Doug Harvey won over one hundred races in his fifteen years of stock-car racing and demolished a total of eight cars. He was a fan favorite.

Bolstered by his popularity, he made a run for Washtenaw County sheriff and won on the coattails of President Lyndon B. Johnson's landslide Democratic win. Harvey was the second-youngest man to hold this elective office in Washtenaw County, a conservative stronghold that had not elected a Democrat sheriff in thirty years. On January 1, 1964, thirty-two-year-old Douglas Harvey took office when he beat his former boss out of his job.

It did not take long for Sheriff Harvey to make his influence felt. The county jail under his reign was called Harvey's Hotel because longhairs booked for the night—or longer—could expect a haircut at the taxpayers' expense. After getting out of jail, some of Harvey's first customers complained publicly that a murderer had cut their hair.

"True enough," Sheriff Harvey explained to the press, "but the man was also a barber."

After that bit of publicity, the sheriff kept a professional barber on call who specialized in buzz cuts. Harvey told the press the haircuts were for lice control. The sheriff enjoyed his notoriety, and his constituents generally approved of his methods. Conservative residents were tired of the glut of young outsiders whom they viewed as nothing more than vagrants and troublemakers drawn to the local universities by the drugged-out hippie subculture. Many county residents felt these interloping punks needed some head busting. Sheriff Harvey did not disappoint them.

Tired of the persistent harassment focused upon him and his followers, John Sinclair entertained an idea from a member of his group Archie Allen. Allen thought it somehow supernatural that so many young women were being murdered by a phantom not leaving so much as a clue in his wake. Allen informed Sinclair he recently read a book called *Psychic* by Peter Hurkos. The idea of contacting Los Angeles psychic Peter Hurkos originated at this time. Maybe the psychic could help the bungling police. What harm could it do? The popular belief was that since Peter Hurkos was instrumental in helping the Boston police solve the Boston Strangler killings, he might be able to help with these cases.

The group started raising money to lure the Dutch psychic to Ann Arbor. The recent depiction of Hurkos in *The Boston Strangler* movie and his show-business hype of being the world's "first police psychic" made him the perfect choice. Trans-Love Energies could get some positive publicity and embarrass the local police at the same time. If there was a break in this case, who would be the heroes then?

Twenty-nine-year-old business entrepreneur Archie Allen was the front man for the group. He called Peter Hurkos's agent and business manager in Los Angeles— Barbara Silver. Allen asked her if Hurkos might be interested in looking into a string of unsolved murders of young women in Washtenaw County. Barbara Silver said she would ask and get back with him.

The *Detroit Free Press* reported on Sunday, July 6, that Hurkos initially wanted a guaranteed minimum of $5,000 plus expenses before he would get on a plane and fly to Ann Arbor. The psychic injured his leg the month before while searching for a lost hunter in the Sierras and was still walking on crutches. Hurkos did not want to fly to Ann Arbor, but Barbara Silver convinced him to do it. She also agreed to send her husband Edward to act as his spokesperson and relieve some of the pressure.

The Ann Arbor group did not have that kind of money, so the deal fell through. A week later, Archie Allen called back offering $1,100 with no added expenses. It was all they could raise. Archie Allen put up the bulk of the money himself.

Barbara Silver knew there was no real money to be made for her client, but she was finding it harder and harder to book nightclub and talk-show appearances for him because he was suffering from media overexposure, and his nightclub act was getting stale. There was a glut of celebrity psychics in the sixties and the public was losing interest. The Dutch psychic relied on his nightclub act and $200 private readings to Hollywood celebrities to pay expenses. Silver knew she needed something to bolster Peter's sagging career and thrust the fifty-eight year old back into the spotlight. With some coaxing, she got Hurkos to accept the $1,100 to cover airfare and expenses for a week. Hurkos agreed this Michigan case might get his name back in the papers.

Later that day, Silver called Ann Arbor from Los Angeles saying Peter Hurkos had agreed to look into the case. Archie Allen headed over to the Trans-Love Energies commune with the news. Tired of being harassed by the Washtenaw County sheriff, John Sinclair and his group of self-styled psychedelic rangers wanted to show the public they had a sense of civic duty and responsibility. They hoped their participation in capturing the serial killer might make them less suspicious, given that the police, the press, and the public generally assumed the killer was a drug-crazed hippie. Sinclair and his tribe did not want or need the unwarranted attention. They hoped this show of public cooperation might improve the group's public image.

Dutchman Peter Hurkos was the world's foremost psychic according to his advertisements. In 1941, he fell from a ladder while painting a building and took a four-story plunge to the street. Hurkos was rushed to Zuidwal Hospital where he spent three days in a coma. He allegedly awoke with the gift of inner vision, popularly known as extrasensory perception (ESP). His publicity material claimed he had the ability "to pierce the barriers separating the past, present, and future."

He originally garnered public notice when he was arrested for his participation in the Dutch resistance during World War II. Despite his extrasensory gift, he was captured and imprisoned in Buchenwald, the Nazi prisoner-of-war camp. After the war, Queen Juliana of the Netherlands decorated Hurkos and seven other Dutch underground war heroes. A sculpture dedicated to them was erected in Rotterdam that still stands in the public square.

As the recipient of many honorary police badges from around the world for his meritorious service in helping solve crimes, Hurkos leveraged his European notoriety and began billing himself as the world's first psychic detective. The most notable case early in his career was the Stone of Scone theft from Westminster Abbey in 1950. Hurkos and several others were allowed to view the crime scene.

Hurkos did so at his own expense without official authorization and made a cold reading of the area. Thanks to the French press and Hurkos's adroit self-promotion, his movements were described in great detail as he investigated the scene. Peter Hurkos told reporters the theft was a prank, and the stone would soon be found. In just over a week's time, Scotland Yard recovered the stone, and Hurkos was proven correct. The French public was impressed with the psychic's predictions and helped make him a celebrity in Europe.

By the end of the decade, Hurkos migrated to the United States and developed a supper-club act based on his notoriety in solving crimes from around the world. Most of his claims were anecdotal and lacked documentation. Peter Hurkos gained widespread media attention in America after he was the subject of a *One Step Beyond* episode—ABC television network's version of CBS's popular *The Twilight Zone*.

In 1961, Peter Hurkos wrote an autobiography with a ghost writer entitled *Psychic*. He told of the origin of his gift of second sight and then related numerous examples of his most notable cases. Early in his book, Hurkos informs his readers that his strange gift has baffled and astounded scientists and researchers throughout the world. "I am what parapsychologists refer to as a psychic. I am sensitive to people and events that concern them. I have been told by scientists that my psychic gift is—so far as they know—the most highly developed in the world."

Hurkos claimed to read vibrations through a phenomenon known as psychometry. He compared his gift with the famous 'Sixth Sense' of history and legend. He defined psychometry as the ability to visualize past associations of physical objects by touching them to create a mental image from vibrations given off by the objects. Hurkos's method fell awkwardly within the psychic realm of ESP, which was a popular belief of New Age proponents in the 1960s. Hurkos claimed to be sensitive to emanations that were similar to heat waves, radio waves, and electric impulses. These vibrations could come from:

- an object a person has touched
- a piece of clothing a person has worn
- a bed a person has slept in
- anything a person is associated with
- even a photograph of a person

Sometimes, Hurkos would get a strong reading from objects; other times he would not. His disclaimer was he had no control over his gift. In his book, Hurkos cites other people from history who had inner vision. He mentions the prophet Isaiah in the Bible, the prophecies of Nostradamus four hundred years ago, and Edgar Lee Cayce, a famous twentieth-century sensitive. Hurkos actually criticizes Nostradamus for vague predictions, saying "I have never claimed more than 85.5 % accuracy in my readings, as established by scientists performing thousands and thousands of tests with me."

––––––

In 1964, Hurkos interjected himself in the Boston Strangler case much to the displeasure of the Boston Police Department. Hurkos hoped to scare up a lead and solve the case. After impersonating a police investigator, he harassed a troubled but innocent man who had to be institutionalized afterward. Hurkos was arrested by the Boston police and warned charges would be pressed if he did not leave town. According to a Boston police spokesperson, the department did not call Hurkos to consult on the case, and he added nothing positive to solving the case.

Hurkos projected his failure onto an uncooperative Boston Police Department and then left town under duress, but not before proclaiming to the press that Albert DeSalvo was innocent of the Boston murders. A few years after this public defeat, Hurkos was hired for one day as a technical advisor on *The Boston Strangler* movie while actor George Voskovic portrayed him on the screen. Whether Hurkos helped on the Boston Strangler case or not, he was reaping the rewards of free publicity doing much to rehabilitate his media reputation. This movie depiction helped convince Trans-Love Energies to invite Hurkos to Washtenaw County and try his hand at solving this case under the noses of the local police.

––––––

On the evening of July 21, 1969, Archie Allen drove to Detroit's Metropolitan Airport to pick up Peter Hurkos and drive him to the Inn America motor lodge. Hurkos hobbled off the commercial jetliner and down the runway ramp on his crutches accompanied by Edward Silver as prearranged. The predictable media circus erupted, and Hurkos snapped to life after his six-hour flight. "This killer knows I come for him," the psychic was quoted in the *Detroit News*. "And I get him! Maybe he comes after me, so. But Hurkos is not afraid." With only one foot firmly planted on the ground, the boastful Hurkos jumped into the middle of this three-ring circus.

This bit of bravura amid the snapping of photographers' flashbulbs got Hurkos off to a rousing good start. There was no way he could afford all the publicity he was receiving, so he made the most of it. He was there "to exorcise the demon from Washtenaw County" and free its anxious residents from the grip of fear. Predictably, the local police were annoyed and resentful while the Washtenaw County Prosecutor's Office was cautiously skeptical.

After the press conference, Archie Allen drove Hurkos and Silver to the motor lodge on the southeastern outskirts of Ann Arbor and helped Hurkos with his luggage. As soon as they were safely in their first-floor suite, Hurkos threw the crutches on the bed and walked around the suite normally. That was the last time Archie Allen saw Hurkos for the rest of the psychic's visit.

The following morning after viewing photographs brought by police, Hurkos and Silver went with Prosecutor William Delhey and a small police escort to tour the murder and drop sites north of Ypsilanti. Nothing new was discovered. Hurkos told reporters the sites were cold. The psychic wanted to handle evidence, but the prosecutor explained that legal issues involving chain of custody precluded that possibility.

From there, the small entourage went to McKenny Union on Eastern Michigan's campus where Hurkos picked up some vibrations from a pay phone in the lobby. Afterward, they cruised Depot Town in Ypsilanti and turned down River Street. The youngest victim in this string of murders was last seen walking down the railroad tracks leading to her home. Hurkos tried to use his psychometric sixth sense to pick up vibrations, but nothing happened. Hurkos wanted to handle evidence belonging to the victims to see if he could read something from it. Prosecutor Delhey politely refused again. Arrangements were made with Dawn Basom's mother for Hurkos to see Dawn's bedroom and allow him to handle some of her clothing hanging in her closet. Try as he might, Hurkos could not pick up any vibrations and became frustrated.

On Wednesday morning, Hurkos received a phone call in his suite from a male warning him to get out of town before he had "fresh blood on his hands." Whether this phone call was a prank or a taunt, Karen Sue Beineman disappeared sometime before one o'clock that afternoon.

Hurkos interpreted the call as a personal message to him. He now became a player in this Greek tragedy. He hoped to become a modern-day Tiresias, the blind prophet of ancient Thebes tapping his way to the truth. For the police, this was an affront that became a horrible premonition. For the murderer, it became the self-fulfilling prophesy of a man who would play God.

———

At 11:15 p.m., Mrs. Verna (Ma) Carson, resident advisor at Downing Hall, a women's residence dormitory at the university, phoned the EMU campus police. One of her girls was missing—Karen Sue Beineman, a freshman out past curfew who had not been seen since lunchtime. A report was taken and tacked on the bulletin board at campus police headquarters with a copy sent over to the Ypsilanti police. It was not until the next morning that action was taken on the missing-person report.

Friday evening, Hurkos and Silver—with an undercover police escort—went out to observe the Ann Arbor nightlife. Maybe the murderer would strike at Hurkos himself. The small cadre of men toured the areas of town connected with the two University of Michigan victims who lived in the campus area.

The *Detroit News* reported in their Saturday morning, July 26, 1969 edition that at one o'clock in the morning, "Peter Hurkos left his motel room with five policemen for a meeting with John Sinclair, the man responsible for bringing Hurkos to town. Hurkos wanted to meet his benefactor, and Sinclair wanted the psychic's take on the murder situation. The two men were known to discuss police harassment, but no report of what else they talked about was made known." A *Detroit News* photographer took a picture to commemorate their brief meeting.

While Hurkos and Silver were observing the Ann Arbor nightlife, a note addressed to "Dutch psychic/Peter Hurkos" was left at the front desk of the Inn America. When Hurkos finally returned, the desk clerk told him that shortly after midnight, a man about six feet tall with short hair slid the note across the counter. The clerk said she did not get a good look at him because she was busy helping someone else. "He said it was important and left," she said.

The note stated there was "something interesting" at a burned-out cabin on Weed Road north of Ypsilanti.

Hurkos felt strong vibrations emanating from the paper, so he notified the police. On the merits of Hurkos's positive feelings, a squad of investigators made a midnight run in a driving rainstorm to the remote area where most of the bodies were dumped. After an hour of riding up and down Weed Road looking for a burned-out cabin that didn't exist, the police were tired of Peter Hurkos and his clairvoyant act.

———

Saturday afternoon, July 26, at 4:21 p.m., while going out to the road with his wife to get the mail, Dr. Conrad Mason spotted the nude body of a young woman about twenty feet off Riverside Drive in a deep gully. The body looked like it had rolled down the embankment with some force. Dr. Mason rushed to his house and phoned the Washtenaw County Sheriff's Department. Within minutes, Sheriff Harvey was on the scene in an unmarked car. Radio silence was immediately established. Harvey used Dr. Mason's private telephone to call the Ann Arbor police and the county medical examiner.

The discovery of the body was kept from the press. Operation Stakeout was implemented. As soon as the body was found, Sheriff Harvey saw an opportunity to trap the killer. Twice before, he wanted to do this with earlier victims, but both times the plan was leaked by the press. Police knew the killer had returned to the drop site of Mary Fleszar and to the farmhouse basement where Dawn Basom was murdered. The police planned to stake out the wooded area and wait for the murderer to return, then they would spring their trap. The plan seemed simple enough.

After the medical examiner determined the cause and

approximate time of death of the victim, the state police crime lab forensic team arrived. While they were collecting evidence and flinching at the brutality of the killing, Prosecutor William Delhey showed up unexpectedly to survey the scene. He listened patiently to Sheriff Harvey's plan and reluctantly agreed to it. The sheriff wanted to use the body as bait, but the beleaguered prosecutor would not allow the body to remain prey to nature and the elements. Out of common decency and compassion for the family, the body needed to be removed.

Insect infestation was extensive, and there was another issue troubling the prosecutor. It had been four hours since Karen Sue Beineman's body was found, and her parents had not been notified. The body was officially a Jane Doe, but everyone knew who the victim was. The sheriff argued for more time, convinced his plan would work and they could end this nightmare. The natural cover was ideal for a stakeout. Prosecutor Delhey agreed to wait until a positive identification came from the coroner's office, and then Karen's parents would be notified.

The revised plan was for prosecutors William Delhey and Booker T. Williams to go over to the J. C. Penney at nearby Arborland mall and borrow a female mannequin. Because the area was heavily wooded and it would be dark, the prosecutors hoped the murderer would be fooled. Sheriff Harvey was frustrated and told the prosecutors to do whatever they wanted. The stakeout was their show now. The sheriff later insisted he was not involved with the mannequin part of the plan, though some of his men did participate in the stakeout.

After prosecutors Delhey and Williams explained the situation to a confused J. C. Penney manager, they chose a mannequin about the same size and hair color as Karen. They personally carried the decoy down the ravine and positioned it in the same configuration as Karen's body. They hid the jointed areas with loose ground cover to make the mannequin look more real. Everyone hoped it might deceive the killer and draw him into their trap. The prosecutors looked up from the gully at the figure of Sheriff Harvey looking down on them.

"It might work," he said.

A surveillance team of nine officers staked out the area to see if anyone approached the gully. Seven of them hid behind the natural cover, while two stayed on Dr. Mason's screened front porch which became the command center. The area was cleared of all police cars except for a couple of strategically parked, unmarked cars. Everyone took their places.

What happened next is open for dispute. After a miserable evening of swarming mosquitoes, the clouds burst forth about 11:30 p.m. Half a dozen officers dressed in SWAT uniforms were being eaten alive when one of them asked over the walkie-talkie for some insect repellent or some netting or something. The terse reply was, "No! Don't reveal your positions."

Then at about 12:15 a.m., Eastern Michigan University officer John Maxwell saw a lone runner jog by the gully and disappear in the downpour. The jogger was wearing a jacket or a loose-fitting shirt. He ran up Huron River Drive, where other officers should have been ready to apprehend him. Sheriff's Deputy Basil Baysinger, who was stationed near Maxwell, said he may have seen something also, but he could not be sure with the heavy rain. They radioed it in, but there was only static on the air. The police radio malfunctioned or the receiver was turned off.

By the time the other officers were alerted, the two drenched officers ran after the suspect. Then they heard a car start up around the bend of Riverside Drive and fade off on Huron River Drive. By the time a squad car was in pursuit, the phantom runner and car were gone.

When Sheriff Harvey heard about the bungled operation, he was not interested in excuses. Three officers swore they saw a jogger but were unsuccessful in apprehending the suspect. When the press found out the next day, they freely ridiculed the farce. Sheriff Harvey took it personally when *Detroit Free Press* reporter Walker Lundy wrote an editorial account on July 27, 1969 of the botched stakeout:

> Governor Milliken acted not a moment too soon in taking charge of the Washtenaw manhunt. He has put Colonel Frederick Davids, state police director, in command of all the police forces and asked the FBI to join the search.
>
> Despite the fact that seven young women have been murdered in the Ann Arbor-Ypsilanti area in slightly more than two years—the last five at a rate of one a month—the governor gave local police every chance to find the murderer or murderers. But the Keystone Kops atmosphere of the past few weeks, especially since the seventh slaying a week ago, was too much.
>
> Sheriff Douglas Harvey, Ann Arbor Police Chief Walter Krasny, and Washtenaw Prosecutor William Delhey have apparently been barely on speaking terms. Though Delhey was officially in charge, he was not told what Harvey's department was doing. Chief Krasny was frequently left in the cold. The

sheriff's stake out Saturday night, using a department store mannequin in place of the body of the seventh victim, flopped although a suspect came within touching distance of the "body."

The problem seems to be one that could not be solved without state intervention. Prosecutor Delhey cannot afford to anger Sheriff Harvey simply because he must work with him. Sheriff Harvey, despite his limited police experience, is considered one of the most powerful political figures in the county. Both are subject to mandates of the electorate.

What was required was a coordinated search by experienced experts who are not involved in the local politics, not running for office, and not looking for glory. This the search will get under the direction of Col. Davids.

Governor Milliken's action certainly is no guarantee of an early solution to these cases, or even a solution at all. But at least the people of Washtenaw County can now know that they have the best possible help, and the people in charge are looking for killers, not glory.

The original plan was Doug Harvey's, but the stakeout was an embarrassing failure for local law enforcement. Several theories were developed to explain what happened to the lone runner. The most dramatic was that the suspect waded through the cattails and marshland until he swam across the Huron River to safety. Nobody knew what happened to the jogger. The evening was a public relations disaster for everyone connected with it. The "Keystone Kops" remark hit home the hardest for the presumed mastermind of this failed attempt at sleuthing—Sheriff Harvey. Rather than issue no comment to the press or shrink into the background, those involved called a press conference for 8:00 a.m. Sunday in which Sheriff Harvey and the rest of the crime center leadership would own up to their mistakes.

Later Sunday morning at Inn America, a reporter who was at the press conference informed Hurkos another body was found on Saturday. The reporter asked Hurkos for a statement because he was so close to the investigation. Hurkos became enraged. Twelve hours had passed since the body was discovered. Hurkos felt he was deliberately kept out of the loop and took it personally. He called Ann Arbor police chief Walter Krasny and asked to be taken to the body drop site for a fresh reading. Hurkos was convinced he could find something the police with all their training could not.

"That is out of the question!" said Sheriff Harvey, and he further instructed Ann Arbor police chief Krasny to "keep that gentleman away from this crime scene until it is finished being processed. It's my case!" Chief Krasny, not wanting a confrontation with the aggravated sheriff, simply ignored him and left to pick up Hurkos.

To pacify and calm the Dutchman, Krasny allowed him to view the drop site, but under the glaring eyes of Sheriff Harvey. Hurkos did not sense any revelations—only resentment. Hurkos got down on all fours with his hands spread wide and surveyed the area where Beineman's body had been. Try as he might, the psychic's ESP powers could not get past his anger and contempt for Sheriff Harvey. The tired Dutch psychic was frustrated and insulted the sheriff had given him the brush-off. Hurkos told Silver, "We go now."

On Sunday evening, Peter Hurkos and Ed Silver boarded

a plane to Los Angeles. In a brief Metropolitan Airport interview, Hurkos said overall he was pleased with how he was treated by authorities, but the county sheriff's attitude was intolerable and interfered with his methods. Nonetheless, Peter Hurkos vowed to return.

Other than a sideshow distraction giving the press something different to write about, Peter Hurkos's visit was inauspicious. He went back to California without the fanfare of the conquering hero. Once again, he was no help to the police. But Peter Hurkos was true to his word: when the money ran out, he went home, but apparently without paying his hotel bill. After some bad publicity, Archie Allen cleared the debt at the Inn America.

— 8 —

A Break in the Case

KAREN SUE BEINEMAN WAS an effervescent eighteen-year-old graduate of Criston High School in Grand Rapids, Michigan. Rather than enjoy a leisurely summer before beginning her college career, Karen attended Eastern Michigan University's summer session, so she could get her choice of dormitories and rooms for the fall semester. Karen chose Downing Hall, one of the newest dorms. It had a great location facing the heart of EMU's campus.

Karen was eager to prepare for a career in special education. She was determined to make a difference in the lives of handicapped children and was overjoyed with the promise and freedom of her new life. Karen was also in a steady relationship with James "Duffy" Dwyer—a twenty-four-year-old high school counselor at Saint Clement Catholic School. She considered herself engaged, but they had no immediate plans to marry. Karen wanted to finish her college education first.

On Wednesday, July 23, 1969, Karen Sue Beineman and her dorm roommates ate lunch at Downing Hall's communal dining commons until about 12:15 p.m. After they finished lunch, Karen asked Sherrie Diane Green to walk downtown to the wig shop with her. Her roommate declined, saying she needed to prepare for an afternoon class.

According to Kay Ann Knowles, another of Karen's roommates, Karen began her mile-long trek to Wigs by Joan at 18½ North Washington Street right after lunch. The summer had been a rainy one, but this was a lovely afternoon to walk down Ypsilanti's tree-shaded streets. The temperature was in the mid-eighties.

The previous day, Karen purchased a hairpiece she was picking up for a weekend wedding she planned to attend. The petite brown-haired coed was approached by a young man on a flashy motorcycle and asked if she needed a ride. The stranger must have looked nonthreatening enough because Karen Sue Beineman got onto the motorcycle and rode the two blocks to the wig shop with him. The ride took under a minute.

The previous day, Karen sent a letter home reassuring her parents she was aware of the danger on campus and wrote, "Don't worry, I'm careful." Included inside the envelope was a full page *Eastern Echo* article on the murders warning coeds to be cautious. The next day the unthinkable happened: Karen hopped onto a stranger's motorcycle and disappeared.

The motorcyclist swooped into a parking space in front of the Chocolate Shoppe next to Wigs by Joan. He parallel parked and offered to take Karen back to her dormitory. Karen climbed off the bike and walked into the wig shop to pick up her hairpiece. The shop owner, Diana Joan Goshe, and her wig stylist, Patricia Spaulding, were on hand to show Karen how to wear her hairpiece. As an aside, Karen mentioned she had done two foolish things that day—buying a hairpiece and accepting a motorcycle ride from a stranger.

Hearing this made the hair on the back of the women's necks stand on end. By this time, everybody in Ypsilanti was on alert, especially women. The young coed standing before them fit the victim profile released by local law enforcement. She was a petite white female with brown hair and pierced ears—Alice Kalom was the only victim without pierced ears. Their maternal instincts warned them something was not right about the young man waiting for the girl's return. Joan Goshe stepped outside her shop and took a good look at the person. When he noticed her, the motorcyclist lowered his head and tilted his face away. Goshe went inside her shop and cautioned Karen not to get back on the motorcycle.

"Tell him the wind will mess up your new hairpiece," she said. Goshe offered to drive Karen back to the dorm. Karen said it was a nice day, and she would walk back to campus. Karen may have been a little embarrassed to put these well-meaning women through any special bother on her account.

Karen left the wig shop and appeared to decline the ride back to her dormitory, but after some coaxing, she climbed back on the motorcycle. The wig-shop ladies watched the couple zoom to Michigan Avenue and turn right. They looked at each other and shook their heads, hoping nothing bad would happen to the foolish coed.

———

When Karen did not show up for dinner, her roommates thought she might be with her boyfriend Duffy. The girls went to the campus grill for snacks and returned to the dorm at 10:00 p.m. There was still no trace of their roommate. The coeds were worried but agreed to wait until curfew at 11:00 p.m. before reporting Karen missing to the Downing Hall front desk.

At 11:15 p.m., Downing's resident advisor, Verna Perkins, called EMU campus police and reported Karen missing. The EMU policeman on duty took the information from the anxious dorm mother and passed the report on to the Ypsilanti police. Ma Perkins, as she was known by Downing Hall residents, took it upon herself to call Karen's parents in Grand Rapids at midnight asking if they knew of their daughter's whereabouts. Alarmed by Verna Perkins's phone call, Roland Beineman immediately called in a report to the Michigan State Police post in Ypsilanti. From there, a copy of the report was sent to Ypsilanti police headquarters and stapled to the earlier EMU campus police report.

Sergeant Herb Smith arrived for work Thursday morning and found both reports lying on his desk. He and another officer named Howell immediately went to Downing Hall, which was a mile from the Ypsilanti police station. They interviewed Karen's roommates. In the presence of Downing Hall Assistant Advisor Sue Neibling, the detectives searched Karen's room for any evidence. They seized Karen's English, history, and fine arts notebooks and several letters hoping to find some clues. Sergeant Smith asked the coeds if they had any photos of Karen. The girls offered one the officers could borrow.

The detectives retraced Karen's probable walking route and pulled up in front of Wigs by Joan where they found Diane Joan Goshe and Patricia Spaulding. The detectives identified themselves and asked if the women recognized the girl in the photograph as the young woman in their shop the previous afternoon. Both women had difficulty making a positive identification from the grainy photograph.

But when Smith and Howell asked the women to describe the person they saw in the shop, they did so in great detail. The girl wore "a blue and white striped, sleeveless lightweight top that showed off her figure real well and some cutoff blue jeans." They also noted she was wearing leather sandals. When Smith asked why they remembered her so well, Joan Goshe said it was because of the guy on the motorcycle. This detail captured the investigators' attention.

"What guy on a motorcycle?"

The wig-shop owner described a young guy on a flashy blue motorcycle wearing a green and yellow striped, short-sleeved T-shirt. The detectives finally stumbled on some valuable information about the suspect. Sergeant Smith asked Goshe why the driver caught her attention.

The shop owner explained, "While the girl was paying for her purchase, she said something odd. 'I've done two things today I thought I would never do. One was buy a hairpiece and the other was accept a motorcycle ride from a stranger.'"

Joan Goshe told the police they asked the young woman if she was aware of the murdered girls in the area. She was. While Patricia Spaulding showed the girl how to wear her new hairpiece, Goshe stepped outside to take a better look at the guy on the motorcycle.

"So, you got a good look at him?" Officer Howell asked.

"I looked right at him. He was parked in front of the Chocolate Shoppe—next door about fifteen feet away. He appeared to be in his early twenties, nice build, about six feet tall maybe. He looked clean-cut with short brown hair. When he noticed I was checking him out, he looked away."

The wig-shop owner could not identify the make or model of the motorcycle, but Patricia Spaulding said her boyfriend rode motorcycles and the bike was maybe a Honda 450 with a square mirror. Sergeant Smith wrote down the information.

Both women felt terrible. Even though they did not fit the victim profile, they shared every local woman's fear of being caught out at night by this vicious killer. To make matters worse, this young woman was abducted in broad daylight in front of their shop.

The investigation had no corpus delecti, but when a body turned up, the police would have something more than conjecture to go on. The call went out to check all campus registrations for Honda 450s with square mirrors. This approach was problematic. Most off-campus students did not register their motor vehicles unless they wanted a campus parking permit. Still, it was the best lead police had in this series of murders that bore few leads.

Later in the afternoon, investigators interviewed other people who worked in the shops near Wigs by Joan. Carol Wieczerza—a clerk at the Chocolate Shoppe next door— was working that afternoon. She told detectives she noticed the motorcycle and its rider. Her account differed from the wig-shop ladies. Wieczerza was a bike enthusiast and showed little or no interest in the rider. She recognized the motorcycle as a blue British-built Triumph with lots of "gingerbread" (chrome) and "juiced up." She was certain of that. This proved to be a valuable piece of evidence later in the investigation. But the press and police were fixated on finding a Honda 450 from an earlier leaked report.

At roughly the same time, another line of inquiry opened on a hunch at the crime center. A twenty-two-year-old rookie EMU campus patrolman attended a Thursday morning briefing the day after Karen Sue Beineman disappeared. Patrolman Larry Mathewson told Senior Assistant Prosecutor Booker T. Williams he remembered seeing a guy in a horizontal striped shirt on a motorcycle the afternoon Beineman went missing. The motorcyclist was talking to a young woman Mathewson took to be a student because she was carrying books. Mathewson could not remember the person's name but thought he recognized him from playing interfraternity football against him the previous year. The young patrolman remembered the person was in the Theta Chi fraternity. Prosecutor Williams asked Mathewson to pursue the lead.

Dressed in street clothes, Larry Mathewson went to the Theta Chi fraternity house on West Cross Street, across the street from the southern border of Eastern Michigan's campus. The aging gray frame house needed repair, but it suited the Thetas. They cultivated their reputation as the animal house of Eastern Michigan's fraternity row. Several Thetas were sitting on the sagging front porch watching the coeds walk past. Mathewson approached the guys and described the person he was looking for. One of the frat brothers said he sounded like John Collins—a former member kicked out of the Thetas for stealing forty dollars from the fraternity's social fund. Now Collins rented a room around the block on the corner of Emmet and College Place.

Mathewson took the short drive around the block and parked in front of the two-story wood-frame house built in 1870. He knocked on the front door and the elderly landlady, Catherine Baker, answered. Mathewson asked if John Collins was home. She grumbled something and told him Collins was working on his motorcycles around back. She directed Mathewson to the right side of the house to what was once a carriage house now used as a ramshackle garage where Collins stored and worked on his motorcycles.

Larry Mathewson could not help but notice directly across College Place Street—less than sixty feet away—was the apartment where Joan Schell lived the previous summer before she was murdered.

Collins was hunched over one of his motorcycles tinkering as Larry Mathewson approached him. Another student named Dave Lee Myers was with Collins. The young patrolman recognized Myers from taking a class with him. They greeted each other, and Myers introduced Larry to John, mentioning that Larry was "campus fuzz."

Larry Mathewson made some small talk about playing interfraternity football against Collins the year before. Collins remembered him. Mathewson got down to business and asked if either of them had seen the girl who had been missing for two days. Then he produced a photograph of Beineman. Mathewson explained the coed was last seen riding off with some guy on a motorcycle. Both of the young men took a good look at the snapshot and said they never saw her before.

John Collins returned the photograph and proffered maybe she just took off some place. At that very moment, another of Collins's friends—Arnie Davis—showed up saying, "John, I have your new plate." Collins's forehead furrowed. He snatched the license plate from Davis without thanking him. Dave Lee Meyers filled the awkward silence. "Officer Mathewson is investigating the latest missing girl."

Directing his remarks at Collins, the young patrolman said he saw John on his bike Wednesday afternoon talking to an attractive young woman on Ballard Street near Eastern's campus. Mathewson asked if either of them saw anything or anyone suspicious. Collins relaxed a notch. He said the girl's name was Lorraine Kellogg, and she lived at the Americana Apartments on Ballard Street. Mathewson thanked Collins while he wrote the information down in a small notebook. Then he began to write down the license plate numbers from the four motorcycles in Collins's possession.

Collins asked Mathewson what he was doing.

"That's my job today," he said. "Writing down plate numbers for motorcycles in the area."

Collins snarled, "Well, you can fuck off and play policeman someplace else."

As Mathewson walked away, he noticed the plate on the blue Triumph motorcycle was bent upward at the bolts making it difficult to read from behind. That in itself was suspicious.

Larry Mathewson went to Lorraine Kellogg's apartment and found her home. He wanted to question her before Collins had a chance to establish an alibi. After he identified himself, Kellogg invited him in. She confirmed what he already knew. Collins was sitting astride his motorcycle and struck up a curbside conversation with her in front of her apartment house at about 12:05 in the afternoon. The brunette coed added she had just returned from a class that ended at 11:50 a.m. John approached her on his motorcycle while she was walking home.

"He was just sitting there watching people go by when he saw me. He asked if I wanted a ride. I said no, but he slowly followed me the rest of the way to my apartment. He asked where I lived, and I said 'Right here.'"

Kellogg said they talked about motorcycles and mutual friends. Collins had dated a couple of her friends, so she treated him like an acquaintance. Kellogg thought he was a mover. She told Patrolman Mathewson, "My roommate Vicki went on a date with him once to watch color TV in his room and he kept trying to get her pants off."

"Did he ask you for a date?"

"We talked for about twenty minutes, but he didn't ask me to go for a ride or anything. He mentioned something vague about going out sometime."

Lorraine Kellogg added that about ten minutes into their conversation, her next door neighbor Joe Westmore pulled up and parked his car. He came over and spoke with them for a short time and went inside to make lunch. A few minutes later, he called out to her saying lunch was ready.

Given the tight time frame, Mathewson surmised Karen Sue Beineman walked south on Ballard Street and over to North Washington Street—the shortest and most likely route to the wig shop. She might have passed Collins and Kellogg on her way. Mathewson asked if Kellogg noticed a petite young woman walk past them while she was talking to Collins.

"No. Several people walked passed us. He may have smiled and said hello to someone. I don't remember. I wanted to say good-bye and eat lunch."

Mathewson asked if she remembered the exact time Collins left her.

Lorraine Kellogg was certain it was before 12:30

because she remembered seeing her entire soap opera that afternoon. It was her daily ritual.

Mathewson asked Kellogg if she knew of anyone other than her roommate who dated John Collins. Kellogg knew of one person for sure, Linda Campbell, who lived on Jarvis Street. Mathewson wrote down Campbell's address. He thanked Lorraine Kellogg and left to interview Linda Campbell.

The coed was at her apartment relaxing before work. She agreed to answer of few quick questions. Campbell told Mathewson she knew John for only six months and maybe dated him ten times. When asked what they did on their dates, she said they went back and forth to Ann Arbor on his motorcycle taking the country roads. Mathewson asked if there was anything peculiar or suspicious about Collins. Campbell remarked he seemed to like motorcycles better than girls. Collins was preoccupied with them, so she quit dating him.

Linda Campbell needed to leave for work soon, so Mathewson did not want to be a nuisance. As he was about to leave, he casually asked where she worked. She said as a waitress at the Camelot Room in the Inn America. The young policeman knew the Camelot Room had been a madhouse for the past week since the psychic Peter Hurkos checked in and began holding court with the local press in the restaurant.

"I bet it's been crazy over there," Mathewson said.

Linda Campbell rolled her eyes. Without prompting, she told how Collins came to the Camelot Room to hear if Hurkos had any revelations regarding the murders. "John said he was hoping to get some inside stuff from the psychic." Campbell said Hurkos did his nightclub act with what local press still followed him. "Hurkos didn't discuss the murders," Campbell said, "but he was still entertaining to watch." Campbell described the night John and two friends sat in a booth that was back-to-back with Hurkos. Afterward, she said John dismissed Hurkos as a clown.

Mathewson found what Linda Campbell had to say interesting, but she was about to leave for work. He asked if she had any photos of Collins he could borrow. She had a photo of him standing by a Christmas tree from the previous December when they were dating.

The quality of the photograph was not great, but it would have to do. Mathewson headed to the wig shop to get a positive ID of the motorcyclist from the wig-shop ladies. Neither woman would commit to a positive identification based solely on a grainy photograph. Both of them insisted it was too easy to mistake someone in a photograph. There was something different about the hair. Disappointed, Mathewson thanked them for their help and left.

The young officer went next door to the Chocolate Shoppe to show the photograph to the witness who worked there. The counter clerk told him the person he was looking for would not be back to work until Monday, so Mathewson was thwarted a second time. Then he remembered a young woman, Mary Martha Thompson, who worked on Washington Street at Marsh's Office Supply. Mary reported to police that a motorcyclist approached and offered her a ride to work on Wednesday afternoon, but she had refused him.

Larry Mathewson found the young clerk eating her lunch and reading a magazine in the basement storeroom. He politely introduced himself, but the girl was annoyed. She had already given a written statement to the Ypsilanti police. Mathewson apologized for interrupting Thompson during her lunch break but asked her to take a look at a photograph. She glanced at it and dropped her sandwich and exclaimed, "Shit! That's him."

Thompson told Officer Mathewson she was walking down College Place Street near Pease Auditorium when a young man on a motorcycle offered her a ride. She described him as the wig-shop ladies had—except his hair was straighter than on the most recent composite drawing of the suspect. She said he was very good looking and pleasant with a nice smile but no discernible accent. He seemed surprised she would not take a ride from him and wanted to know why.

Mary Thompson said the man wore a green shirt with horizontal yellow stripes and cut-off shorts, but she could not describe his shoes or anything else. The motorcycle was clean with lots of chrome, but it was not excessively noisy. When the motorcyclist was rebuffed, he took off down West Cross Street. Thompson felt certain she could identify him again if she saw him. Mathewson returned to the crime center to write a complete report of everything he had discovered that afternoon. At roughly the same moment, the nude body of a young woman was found by Dr. Conrad Mason and his wife as they were getting their Saturday afternoon mail at 4:40 p.m. The body was lying facedown with legs crossed at the ankles at the bottom of a steep gully. It had been rolled off the shoulder of Riverside Drive in Ann Arbor Township.

———

On Sunday, July 27, 1969, Chief Assistant Prosecutor Booker T. Williams reviewed the latest reports that pointed to John Norman Collins as a possible suspect. He ordered that Collins be placed under twenty-four-hour surveillance but made it clear that he should not be picked up until they learned more about him or caught him in a crime. Collins was not seen all day at his boardinghouse room. Several surveillance teams came and went. Earlier that morning, Arnie Davis—one of Collins's friends—bounded down the front porch stairs of their Emmet Street house and boldly walked up to one of the surveillance teams. Davis asked if they were watching his house.

The officers felt foolish they were flushed out but soon recovered. "We want to question John. Is he home?" Davis said Collins was spending the weekend at his mother's house. The police thanked him for the information and pulled away.

The next surveillance team pulled into position shortly afterward and chose a less obvious site. To verify Arnie Davis's statement, the Center Line police were contacted and asked to check out 7327 Helen Street and place John Norman Collins under surveillance. The Center Line police reported back later that afternoon. Collins was seen washing and waxing a silver Oldsmobile Cutlass inside and out—including the trunk—in the driveway of his mother's house.

When Collins returned home to Ypsilanti at eleven o'clock Sunday night, the officers on the night-shift stakeout were not told of Booker T. Williams's directive that Collins not be apprehended. This team was acting on new orders to pick him up for questioning. Collins was now a person of interest and considered a flight risk. The police did not want to look foolish again. This would be the second time police questioned John Collins in the last year.

After two hours of interrogation at the crime center,

Collins agreed to take a lie detector test in the morning, but now he was exhausted and needed some sleep. Besides, it would take some time to arrange for the polygraph examination. Collins was driven home and released on his own recognizance. Arnie Davis overheard Collins calling his mother and telling her he was in trouble. Loretta Collins arranged for a defense attorney the first thing in the morning.

When the state police arrived at his boardinghouse Monday afternoon, Collins was waiting for them with his Ann Arbor lawyer Robert Francis, a twenty-nine-year-old former marine and graduate of U of M's law school. He had worked for the Washtenaw County Legal Aid Clinic before hiring on as a junior partner with John M. Toomey. Francis had been in private practice only six weeks when he was given the Collins case.

Francis advised Collins not to take the polygraph test, and he challenged police to charge his client or leave him alone. They had no choice but to leave. They needed more evidence before they could get an arrest warrant. The search intensified for the site where Karen Sue Beineman was murdered.

——◆——

The David Leik family arrived back home from a twelve-day family camping vacation on Tuesday night, July 29. Leik and his wife Sandra had entrusted the care of their German shepherd to Sandra's nephew, John Collins. The dog was kept in the garage. Collins cared for the dog daily but had no household responsibilities.

When Sandra got up the next morning to make breakfast for the kids, she noticed scuff marks on her kitchen floor. She had mopped and waxed the floor before the family left on vacation. Sandra was a fastidious housekeeper and did not like returning to a messy house. Her nephew had no reason to enter the house, but they gave him a key anyway. Sandra would ask John about the errant scuff marks when she called him later.

Sandra Leik went down to the basement laundry room to wash the dirty vacation clothes. She noticed black blotches of spray paint on the floor from the doorway of the recreation room to the right corner of the laundry room. She was absolutely certain that the paint was not there before because she had swept the floor of hair clippings after she cut her sons' hair. Everything was clean and tidy before the family left on their vacation.

She looked around and noticed that an empty king-size box of Bold laundry detergent she had planned to use as a waste container was missing. She looked over her laundry supplies and saw that a bottle of ammonia was also gone. Something was odd. She went upstairs and asked her husband what the black paint on the basement floor was all about.

David Leik went down to the basement, took a look at the cement floor, and then rummaged through his paint shelf. Something else was missing—a partially used can of flat-black spray paint. Perhaps John had some explanation, but now the Leiks were more annoyed than angry. They wondered what their nephew was doing in their basement while they were gone.

Corporal Leik went to the Ypsilanti state police post the next morning as scheduled to report back for active duty. Post Commander Carl Freedborn wanted to brief David Leik personally to tell him his nephew was under suspicion for the sexual assault and murder of Karen Sue Beineman, the latest unsolved case that occurred while the Leik family was on vacation. After Trooper Leik listened intently to what Commander Freedborn reported, he did his duty and revealed the irregularities he discovered in his basement. The post commander thanked Corporal Leik, realizing how difficult the family situation was going to be for the young state trooper.

The crime center was contacted with Lieutenant Leik's latest information. For two years, police investigators made little or no progress on these murders. Now, credible leads were developing at a remarkable pace. John Norman Collins's alter ego was about to be unmasked by police and revealed to the public.

John's Aunt Sandra was unsuccessful phoning her nephew. Since he was not answering, she decided to call her sister Loretta in Center Line. Loretta Collins told Sandra that John was at home visiting but not there at the moment. Loretta said she would tell John to call Sandra later when he got home. Later turned out to be 10:30 p.m. The Leik phone rang and Sandra answered. She quickly asked John what he was up to while they were gone. Under different circumstances, it might have been an innocuous question.

"What do you mean, Aunt Sandra?"

Sandra Leik was unaware her husband had been briefed that morning on her nephew's possible involvement in the Beineman murder. Corporal Leik did not know how to tell his wife her nephew was under police surveillance as their prime suspect. Leik picked up the extension in the kitchen and broke into the conversation, "Hey, John! How's it going?"

Collins asked his uncle how the vacation went. After some small talk, David Leik asked his nephew if he had spray-painted anything in their basement while they were gone.

After a slight pause came a flat denial.

Then Sandra jumped back into the conversation saying "I noticed there were a couple of things missing in the basement. Did you throw anything out?"

John became defensive and swore he never touched anything. It was late, so his aunt thanked him for taking care of their dog and said good night. After the phone call, David told his wife he was not sleepy and wanted to have a couple of beers with a police friend.

Officer Stu Lucky was nearing the end of his shift, and David Leik needed to talk to someone about his nephew. The two of them went to the Tap Room—a downtown Ypsilanti bar on Michigan Avenue. They chose an out-of-the-way booth to drink a couple of beers and talk privately. Several things were gnawing away at David Leik. Had his nephew lied about the spray-painting? Or had someone else entered their house and done it? But why? He found no forced entry when he checked the house and basement windows. John was the only person with a key to their house. That was the level of trust he and his wife placed in John.

And if that was not enough, several more items were missing from the basement that John denied any knowledge of. John's defensive posture unsettled the state trooper. There had to be some explanation, but John offered none. David Leik tried to assimilate everything he had learned since his morning briefing. Was it possible his wife's nephew was the Ypsilanti Ripper? He could not get his nephew's reaction out of his mind. John was never evasive with him before.

"Have you scraped under the spray paint?" Stu Lucky said. "Maybe it's hiding something." Just after midnight, the two men quietly went down to the Leik basement. David took a screw driver and loosened the largest of the paint blotches. Both men suspected the semidry, sticky substance beneath the spray paint could be blood.

At the beginning of his next shift, Corporal Leik briefed Commander Freedborn about what he discovered in his basement. A call was made to the crime center in Ann Arbor. Prosecutor William Delhey and Colonel Frederick Davids—newly appointed commander of the crime center task force—agreed to send in state police crime lab technicians. Corporal Leik was instructed to go home and wait for them.

When he got home, Sandra was on the phone with her nephew again. She covered the receiver with her hand. "It's John," she whispered. "He wants to know about the paint." This is when Leik whispered to his wife that the crime lab unit was on the way over. Sandra's eyes widened. Before her husband could stop her, she told her nephew the crime lab was on the way over. This was supposed to be a secret police operation, and now it had been leaked to the last person who should have known. David Leik winced.

"Let me know how it comes out," John replied.

"Sure, honey. I will. Say hello to your mom for me." Sandra hung up the phone and asked her husband what was going on. Leik told her as gently as he could that her nephew might be the person responsible for the murders in Ypsilanti and Ann Arbor over the past two years. The Leiks considered John more of a son than a nephew. It was unthinkable her sister's son could be capable of these horrible murders.

Sandra Leik went into shock. David did what he could to comfort her, guiding her upstairs to their bedroom where she fell into a heap of inconsolable sobbing. Now the children were concerned since they were not accustomed to seeing their mother cry. David shut the door and ushered the kids outdoors to play with friends. He did not want them around when the crime lab unit arrived.

"Your mother heard some bad news about someone she cares about very much," he explained. "Now go outside and play baseball or something with your friends. Your mother just needs some quiet time." The three kids obeyed their father and went to the nearby park which temporarily simplified the situation. The boys would need to be told before they found out on the television news or from someone at school.

At 11:00 a.m. on Thursday, July 31, the state police crime lab team arrived as quietly as possible to avoid alerting the press. They scoured the laundry room for what evidence they could find. The original blotch of black paint David Leik removed turned out to cover varnish from a do-it-yourself project Leik had worked on before vacation. He was embarrassed he had forgotten about it.

But the lab techs found other blood evidence in the basement. There were several blood spots on a laundered shirt and a blue dental hygienist tunic hanging in the basement laundry room. Friction marks on the copper water pipes running above and along the floor joists showed abrasion signs of a possible struggle. Karen Sue Beineman's wrists had deep impressions on them from being tied with an electrical cord like one found in the Leik basement. It was obvious her wrists supported her body weight as she hung there. Her ankles were also bound.

Investigators found more blood splatter under the clothes dryer which was tucked into the southwest corner of the cramped laundry room. But the most profound evidence would also be the most contentious. Hundreds of short hair clippings discovered under the dryer would become more incriminating than the blood evidence for connecting the body of Karen Sue Beineman to the Leik basement.

Just before their vacation, Sandra cut her sons' hair with electric barber clippers. She sat each son in turn on a stool placed in a nook under the basement stairs directly in front of the clothes dryer. Sandra used one of her dental hygienist tunics as a barber gown and trimmed them up. She was in a hurry preparing for their vacation, so she quickly swept the shorn hair into a pile and disposed of it. In her haste, some of the hair clippings made their way under the dryer. These recovered hair clippings matched in every significant detail hair clippings recovered from panties that the Washtenaw County medical examiner found stuffed into Karen Sue Beineman's vagina.

The prosecutor now had enough evidence to link Karen Sue Beineman with the Leik basement. Thursday evening, July 31, 1969, three state police officers picked up Collins and took him to the crime center. One of them was David Leik. Collins telephoned his attorney Robert Francis and wanted him present for the interrogation. Collins was led to an interview room and offered cigarettes, coffee, Coca-Cola, and water while everyone waited for Francis to arrive.

Police investigators wanted Collins in custody while they waited for a phone call from the Washtenaw County prosecutor. When Francis arrived at the Plymouth crime lab, he asked if his client had been booked. When told no, the attorney demanded to know why his client was being held. The police told Francis they wanted to take a couple of photos and get John's fingerprints. Investigators also wanted to ask Collins a few questions with his lawyer present. Francis refused to allow photos or fingerprinting, but he had no choice but to comply with the questioning.

At the Washtenaw County Building in Ann Arbor, Prosecutor William Delhey was waiting to hear from the state police crime lab in East Lansing if they had any solid physical evidence against Collins. If they did have physical evidence, then the prosecutor needed to convince a judge to charge Collins and issue an arrest warrant.

After a state policeman took an unauthorized snapshot of Collins, defense attorney Francis and his client began to march out when the call came through. Sheriff Douglas Harvey signed a first-degree murder complaint against Collins, and district court Judge Edward Deake signed the arrest warrant. Collins was taken into custody and arrested at 8:40 p.m. He was brought to the Washtenaw County Jail and booked for the murder of Karen Sue Beineman.

— 9 —

A California Connection

IN CALIFORNIA OVER TWENTY-FOUR hundred miles across the country, Monterey County district attorney investigator Robert L. Taylor was sitting in front of his television watching the national news about the arrest of a suspect in a series of unsolved Michigan murders. An Eastern Michigan University senior named John Norman Collins was under close police scrutiny since the discovery of eighteen-year-old Karen Sue Beineman's battered body in Ann Arbor on July 26, 1969.

Taylor was working on the strangulation murder of Roxie Ann Phillips and quickly drew parallels between the case he was working on and the Beineman case in Michigan. Both victims died of strangulation and were found nude except for their sandals. Their bodies were dumped in secluded areas—one in a canyon, the other in a gully. Most striking of all was the Salinas investigators were looking for a twenty-something male named John from Michigan last seen driving a late-model silver car. The Monterey County Prosecutors' Office contacted the Michigan State

Police informing them the man they had in custody for the Beineman murder was their prime suspect in the Roxie Ann Phillips murder in Salinas, California, at the end of June. The Monterey County prosecutor notified Washtenaw County authorities and asked for further information about Collins.

Seventeen-year-old Roxie was visiting Salinas from Milwaukie, Oregon, where she lived with her mother. The high school senior was spending the month of June in Salinas in exchange for babysitting the children of Mrs. Norman Kunnas, a family friend. Just after noon on June 30, 1969, Roxie left the Kunnas residence at 38 East Acacia Street to mail a letter home and visit her friend Nancy Albrecht, who lived several blocks away. Roxie said she would return by 4:00 p.m. to babysit the children. When she did not return by 7:00 p.m., Mrs. Kunnas filed a missing person report with the Salinas police.

When Roxie left the Kunnas's home, she was wearing a red pants-dress with a small white flower design printed on the fabric. Mrs. Kunnas identified the cloth belt found around Roxie's throat as made from the same material as the missing dress.

Roxie mailed her letter, but she never showed up to visit her friend Nancy Albrecht. On July 18, Investigator Taylor interviewed Albrecht and asked when she last saw Roxie. Albrecht answered she visited Roxie at the Kunnas's home the day before she disappeared. Afterward, Nancy walked home to Pajaro Street at 2:00 p.m. En route, a car pulled up alongside her. A pleasant-looking young man asked for directions. He said he was new to the area and identified himself as John, adding he was studying to be an elementary schoolteacher. He told Albrecht he and a friend pulled a house trailer all the way from Michigan.

John made a date with her for the following day. Nancy described John to police as a white male in his early twenties with short brown hair. He was wearing Levi jeans and a T-shirt. When Nancy arrived home, she called Roxie and told her about meeting a guy with a flashy silver car. John never kept his date with Nancy. Both he and Roxie vanished the next day.

Upon further investigation, it was learned Collins had a traveling companion, Andrew Manuel, originally from Salinas. They were visiting California in a fraudulently rented house trailer at the time of Roxie's death. The trailer was found abandoned in an alley behind the home of Andrew Manuel's elderly grandparents. When eighty-year-old Silver Manuel was questioned about his grandson and his friend, all he knew was they left suddenly without saying good-bye. The trailer was towed to a secure location and sealed.

Two Michigan State policemen from the state police crime lab in Plymouth, Michigan—Detective Tom Nasser and Sergeant Kennard Christensen—flew out to Salinas on the next available flight. They joined forces with Salinas police investigator Vic Collins and searched every inch of the trailer. They found it wiped clean, inside and out—a suspicious act but not proof of murder.

Once the Salinas police got the vehicle identification number for Collins's Oldsmobile Cutlass, they soon discovered it was serviced—and a trailer hitch taken off—at Tolan Cadillac-Oldsmobile in Salinas on July 3. The vehicle was registered to Loretta Collins of Center Line, Michigan.

During the investigation of the body drop site, one of the Salinas police investigators contracted a bad case of poison oak. He surmised the murderer may have also. It was a long shot, but he canvassed doctors in the area asking if anyone fitting John's description was treated for poison oak recently. The detective's hunch paid off. He located a doctor who identified John Collins as someone he treated for poison oak.

Michigan State Police forensic investigators shared information about evidence they collected from John Collins's vehicle the day after his arrest for the Beineman killing. Forensic investigators found blood residue on the front seat, the seat belt, and the seat-belt channel. The bucket seat was removed and taken to the Michigan Department of Health Laboratories in Lansing and examined by Dr. Curtis Fluker. He determined the blood was of human origin. Blood evidence was inconclusive in the days before DNA positive identification, but the type O samples matched Roxie's blood type.

Caught up in the seat's undercarriage was a piece of red fabric about the size of a dime. The Salinas police gave Sergeant Christensen a sample cut from the red belt removed from Roxie's throat. With a compound microscope, Dr. Fluker compared the belt sample with the swatch of fabric recovered from the Cutlass. Fluker's laboratory report issued August 7 determined the samples were similar in all respects. Both were 100 percent cotton fabric woven the same way with the same thread diameter. Both samples were rolled with identical dyestuff, and the white floral pattern on the fabric was the same size. The red swatch found in Collins's Cutlass linked Roxie to his car.

Dr. Fluker also examined a brown sweater taken from Collins's closet by forensic investigators after Collins's arrest. Twenty-two pubic hairs were embedded in the yarn fibers. The hair samples did not match any of Collins's other alleged victims. By this time, Roxie Ann Phillips's body was buried in her home state of Oregon. Washtenaw Country officials asked that her body be exhumed to get pubic hair samples, fingerprints, and blood evidence from her remains. The collected hair samples from the sweater were found by microscopic examination to be similar in all respects to hair samples from Roxie's body. This was physical evidence linking Collins with Roxie's body.

Investigators believed Collins hefted Roxie's 130-pound body over his head and carried her on his shoulders from his car to a secluded spot used as a trash heap in Pescadero Canyon before daylight on July 1. The shifting movement of Roxie's nude body forced her pubic bone to work her hair into the knit yarn of Collins's sweater. There was no other explanation.

On the strength of a Monterey County grand-jury investigation, the state of California indicted John Norman Collins for the first-degree murder of Roxie Ann Phillips on September 29, 1969, only two months after Collins's arrest for the strangulation murder of Karen Sue Beineman.

When Russell H. Phillips was notified John Collins was indicted for the murder of his daughter, he responded to an *Ypsilanti Press* reporter on April 17, 1970. "There is no possible way of getting any pleasure out of this. As long as the person who did this is in prison and cannot hurt anyone else, it's all that can be expected. Roxie played the violin very well, and she always sang in the church choir. She is much better off than the person who took her life."

Michigan law enforcement was more convinced than ever that John Collins was the serial killer they were seeking.

Now, the Beineman murder charge needed to be proven beyond a reasonable doubt in a Michigan court of law. The Monterey County indictment would have to wait until the Washtenaw County case played itself out.

—10—

In the Shadow of the Water Tower

ONCE THE ARREST OF Collins was announced, the *Detroit News* made it their business to discover as much as possible about him. The paper sent a team of four reporters (Thomas F. Pawlick, Suzanne Hemmen, Al Stark, and Nancy Abner) to question people who knew Collins. Robert A. Popa compiled their reports in an extensive article for the paper's Saturday edition on August 2, 1969.

Reporters discovered Collins was a twenty-two-year-old senior at Eastern Michigan majoring in English and preparing to be an upper-elementary schoolteacher. By all outward appearances, Collins was progressing well with his studies and looking forward to working with kids. He needed to earn twenty-four more credit hours for graduation. On the surface, he appeared to be "the living embodiment of the All-American boy," Popa wrote.

After graduating in 1965 from Saint Clement Catholic High School in Center Line, Michigan, Collins followed his older brother to Central Michigan University on a sports scholarship. He played football but soon realized he was not large enough for college-level ball. When Collins's brother graduated from Central Michigan in Mt. Pleasant, Collins wanted to be closer to friends and family. He transferred to Eastern Michigan in Ypsilanti, which was less than fifty miles from Center Line—and only an hour's ride home.

At Eastern Michigan, Collins played intramural football in a campus fraternity league. At that level, he was a standout and enjoyed playing the game again. Collins wasted no time joining Theta Chi—a sports and social fraternity known for its massive rush parties. While a member of the Thetas, he wrestled for EMU's Greco-Roman team.

Reporters soon found that Collins had a busy dating life and showed an active interest in the opposite sex. Some girls described him as a respectful, hands-off type, while others said he was as sexually aggressive as other single men his age. Nineteen-year-old sophomore Victoria Waite went on one date with Collins. He took her to his room to watch his new color TV. "He was kind of a mover," she said. "He pressed me to have sex with him." Jo Ann Fitzsimmons, a sophomore at EMU, met Collins when the university ski team took a semester break trip to Aspen, Colorado. "John was kind of fresh with me. He kissed me in a public lounge. My reaction wasn't favorable. He was a flirt."

Asking that her name not be used, another EMU coed told *Detroit News* reporters she dated Collins the month before and rode with him on his motorcycle a few times. On the Tuesday before he was arrested, she saw Collins riding in front of her dormitory and yelled out to him, "Hey, John, you look like the guy in the picture (on the latest composite drawing)."

He yelled back, "You look like the other picture (photo of Karen Sue Beineman)." She said they kidded each other about the murders when they were dating.

EMU senior Barbara A. Stevens remembered Collins asking her to go on a motorcycle ride at 1:00 a.m. "He nearly had me talked into it," she said. "The only reason I didn't go was I was wearing a skirt." Seeing the most recent composite drawing of the suspected killer in a striped T-shirt made her feel uncomfortable. "I immediately thought of the time John asked me for that bike ride," she recalled with a shiver. "I remember him wearing a similar T-shirt."

Ken Roe worked with Collins the previous year at the EMU Alumni Office. "He was really a nice guy," Roe said. "The kind of guy you would let your sister go out with. He was an open and friendly person who had no trouble meeting girls."

Bill Freer—an EMU freshman who worked with Collins at Motor Wheel Corporation—said Collins was a nice guy. "He's real straight. The only time I saw Collins upset was when he learned a friend had been killed in Vietnam. Collins dreaded the thought of being drafted and sent to fight in Vietnam."

———

Collins's Saint Clement High School record showed he was a model student who was consistently on the honor roll. He cultivated his jock persona by becoming a star athlete lettering in football, basketball, baseball, and wrestling. Collins was one of three captains of the football team his senior year. A profile written for the yearbook *Crest* described him with typical high school zeal:

> Collins, sparkling end for the Green-and-Gold, has been a letterman since his sophomore year. His fine blocking has resulted in many extra yards for *Crusader* ball carriers. Leading the way, he pokes holes in opponent lines, smashing through to open the field for a touchdown.
>
> Collins pokes holes in other things besides the opposing football lines, as any of his classmates will tell you. An alert debater, he is a ready participant in class discussions where instead of an opposing lineman another student's argument is his target.
>
> Naturally curious, Collins digs through to something until he is satisfied he has reached an answer. This vitality is present in other activities too; for instance, his eye-catching dancing ability and his participation in all high school events. His pride outside of sports is his car, which he keeps in top-flight condition, indicative of his natural attraction to cars. His interests run the gamut of teen interests. He is extremely meticulous in his appearance, with tastes a little unusual. Collins tries to dress with a certain flair which makes him stand out in a crowd.
>
> Like most boys, he loves food, flavorful "stick to the ribs" dishes such as steak. But when it comes to his one idiosyncrasy, potatoes, they must be just so, either French fried or whipped. Any other style is liable to result in a disgusted look at the dish and a "What do you call that?" expression.
>
> A real fighter on the field, Collins seems to carry

his image with him wherever he goes—physically at least. His jaw firmly set, he gives the impression that he is always on the lookout for action. But this "tough-guy" appearance is misleading. As any of his friends will tell you, he is easy to get along with and sports a gay sense of humor. Not only athletically and socially does Collins stand out, he also makes his mark scholastically, as he maintains a nearly consistent status on the honor roll.

But even during his time at Saint Clement's young women who dated Collins reported he was often sullen. Not once does he have more than a tentative grin in any of his high school yearbook pictures. As Collins became a young man, he was more attached to his cars and motorcycles than the girls he dated—with the possible exception of his high school sweetheart.

Bernadette Hudak and John Collins met at homecoming during their freshman year and went steady off and on throughout high school. Even with Bernie, a wall separated Collins from any lasting relationship. They broke up after high school when college sent them in different directions. Hudak told the *Detroit News* that on September 28, 1968, Collins phoned her asking for a date. Instead of going to a movie as planned, they went for a ride. Collins wondered if she still loved him, and Hudak answered no. Collins took her home. Several days later, Collins called back and said, "If you ever change your mind, write to me."

Hudak described Collins as "level-headed, smart, and on the honor roll. English and Spanish were his favorite subjects. John was an avid weightlifter who worked out almost every night." She continued, "When others disagreed with John, he was inclined to become moody—sometimes for a day or two. He came from a broken home with very little fatherly influence but always spoke of his mother with great respect."

John Collins's high school football coach, Al Baumgart, described Collins as "a real competitor who liked strong discipline and wanted to be disciplined. He was a winner and didn't want to lose. He gave one hundred percent." The coach attributed many of Saint Clement's victories to Collins's playing spirit, which earned Collins an all-state honorable mention as an offensive end and safety. "I never thought anything like this would happen. Evidently something was disturbing him. That's all I can think of."

Tri-captain of the *Crusaders* football team Chris Diliberti said Collins was "nothing but a great guy. I just can't believe he's connected with any of this. He was a good, strong football player, but he wasn't violent. I believe he is innocent. I am really shocked."

Collins graduated from Saint Clement with accolades at the top of his class. Never again would he hear the roar of an admiring crowd or wear the mantle of local sports hero. Those days were over for him.

———

While searching the glove box of Collins's Oldsmobile Cutlass after his arrest, police found a copy of *Cliff's Notes* for Fyodor Dostoyevsky's novel *Crime and Punishment*. EMU campus police interviewed Collins's world literature professor who was able to produce a composition Collins had written on the main character Raskolnikov and his extraordinary man theory. One passage especially drew the investigators' attention:

If a person wants something, he alone is the deciding factor of whether or not to take it—regardless of what society thinks may be right or wrong. For example, if a person sees a piece of jewelry, or something that he likes in a store window, it is up to him to smash the window or not, or to take it or not. It is the same if someone holds a gun on somebody—it is up to them to decide whether to take the person's life or not. The point is: It's not society's judgement that's important but the individual's own choice of will and intellect.

Collins's professor, Dr. Franklin Case, accused Collins of plagiarism for his half-digested rehash of *Cliff's Notes*. The police were more interested in Collins's sociopathic explanation that some people in society were expendable. It was a crude mix of Friedrich Nietzsche's superman theory and Charles Darwin's survival of the fittest theory. When Professor Case confronted Collins about his dishonest attempt at scholarship, Collins was arrogant and argumentative. Then he quit coming to class.

———

Little is known about the early life of John Norman Chapman (Collins). John's birth father Richard Chapman was a twenty-two-year-old bus driver in Windsor, Ontario, when he married nineteen-year-old Loretta Marjorie Girard on May 15, 1943, in Detroit, Michigan. Her occupation listed on their marriage license was clerk. John Norman Chapman was born in Riverside, Ontario, Canada, on June 17, 1947, the youngest of three children born to Richard and Loretta. John was preceded by his brother Jerry and his sister Gail.

A year after John's birth, Loretta filed for divorce on the grounds of "extreme and repeated cruelty." In the decree, she demanded Richard Chapman never contact the children, and in exchange she would not ask for child support. Loretta did ask for and was granted alimony. The story Loretta handed down to her children was their birth father deserted them.

Collins's last Canadian blood relative, first cousin John Philip Chapman, disagrees with the assertion his Uncle Richard abandoned his children. He said his aunt's family came from money and felt their son-in-law was not good enough for their daughter, and he was not a Roman Catholic. This is what Richard Chapman told his brother, John Phillip's father.

In further defense of his deceased Uncle Richard, John Philip Chapman said in a phone interview, "Richard Chapman was a light-infantry, noncommissioned officer in His Majesty's Canadian Services during World War II. He was an explosives and demolition expert who lost his left leg in 1944 fighting the Nazis in Europe. He spent many weeks recuperating in a European military hospital before shipping home with the condition military doctors diagnosed as Battle Fatigue. The term in use today is Post Traumatic Stress Disorder."

John Philip Chapman further explained, "War changes people, and my Uncle Richard and Aunt Loretta were no exceptions. My uncle loved his wife and their children and was never abusive towards them. Not wanting to put his children at the center of an ugly divorce, Uncle Rich simply left Windsor and moved to North Kitchener, Ontario, agreeing to fade into the background."

In 1949, Loretta and her young family crossed the

Ambassador Bridge to Detroit and settled in Center Line, Michigan, a small municipality surrounded by the city of Warren. There she met William Collins and married him in 1952. Collins held a steady job as a local mechanic. He formally adopted Loretta's children, and they took his last name.

William Collins was a heavy drinker and an angry drunk. It was rumored he once threw toddler John across the hood of his car at his mother. On another occasion, he used the toddler as a human shield when confronted by a man with a gun over a gambling debt. Neither incident has been confirmed but accounts survive in print. Loretta and William separated in 1955 and divorced in 1956. This marriage lasted four years before Mrs. Collins found herself single again.

A person associated with the Collins's family who wishes to remain unidentified shared information about Loretta's early life in Michigan after she left Canada with her children. She agrees the loss of Richard Chapman's leg was a factor in their divorce. But she disagrees the divorce was forced upon Loretta by her Catholic family. She maintains that Richard Chapman's violent flashbacks made Loretta afraid of her husband. She left and took her children to Detroit. According to this confidential source:

> If Loretta's parents were well-off, it was news to me. She never had any money as a single mother of three children. When they needed a place, her family in Center Line took them in. They cared for the kids while Loretta worked. Without a college degree or serious work experience, Loretta took the only job open to her, waitressing. She learned the trade

and worked some of Detroit's high end restaurants like Stouffers, Top of the Flame, and Greenfield's in Southfield. The hourly wages were minimal, but the daily tip money was good.

Loretta was able to make ends meet and provide materially for her children, but at a high personal cost. Her work hours conflicted with her home responsibilities, and she was forced to make the same compromises most single working mothers face—not always being at home when the kids came home from school.

Basically, she knew the lifestyle she wanted and worked her butt off as a waitress to get it. She came from nothing and wasn't going to leave earth that way. She wanted to be somebody with enough money to support her and raise her children. She was so sweet and nice, and always there to help a friend.

Being a wife and a stay-at-home mom were the expectations in the 1950s for American women. Wives were supposed to take care of their husbands and raise their children. Loretta's life did not follow that pattern. She had a job outside the home, worked odd hours, occasionally dated men, and had her own money. To compensate for the less-than-ideal home life, Loretta enrolled her children in Saint Clement Catholic School only four blocks from their home. She was proud her daughter was on the honor roll and her sons were talented athletes.

Loretta attended mass rarely because she claimed she was excommunicated for being divorced twice. She was the object of neighborhood gossips spreading rumors about the woman who always wore nice clothes and lots of jewelry and never left the house without full makeup and her hair done. Mrs. Collins was not active in parish events at Saint Clement Church, which was a major strike against her in their heavily Catholic community. Despite her real and perceived flaws, Loretta Collins was a complicated person devoted to her family.

———

Sometime during the second semester of his sophomore year in college, something went terribly wrong for John Collins. Before the semester was over, he was thrown out of the Theta Chi fraternity house. Like so much about Collins's past, there are conflicting stories. Wayne Patterson, spokesperson for Theta Chi, told the *Detroit News* that Collins pledged the fraternity in the fall of 1966 and lived in the frat house at 603 West Cross Street. He said, "Collins was expelled about a year ago for nonpayment of dues and nonattendance at fraternity meetings." When asked about Collins himself, Patterson said, "He was good looking and had no trouble meeting girls. He didn't seem more preoccupied with sex than anyone else here."

Unofficially, several of Collins's former fraternity brothers complained there was a pattern of theft in the house while Collins lived there. They suspected him of stealing cash from the group's social fund. Other valuable personal items turned up missing as well—golf clubs, hunting rifles, jewelry, and other sellable items. A former fraternity brother and friend confirmed John disassembled stolen motorcycles for parts in the basement of the fraternity house and disposed of the stripped frames in dumpsters around Ypsilanti.

After Collins left the frat house, he sublet an apartment over the summer at Woodland Hills—a complex between Ann Arbor and Ypsilanti. When the fall semester began, Collins rented a room in a small boardinghouse at 610 Emmet Street on the corner of College Place Street. The rent was cheap and the view from the second-story room provided a great vantage point for watching off-campus coeds walk up and down the street between classes. Collins had a daily look at who was who in the student ghetto—a neighborhood of cheap, substandard rentals just off campus. Lovely in the spring and summer, the aging neighborhood was fully shaded with mature trees, making the streets especially dark at night. The neighborhood where John Norman Collins lived in plain sight was peaceful and quiet, with the exception of traditional weekend college parties and the occasional coed murder.

PART TWO

—11—

The Preliminary Hearing

ON AUGUST 1, 1969, John Norman Collins stood mute before Washtenaw County Fourteenth Circuit Court judge Edward D. Deake. The judge set a preliminary hearing for August 7, 1969, to determine if the prosecution had enough evidence to bring Collins to trial for the first-degree murder of Karen Sue Beineman. Collins was dressed in a light-blue sports coat, dark-blue trousers, a light-yellow shirt, and a dark, narrow tie. His hair was neatly combed except for the single lock that tumbled down his forehead—an identifying feature in the composite drawings of the suspected killer. His lawyers entered an innocent plea, and Collins was held without bail in the Washtenaw County Jail in Ann Arbor.

John M. Toomey of the Ann Arbor law firm Toomey and Francis explained to Judge Deake that Mrs. Loretta Collins wanted to have a court-appointed attorney represent her son because she could not afford counsel. Toomey indicated that John Collins agreed to whatever his mother wanted. Attorney Hale Saph III—representing Mrs. Collins—requested the court provide "the financial resources of Washtenaw County be used for proper legal counsel because of the seriousness of the charge."

Next, Judge Deake swore in Collins and questioned him about his financial condition. Collins stated he owned no property except a motorcycle, and he had not worked since leaving his job at Motor Wheel Corporation in June. The judge explained to Collins he was entitled to a preliminary hearing within ten days after his arrest. If he wanted a court-appointed attorney, the hearing would be delayed. Collins agreed to the postponement on the advice of his lawyers. This was the first of many delays that would make this case the longest and most expensive criminal trial in Washtenaw County history.

Toomey petitioned the court for his firm to be released from the case. Judge Deake granted his request. The judge adjourned the case until the following Thursday to enable the defendant to obtain an attorney and prepare a defense. According to the *Detroit Free Press*, the initial proceedings took twenty-one minutes before Collins was rushed out a side door, placed in an unmarked sheriff's patrol car, and returned to the county jail.

Tight security surrounded the old Fourteenth District courthouse, a stately nineteenth-century mansion at 206 North Huron Street in Ypsilanti's historic district. Policemen from the Washtenaw County Sheriff's Department, the Michigan State Police, the Ypsilanti city police, and the Eastern Michigan University campus police—forty in all—held the crowd of two hundred people away from the court-house.

Judge Deake charged Sheriff Harvey with the task of maintaining security in and around the historic building known as the Quirk House—built in the 1855. Daniel

Lace Quirk, Ypsilanti's most successful businessman of the nineteenth century, bought the home in 1908. After Daniel L. Quirk died in 1911, his son and daughter inherited the property and eventually donated the building to the city. In 1927, an extensive library was added to the north end of the house which now served as the setting for the most notorious criminal trial in Washtenaw County history.

A sniper threat came into the Ypsilanti state police post saying State Trooper Daniel Leik's life was in danger. With characteristic bravado, Sheriff Douglas Harvey told the press he did not want "another (Jack) Ruby incident to take place," alluding to the killing of Lee Harvey Oswald in the Dallas city jail garage on his way to court only six years before. The mob hit was seen by millions of Americans live on television. Policemen with rifles were stationed on the upper stories of the courthouse as Collins was brought in under heavy guard. The threat turned out to be a prank call or a scare tactic. No sniper incidents were reported.

Ypsilanti fire chief Ralph Crawford enforced the courtroom occupancy limit of forty persons with a maximum of ten more on the balcony. Thirteen members of the press corps vied for ten allotted positions. Sitting in the front row of the gallery were Loretta Collins, John's mother; Sandra Leik, Loretta's sister and the wife of Corporal David Leik; Jerry Collins, John's older brother; and Gail Maison, John's older sister. There was also an unidentified family friend in the front row of the gallery. Understandably upset by the circumstances, Loretta Collins cried briefly before her son entered the courtroom.

Three spectators notably not admitted into the courtroom were family members of Mary Fleszar, the first victim in this series of unsolved murders. Her father Chester, his wife Theresa, and their son Jim were left to stand outside the courthouse with the gawkers. Somehow their daughter Sandra made it inside.

No witnesses were called to testify because of the sudden move to get John Collins a new attorney. Prehearing motions calling for a change of venue, a demand for a bill of particulars, and permission to inspect police evidence were voided by the court until a public defender was appointed. The hearing was adjourned after fifteen minutes.

Outside the courthouse, Chester Fleszar met with the press. "I feel sorry for him," Mr. Fleszar said. "I feel no animosity. If the man is guilty, he must be sick." Then he spoke about the possible involvement of others. "But other people who may have been involved, these are the people who could have prevented additional deaths. They are just as guilty as the killer. The public ought to know what silence means.... I hope those who were silent can live with themselves."

Sandra Fleszar told reporters she knew Collins. "I know him from somewhere, but I can't place where." Jim Fleszar told reporters he worked as a stock boy at Montgomery Wards with Arnie Davis, a close friend of Collins. Davis was a salesman there for about two months. Davis and Collins had a scam where Collins purchased a high-priced item with a bogus check and returned the merchandise to Arnie for cash.

Chester Fleszar made a final appeal to the press for anyone with evidence in the case of his daughter to come forward. He also expressed his concern about all the pretrial publicity this case was getting. He hoped a jury could be seated and there would be a fair trial.

Also denied entrance to the courthouse was Dutch psychic Peter Hurkos. After an anticlimactic morning, reporters spotted Hurkos walking to his car. The predictable media frenzy broke out. His driver slowly edged the car through the crowd. Reporters with microphones thrust them through the open window to get a statement from Hurkos. Among other things, he said he believed three people were involved with the coed slayings and as many as nineteen murders might be related. Then the car whisked away from the media circus. The reporters had their story and Hurkos had his moment.

Upon further investigation, reporters discovered Hurkos had been in town earlier in the week doing research and stopped by Collins's rooming house. It was reported that Hurkos sat on Collins's bed and touched the walls, ceiling, and furniture. The psychic was reputed to have repeated "Canada, Canada, Canada" as he rocked back and forth on the bed pounding his forehead. Hurkos discovered Collins was born in Canada. The next time Peter Hurkos showed up in the Ypsilanti area, he would be hired as an actor to play himself in the motion picture *Now I Lay Me Down to Sleep* based on the local coed killings.

In another development Michigan law enforcement hoped would be a relevant feature in their upcoming case, John Norman Collins's alleged partner in crime, Andrew Manuel, was apprehended at his sister-in-law Ernestina Masters's apartment in Phoenix, Arizona. After a nationwide FBI search, Manuel was being held on an interstate flight charge to avoid prosecution on a conversion of stolen property charge in Michigan.

Collins forged a stolen check to rent a seventeen-foot-long house trailer from Hendrickson's Trailer Rental in

Ypsilanti. The young men towed the trailer to the West Coast behind John's Oldsmobile Cutlass. Two weeks later, the trailer was found abandoned in Salinas, California, parked in an alley behind Manuel's grandparents' house.

On the day after John Norman Collins's preliminary hearing, August 8, 1969, four Michigan police authorities flew to Phoenix to question Manuel about the Michigan murders. At the same time, California authorities wanted to interrogate Manuel about the murders of three young women on the West Coast while Manuel and Collins were visiting there.

An FBI spokesperson stepped in and said investigators would not be permitted to question Manuel until extradition was formally requested and agreed upon. Manuel indicated he would fight extradition until his court-appointed attorney explained the difference between a capital punishment state and a state that outlawed the death penalty.

On Saturday, August 9, Andrew Manuel was extradited to Michigan and arraigned on larceny charges. He appeared in court wearing a blue-green sports shirt, dark pants, and black shoes. Unlike his partner, John Collins, Andrew Manuel looked menacing. He was a hulking man of mixed Filipino-Hispanic descent with dark, brooding eyes.

In court Manuel appeared familiar with judicial proceedings. He was represented by public defenders Robert W. Leutheuser and Edwin L. Pear. When the judge asked Manuel if he could afford counsel, he pleaded poverty adding he had a wife but no children. The judge charged him formally on the trailer conversion complaint and scheduled the hearing for August 27. Bond was set at $7,500.

The prosecution also brought a surprise charge against Manuel of concealing stolen property. A diamond ring valued at close to $500 was hidden in his pants when he was searched. The ring was the property of Elizabeth D. Baker, an Ypsilanti Township public schoolteacher. Her apartment was burglarized while she was at work on June 13. A local jeweler's mark inside the ring band helped identify it. The judge set a hearing for the new charge on September 3 and added another $7,500 bond. Andrew Manuel was having a bad day.

———

On Tuesday, August 12, fifty-four-year-old Richard W. Ryan was appointed public defender by the Washtenaw County Fourteenth District Court to represent Collins before the pretrial examination on Thursday morning. Nicknamed Smokey, Ryan was well-known with almost thirty years of experience as a defense attorney in Ann Arbor courtrooms. Ryan asked Judge Deake if Toomey and Francis could be retained as advisors until he became more familiar with the case. With only two days to prepare for the pretrial hearing, the court agreed. Toomey and Francis consented to stay on as advisors at the county's expense this time.

Judge Deake announced that members of the Washtenaw County Board of Supervisors had voted earlier in the day to give the district judge permission to move the preliminary hearing to Ann Arbor—the county seat. The Washtenaw County Building on Main Street was more modern and better equipped to handle a trial of this magnitude. Security was tight, but only twelve deputies were needed to secure the Ann Arbor venue, rather than thirty at the Ypsilanti courthouse in the Ypsilanti City Hall building. The trial shifted to Ann Arbor.

The only female deputy on the county courthouse detail was Jean Devine. Her duty was to search women's purses and pat down the ladies. Everyone entering the courtroom had to submit to a frisking each time before being admitted inside the building. Seated in the front row of the spectators' gallery were Loretta Collins; Sandra Leik, John's aunt and Loretta's younger sister; Jerry Collins, John's older brother; Gail Maison, John's older sister; and an unidentified man.

Judge Deake entered the courtroom and formally opened the proceedings. The witnesses sat outside the courtroom and were not permitted to speak with or hear the testimony of other witnesses. One by one, they came and went.

The prosecution called its first witness, Sherri Diane Green. She testified that Karen Sue Beineman and another coed had lunch at the dining commons of Downing Hall at noon. Karen asked Sherri if she would walk downtown with her to pick up a hairpiece from a shop about a mile from their dorm. Sherri said she had to prepare for an afternoon class and declined. Beineman started for the wig shop alone at about twenty minutes past noon.

The second person to testify was Washtenaw County sheriff Douglas Harvey. He told how a university professor and his wife on their way to their mailbox found the nude body of a young woman at the bottom of a gully in Ann Arbor Township. Harvey told the court that when he arrived on the scene he "discovered the body lying in a ditch." When the sheriff was asked if he could identify the victim, Harvey said he had a picture of Beineman, but it was up to the medical examiner to make a positive identification. Defense attorney Ryan asked Sheriff Harvey what the source of the photo was and how he came into possession of it.

Harvey sidestepped the question, saying, "I don't know. It was just a picture we had at the station. Everyone knew who we were looking for."

The third witness called was Dr. Robert M. Hendrix, the University of Michigan pathologist who performed the autopsy on Beineman and the six other young women who were brutally murdered over the past two years. To avoid jeopardizing the Beineman case, no mention was made of the other victims. The pathologist identified the missing coed from a photograph and gave the cause of death as strangulation. Dr. Hendrix testified Beineman had type A blood, and she had been raped.

There were deep abrasions and bruises on both wrists and ankles, and skin was missing from her front left arm and chest. The trunk of her body was discolored from decomposition and exposure to the elements. Dr. Hendrix said he found a five-inch-square piece of coarse golden cloth lodged "very far back" in her throat which eventually caused death. One of Beineman's front teeth was broken, and she suffered repeated blunt force trauma to the head that caused extensive brain damage. As if all that was not bad enough, the doctor found a pair of white underpants with hair clippings on them stuffed into her vagina. Earlier testimony said Beineman had eaten at noon on the day she disappeared. The doctor estimated her digestive processes stopped about three hours later.

Under cross-examination, Dr. Hendrix conceded that the time when Beineman's digestive processes ceased was not necessarily the exact time of her death. Hendrix admitted the body had been exposed to insects about twenty-four hours before it was found. It was another fourteen or fifteen hours before he saw the body. Defense attorney Ryan asked the doctor about the accuracy of determining blood type after so long a period. Hendrix replied dryly, "Blood types have been determined from Egyptian mummies."

Next in the witness chair was Larry Mathewson, a rookie Eastern Michigan University patrolman. He testified he saw John Collins on a motorcycle on July 23 about six blocks from the wig shop and four blocks from Downing Hall. When asked how he could be sure it was Collins, Mathewson testified he knew John Collins from competing against him when they were in rival fraternities. Richard Ryan asked if Patrolman Mathewson saw Karen Sue Beineman with John Collins that afternoon. He answered no.

Diana Joan Goshe was the twenty-five-year-old owner of Wigs by Joan on 18½ North Washington Boulevard in downtown Ypsilanti. Questioned by Prosecutor William Delhey, Goshe placed Collins with Karen Sue Beineman. She had not seen them pull up together, but she took two separate looks at him. The first was when she went outside to check him out, and the second was after the girl left the shop and took off down the street seated on the back of his motorcycle. Goshe and Patricia Spaulding were no more than fifteen feet away when the pair drove past them.

"What made you take a second look?" Prosecutor Delhey asked.

"Something the young woman said."

"What was that?"

"She said 'I've done two foolish things in my life, buy this wig and accept a ride on a motorcycle with a stranger.'" Goshe said she and her wig stylist tried to talk the girl out of getting back on the motorcycle.

When asked to identify Collins in a lineup of five Arm of Honor fraternity members, both ladies were able to pick Collins out. Under Ryan's vigorous cross-examination, Goshe unshakably maintained her testimony. She and her wig stylist looked at hundreds of mug shots at police head-quarters, and both women were unwilling to commit to a positive identification from a photograph.

When asked if they had seen a photograph of John Norman Collins before the lineup, Goshe admitted a campus policeman showed them a Polaroid of a young man standing alone next to a Christmas tree. Neither lady was comfortable identifying Collins from that grainy photograph. When interrogated by Ryan about the police lineup, Goshe admitted she was watching when Collins's position in the lineup was switched with someone in the middle. Try as he might, though, Ryan could not shake her from making a positive identification of his client.

The sixth witness at the preliminary hearing was Michigan State Police trooper Corporal David A. Leik, John Collins's uncle by marriage. Sandra Leik was in the front row of the gallery sitting next to her sister, John's mother. Corporal Leik began his testimony by saying he and his family went on vacation on July 18, and his nephew John "had the run of the house." The patrolman testified he gave John a key to the front door to his house two years before when the family first purchased the home. He asked John to take care of the family dog while they were away for two weeks on vacation. At that time, Leik gave John a key to the side door. He was not sure if there were any other loose keys out there, but those were the only two he knew about.

When they returned home after vacation, his wife noticed blotches of black paint on the basement floor. David Leik went down to take a look. He found seven spots leading toward the dryer. After the state police crime team was called in, they discovered dried blood under the dryer and hundreds of tiny hair clippings. Leik explained his wife gave their three sons haircuts in the basement laundry room prior to leaving on vacation. During his testimony, Loretta Collins wept quietly. A permanent wedge was driven between the sisters that day, and the seeds were sown for the dissolution of the Leik marriage. With a family tragedy of this proportion, all are punished.

Richard Ryan made a motion to have the charges dropped due to insufficient evidence, which Judge Deake immediately dismissed. The judge set a September 5 date for arraignment on a charge of first-degree murder in the wrongful death of Karen Sue Beineman. As soon as the gavel came down, Collins was rushed out of the courtroom by a contingent of waiting police. It happened so fast his mother burst into tears. She rose from her seat trying to say good-bye. Her adult children restrained her. Mrs. Collins waved to him, but he was gone in an instant.

The *Ypsilanti Press* reported after the hearing that defense attorney Richard Ryan was not surprised the case was not dismissed because of the "loud and boisterous" arrest. Ryan indicated he would move for a change of venue because he felt it would be impossible to get an impartial jury in Washtenaw County. In response to a question from the press, Ryan said he had not determined if his client would undergo a psychiatric examination prior to the trial or if those reports would be used in Collins's defense. Ryan was asked how he felt about defending a client who was the object of so much publicity. "It weighs heavily on my conscience," he said. "But it weighs heavier on Collins's soul."

In a brief statement to reporters, Prosecutor Delhey commented that the key evidence was the hair clippings the crime lab recovered. Their principal witnesses would be from the scientific community. Delhey directed all other inquiries about the case to Michael Devine, the Michigan Supreme Court-appointed spokesperson for the case.

—12—

Sideshow Developments

SEVERAL DAYS BEFORE THE preliminary hearing took place on Thursday, August 7, Edward Carlbom read in the evening newspaper that his Triumph 650 motorcycle had been seized as evidence in the Karen Sue Beineman case. Carlbom was a former Theta Chi fraternity brother of John Collins and recent graduate of Eastern Michigan University. He now worked in Benton Harbor on the western side of Michigan over 150 miles from Ypsilanti.

Three months before, Carlbom reported to the Ypsilanti police that his Triumph 650 motorcycle was stolen from his garage at 311 Jarvis Street. That was the last Carlbom heard from the Ypsilanti police regarding the theft until he called the station declaring he was the lawful owner of the motorcycle in question. Carlbom was told to show up with proof of ownership to make his claim. Because of work commitments, he waited until the weekend to make the long round-trip to reclaim his stolen property.

Carlbom spoke with an unsympathetic plainclothesman about taking possession of his motorcycle. After all, it was lawfully registered to him. The officer was unmoved. He told Carlbom the motorcycle was sequestered and that was all he was authorized to say. Carlbom persisted and explained he was concerned the gas line may not have been turned off properly which could ruin the bike's engine. The officer lost his patience and threatened Carlbom with being locked up if he bothered police again.

In a public relations move to curb bad publicity, Lieutenant Kenneth Holder of the Ypsilanti police confirmed in a press release that Edward Carlbom's stolen Triumph 650 was being held as evidence at the murder coordinating center in the former Holy Ghost Seminary. He added, "Mr. Carlbom will be notified when his property is no longer needed by the court, then it will be released to him." Over one year later, Ed Carlbom's motorcycle was returned to him.

———

In Collins's first public statement since his arrest, Richard W. Ryan told reporters on August 20 that his client said he did not kill Karen Sue Beineman and did not know who had killed her. "He says he simply didn't do it." When asked about a rumor being circulated among the press, Richard Ryan said an anonymous woman called one of Collins's original lawyers, John M. Toomey, and claimed Collins told her before his arrest that Beineman's death was accidental. Collins allegedly confided in her that the young coed had fallen off the back of his bike and was run over by a car. The informant said Collins told her he became frightened and "made it look like a murder" by disposing of her body in a wooded area.

When Toomey asked the woman why she did not come forward earlier, she said she talked to a "nice young man" from the sheriff's department. This was never confirmed or denied. If a hit-and-run driver ran over Beineman, why was there no evidence of tire tracks on her body? The incident was either a prank call or a deliberate attempt to obfuscate the facts. It seemed calculated to confuse the public with spurious news reports to undermine the selection of an impartial jury. If a jury could not be impaneled, further delay for a change of venue hearing would be necessary giving the defense more time to develop its case. Richard Ryan was quick to state his client denied any connection with the claim by the unknown Ypsilanti woman.

———

Monday afternoon before Thursday's preliminary hearing, John Collins had an uninvited and unexpected visitor in his maximum-security lockup at the Washtenaw County Jail. The Saturday edition of the *Detroit Free Press* reported that a sixty-two-year-old man named Joseph Pasic, self-appointed bishop of a two-hundred-year-old Russian religious sect, presented credentials stating he was a clergyman. Pasic talked his way past jail officials and spent two hours with Collins in his cell.

Pasic, also known as Brother Bartholomew, told *Free Press* reporters that Sheriff Harvey was a "wonderful man" who was "very courteous and efficient in allowing me to see John." When apprised of the situation, Sheriff Harvey said he did not have any knowledge of Pasic's visitation but later admitted "by state law I have to let any minister in to see a prisoner any time he wants to."

Ironically, when Pasic talked his way past jail security and signed the visitor's log, Sheriff Harvey and other county authorities were at another location discussing the high-security arrangements for the preliminary hearing inside its cramped courtroom. When Collins's original attorney, Robert Francis, found out from his client about Pasic's visit Monday night, he said he did not think Pasic had anything to do with the case, so he was not going to worry about it. To protect his client, Francis spoke to authorities about security measures at the jail, and procedures were tightened.

Pasic set up a polished wooden crucifix in a stand with two candles and read eight chapters from Matthew and Luke in the *New Testament*. Pasic lived in a rented, 100-square-foot room in a house on Davenport Street in Detroit. He told reporters Friday he talked with Collins about many things including the murders, which was privileged information in his role as clergy. "We talked mostly about his spirit and his soul," Pasic said. "He seems to be a very repentant young man. Several times during my visit, Collins broke down and cried."

The bishop told reporters he was referred to Sheriff Harvey by an assistant of Colonel Frederick E. Davids, state police director, when Pasic went to Lansing the previous week to get permission to see Collins. On the day he showed up at the jail, Pasic was wearing a brown suit and a bow tie. He carried two briefcases and an umbrella into the cell block. He claimed the deputies did not search the briefcases, but his body was patted down before his visit. The two men talked for two hours through a security screen.

When Prosecutor William Delhey found out about the visit, he was upset about jail security. The prosecutor's office made a cursory examination of Pasic. It was soon discovered Joseph Pasic was an ex–mental patient who was a self-styled leader of the Doukhobors religious sect, an eighteenth-century Russian religious group once active in

Western Canada. Their teachings were based on peace and love, much like the Quakers in the United States. There was an active branch of the group in British Columbia known as the Sons of Freedom.

Investigators also discovered Pasic was the welterweight boxing champion of Michigan in the 1930s. "He fought under the name Joe Sharkey," said his older brother Steve, a retired foundry supervisor in Albion, Michigan. "That's when he got a little punchy too, I believe. He had a cataract in his left eye, and he caught a lot of punches he shouldn't have." Pasic fought out of Benton Harbor and moved up to the middleweight rank and then the light heavyweight division. Repeated blows to the head had taken their toll on him.

A search of his criminal record revealed Pasic was once arrested for embezzling $400 from three sisters who gave him power of attorney and the money to pay off their mortgage. He never paid it. Charges resulting from "the collection of fees while impersonating a lawyer" bought Pasic a five-to-ten-year term for embezzlement in 1943 at Jackson State Prison. He served three years of his sentence. While in jail, Pasic studied law books and was said to have convinced Washtenaw County Circuit Judge James R. Breakey that he was a lawyer. In some ways, Pasic was a chameleon-man who could assume roles and convince others he was something he was not.

Whatever his talents, Joseph Bartholomew Pasic was committed to Ypsilanti State Mental Hospital by Jackson County Probate Court on June 16, 1961, where he stayed until March 20, 1963, when he was transferred to Ionia State Hospital and released shortly after.

Ann Arbor police chief Walter E. Krasny revealed to the

press that Pasic's name came to the attention of authorities two weeks before when he telephoned Dutch psychic Peter Hurkos on July 25 at the Inn America two days after Beineman disappeared. Krasny said the motel telephone was tapped and the conversation was recorded with a transcript sent over to the state police officials at the crime center. At that time, they did not know Pasic's name. After the Collins jail visit, the cleric admitted he made the call.

The Ann Arbor police chief reported to the *Detroit News* that Pasic told Hurkos he had "greater psychic powers" than Hurkos and called him a "fraud." Pasic warned Hurkos he was "infringing upon his territory and was bothering his flock." The caller added if Hurkos did not drop his investigation, "The killer may say 'I will kill two or three more girls just to show Hurkos is a fraud.'" The self-styled preacher told Hurkos to "get out of my diocese," but he made no threats. Several days later, Beineman's body was discovered.

After Pasic's visit, Collins told Sheriff Harvey he did not want to talk with him again. The prosecution and the defense finally had something to agree upon: neither wanted anything further to do with Brother Bartholomew Pasic.

—13—

New Person of Interest

EARLIER IN THE SUMMER of 1969, frustrated Michigan authorities requested Federal Bureau of Investigation involvement in this case, but there were jurisdictional problems. No state lines were crossed. In a letter to Republican Congressman Gerald Ford of Grand Rapids, Michigan, FBI director J. Edgar Hoover wrote that his agency found no evidence federal law was violated. Without such evidence, the FBI was not empowered to enter the case. That abruptly changed when federal agents learned a fraudulently rented trailer was driven from Michigan to California by John Collins and Andrew Manuel. This was the first law enforcement connection between Manuel and Collins, who was already behind bars charged with first-degree murder. The FBI issued a fugitive warrant and a nationwide search for Andrew Julian Manuel Jr.—Collins's Motor Wheel work buddy and California traveling companion.

In Detroit, FBI spokesperson Special Agent Paul Stoddard said the federal warrant for Manuel did not mean the bureau was entering the murder investigation. Manuel was merely being sought on a fugitive warrant. "That's where our jurisdiction lies," Agent Stoddard told the assembled press.

To the casual observer, it appeared the theft of the house trailer was more important to the FBI than the murders of seven women, but that was not the case. Without jurisdictional authority, federal interference in a statewide case would make any evidence the FBI discovered inadmissible in court. Any competent defense attorney knew that. The risk of setting the accused murderer free or having a mistrial was too great.

Manuel fled Michigan on July 24, 1969—the day after the disappearance of Karen Sue Beineman. He was actively sought by the FBI at the beginning of August. When the FBI had not apprehended Manuel by August 6, there was growing suspicion he fell victim to foul play or had left the country. "The longer he is missing, the greater that feeling," an unnamed FBI spokesperson said.

At first, Manuel was characterized as a Mexican American, but it was later discovered he was Filipino Hispanic. Described as six foot one inch tall with dark hair and brown eyes, Manuel weighed 270 pounds. He had a tattoo of an eagle on his left forearm. Also known to use the alias Richard Diaz, Manuel had a police record in Riverside, California, and was convicted in 1963 on two counts of burglary.

According to a neighbor in Ypsilanti, Manuel lived with his wife Betty Sue at 785 North Harris Road until recently. When Manuel was at home, he was visited by male friends who rode motorcycles. Manuel moved into a room in the same boardinghouse where John Collins was living before the pair left for California.

The Washtenaw County Prosecutor's Office discovered in their initial investigation that Manuel moved from Salinas in 1965 and took a job with the Ford Motor Company. In the summer of 1968, he worked at Bond Warehouse in Detroit. In September 1968, he took a job as a machinist for Motor Wheel Corporation where he met Collins, who worked part-time as an inspector since August 1968. Manuel worked the full-time night shift until he left the job in May 1969. Collins left his job in June, a month after his friend.

The FBI thought Manuel might be hiding out at his mother's house in Salinas, California, and there were rumors he might have fled to Florida. But he was finally picked up without a struggle at his sister-in-law's house in Phoenix, Arizona, on Monday, August 6. He had been there since Sunday night with his sister-in-law Ernestina Masters and her roommate Nancy McClure—both twenty-two years old. Ernestina was unemployed and Nancy worked as a cocktail waitress.

After two and a half hours of questioning, police discovered Andrew Manuel called Ernestina from his hometown of Salinas on the previous Saturday night. He told her he was in some trouble. He asked if she would wire him fifty dollars for a bus ticket. She did. Then Manuel took the bus to Phoenix, arriving at her apartment on Sunday night. He spent his entire stay inside, sitting quietly in a chair and staring into space. "He never, not once, went outdoors," Masters said. "He was really depressed and acted very strange. He was scared he would be sent to jail for something he didn't do."

"I didn't have anything to do with the killings," he told her. "Andrew claimed he knew Collins for only a few months and was shocked when he learned of the murder charge against him." The truth was Andrew Manuel knew John Collins for eleven months.

FBI agents refused to say how they located Manuel, but one agent commented, "It was just one of those things where we got a tip and everything jelled." When asked by reporters, Ernestina Masters speculated Manuel might have been traced by the telegram she sent him wiring the fifty dollars which seemed plausible. Masters added, "Andrew planned to turn himself in on Tuesday, but on Monday morning, federal agents knocked on the door. They identified themselves and asked if Andrew was inside. He gave himself up without a struggle, and they took him away." Ernestina Masters thought highly of her brother-in-law. "He has always been wonderful to me and my family. I have total faith in his innocence." Andrew Julian Manuel was arraigned on August 6, 1969, and remanded to the Federal Detention Center in Florence, Arizona, sixty miles southeast of Phoenix.

Back in Ypsilanti, Sheriff Harvey reported that Collins owned several guns, a shotgun and two rifles, which were recovered. Manuel sold the weapons to buy a bus ticket out of town. Harvey told reporters "several Collins's associates are believed to have been involved in a burglary crew responsible for a series of thefts in the area." Other stolen items found in Collins's possession were four motorcycles, several wallets, assorted sporting goods, and a camera. Harvey said when he showed the guns to Collins, Collins identified them as his property and added Manuel must have stolen them from his room. One of the deer-hunting rifles belonged to a former Theta Chi fraternity brother who had reported it stolen earlier.

Sheriff Harvey's informant, Gani Elizi, manager of Roy's Squeeze Inn, claimed Manuel sold him three guns and a diamond ring for one hundred dollars. After the sale, Elizi stated he drove Manuel to the bus station in Ann Arbor. Manuel said he was leaving for California. Manuel offered Elizi a .22-caliber pistol which he refused to take for some unspecified reason. "The pistol is currently unaccounted for," Sheriff Harvey said.

When Manuel was extradited to Michigan from Texas, he claimed to have thrown the handgun away somewhere along the highway on his bus ride to California. He conveniently forgot on which stretch of highway. The loss of this gun was considered critical to the prosecution who had two unsolved murders where a .22-caliber revolver was used. Surely, Manuel knew the make of the handgun which would have proved helpful with the case, but he pleaded ignorance.

Different brands of pistols have unique lands (ridges) and grooves in the barrel called rifling. The bullet exits the barrel spinning to give the shot more stability. Colt revolvers spin and mark the bullet one way while Smith & Wesson revolvers spin and mark the bullet the opposite way. Microscopic examination of .22-caliber bullets recovered from Alice Kalom and Jane Mixer identified the handgun as a High Standard revolver. It was Manuel's only asset on the bus ride, and he very possibly sold the gun for cash in a bar or truck stop somewhere along the way.

On September 3, 1969, two witnesses testified before district court Judge Henry D. Arkinson that John Norman Collins and Andrew Manuel used bogus names, a stolen driver's license, and a forged check to rent the house trailer they abandoned in California in June. Witness Carol Blackmer worked at Hendrickson's Trailer Rental. She told the judge that Collins used the name James Skotak to reserve a trailer on June 19. Manuel paid a twenty-five dollar, good-faith cash deposit. On the following day, Collins paid the eighty dollar balance for a week's rental with a forged check and stolen ID.

The trailer was hitched to an Oldsmobile Cutlass with license plate number CW3383. Michigan Secretary of State records indicate the plate was reported stolen on March 4 from a 1968 Plymouth Coupe registered to residents in Belleville. Rather than visit Canada for a week as Collins claimed, the two young men headed west to California with no thought of returning the trailer.

"Is this the check?" Assistant Prosecutor Jerome Farmer asked.

"Yes, it is," Blackmer said. "I asked him [Collins] if it would bounce. He said 'It better not!'"

"Did it bounce?"

"That check is still bouncing."

Next up on the stand was the real James Skotak, a student at Eastern Michigan University from Redford Township. He testified his gym locker was broken into last April and his wallet and identification were stolen while he was taking a class at Warner Gymnasium.

The next witness called was Elizabeth V. Baker. Baker testified the week before against Andrew Manuel on a charge of possessing a diamond ring burglarized from her home. When shown the bogus check, she identified it as having come from a book of checks stolen from her apartment on March 14, 1969.

Virgil Hendrickson, the owner and operator of the trailer renting agency, testified he hitched the trailer, valued at $2,395, to a car driven by Manuel already described by Blackmer as a late-model Oldsmobile Cutlass. He testified the trailer was never returned. Then one day, the police in Salinas, California, contacted him saying the trailer had been found abandoned.

The final witness at the preliminary hearing was Regina Lawson of 4762 Washtenaw Avenue in Ann Arbor. She testified that on July 12, Andrew Manuel tried to sell her and her husband a trailer he said could sleep eight people. She and her husband told him they were not interested. Defense attorney Robert W. Leutheuser tried to impeach Lawson's testimony by suggesting she and Manuel were involved. She insisted they were close friends. "Andrew was someone I could talk to." Leutheuser dismissed Lawson from the stand without further cross-examination.

Assistant Prosecutor Jerome Farmer moved that the case be bound over to circuit court. Leutheuser strongly objected. He argued the state had shown only guilt by association and nothing more. Assistant Prosecutor Farmer reminded the court that at a preliminary hearing, the prosecution does not need to exhibit all of its evidence, only enough to show a crime was committed and the accused may be responsible.

Judge Henry D. Arkinson said these requirements were met, and Andrew Manuel was bound over for a September 26 circuit court appearance. Leutheuser moved that the $7,500 bond be removed and his client released on his own recognizance because he had family in the area—a wife. Since Manuel was the object of a nationwide FBI manhunt and because of the seriousness of the crime, the bond was not rescinded or reduced.

Manuel's wife Betty Sue was described by the press as a pretty brunette. She and Andrew's mother sat through the ninety-minute hearing in the tiny paneled Ypsilanti courtroom. Outside the courtroom, Betty Sue told reporters she did not think her husband was involved in the murders, and she did not know John Collins very well. "He used to visit sometimes, but that's all. I went target shooting with him once," she said.

On Monday, November 16—two days before Manuel was scheduled to be brought to trial—defense attorney Robert Leutheusar told Judge William F. Ager that Andrew Manuel wanted to plead guilty to both counts brought against him and throw himself on the mercy of the court.

Judge Ager asked Manuel where he got the rings. He answered, "From John Collins." Continuing his questioning, Judge Ager asked if he knew where John Collins got the rings. Once again, Manuel pleaded ignorance. He said, "Collins gave me the rings because he had no use for them." Judge Ager accepted the guilty plea and set sentencing for both charges on December 10. Andrew Manuel was sentenced to five years of probation, a fifty-dollar fine, and three hundred dollars in court costs for the conversion case. He received the same sentence for the concealing stolen property charge. In addition, Hendrickson's Trailer Sales was awarded $1,500 in restitution for the abandoned trailer.

In a good-faith attempt to enlist Andrew Manuel's aid in testifying against Collins, Senior Assistant Prosecutor Williams announced in court that Andrew Manuel was cleared of suspicion in the deaths of the seven young women in Washtenaw County. Williams said he felt it was necessary because of the nationwide FBI search focused on Manuel due to his involvement with Collins. With Prosecutor Williams's statement, Andrew Manuel was no longer under suspicion as a murder suspect.

Outside the courtroom, as if to underscore what the prosecutor said, Ann Arbor police chief Walter Krasny told the press, "Manuel has been thoroughly questioned by authorities who are convinced he had nothing to do with the murders in the area." From that moment, Manuel was dealt out of the game until he was called later to testify in the Collins trial.

—14—

Waiting for a Trial Date

By August 31, 1969, John Norman Collins had been in his basement maximum-security cell in the Washtenaw County Jail for one month. *Detroit Free Press* reporter Walker Lundy wrote that "Collins sits on the floor because there are no chairs in the room. His guards say he talks little and cries occasionally. His family and friends insist John is acting like any normal college student would in jail, rather than the portrait of a cold-blooded killer police paint him to be." Collins received regular letters from his mother, and his family visited for fifteen minutes each Sunday.

Circuit court Judge John W. Conlin presided over the hearing on September 5 that lasted only thirty minutes. The judge ordered the prosecutor's representative to meet with the defense for a discussion of state evidence. Richard Ryan requested admittance to the Leik house—the alleged scene of the crime.

"The prosecutor's office has no jurisdiction over this house," Senior Assistant Prosecutor Williams told Judge Conlin.

"I can only recommend that the family permit defense counsel to enter the house, but I cannot order it," the judge added.

The defense wanted all of the scientific evidence taken from the incinerator at 619 Emmet Street, the blood types and Rh factors for all the members of the Leik family, and the names of the witnesses against John Collins. Ryan challenged the testimony of Diana Joan Goshe, owner of Wigs by Joan. The defense attorney argued she identified Collins only after being shown a photograph of him.

On September 17, the judge ruled against all the defense motions except for one meaningful concession. State police trooper Corporal Leik relented and allowed the defense team to visit the basement of his home if the prosecutor's office made no objection. The next hearing was scheduled to take place on October 1.

In a signed police deposition read in court the day of the hearing, Joe Patton, owner of J & J Cycle on Ecorse Road in Ypsilanti, told investigators John Collins was in his shop at 1:00 p.m. on July 23 and left about an hour later. Patton could pinpoint the time because Collins arrived at about the same time the crew ate lunch. The motorcycle-shop owner's deposition stated Collins was in his shop the day before working on his bike, and he came to the shop on Wednesday to pay for a motorcycle chain he had purchased.

This new information was calculated to cast the shadow of doubt over the prosecution's time line. When Judge Conlin asked why Patton was not in court as a witness, neither attorney could offer an explanation.

Next to testify was J & J Cycle mechanic John Lehto. He told the court Collins arrived at the shop as late as 1:30

p.m. and stayed as late as 3:00 p.m. Lehto worked at J & J since April and knew Collins since May. Lehto added, "Collins acted normal. He was in his usual jovial mood."

Of the many people who knew John growing up in Catholic school and at college, words like *moody*, *brooding*, or *edgy* were more likely used to describe Collins than *jovial*. People say he rarely smiled. Photographs of John Collins in his high school yearbooks from 1963 through 1965 bear this out. Collins looks sullen and serious in virtually every photograph he appears in.

When the judge asked Lehto about the whereabouts of his missing boss Joe Patton, he expressed surprise. "The police were there (at the shop) to interrogate us on his (Collins) behavior and habits just this afternoon."

A third witness at the motorcycle shop who gave a police statement was John MacDougail. When Lehto was asked about MacDougal's whereabouts, he told the judge he left for California and could not be reached.

The motorcycle-shop guys tried to help Collins the best they could. The rumor around town was that J & J Cycle fenced hot motorcycle parts, and Collins did business with them. The guys may have been protecting their own self-interests by providing a plausible alibi for one of their compatriots. After the hearing, an unnamed veteran police official remarked to the press, "The Patton angle was a clumsy attempt at an alibi."

In other business, Senior Assistant Prosecutor Williams called the defense motion to see all of the state's evidence a *fishing expedition*. Judge Conlin agreed the motion was too broad to be granted. The judge also denied a defense motion to see all the sworn statements of witnesses. The motion to suppress evidence and testimony of Diane Joan Goshe was adjourned until the next day. Defense attorney Ryan decided not to file a change of venue motion at this time.

On Wednesday, October 8, Judge Conlin imposed a gag order in the case. The judge said there was a "reasonable likelihood that the dissemination of certain information or opinions would interfere with a fair trial for Collins." The penalty for disobeying the court order would be a contempt of court citation.

The hearing resumed on Tuesday with the testimony of Lieutenant William Mulholland, lead detective from the Washtenaw County Sheriff's Department, who revealed statements made by witnesses and other testimony relating to physical evidence.

Lieutenant Mulholland testified he questioned Joseph Patton, who originally placed Collins's visit at between "2:00 p.m. and 3:00 p.m." Patton revised Collins's estimated time of arrival at between 1:00 p.m. and 2:00 p.m. when questioned later. The one hour discrepancy in the time frame was not explained. Mulholland further testified Collins was placed under arrest on the evening of July 31 while undergoing questioning at the crime center in Ann Arbor.

The police detective additionally testified that an unidentified student saw Collins and Beineman leave the wig shop on a motorcycle she positively identified as a blue Triumph 650. She told police she was a bike enthusiast and noticed all of the fancy chrome on the bike.

Officer Mulholland told the court five young women reported Collins attempted to pick them up on the day Beineman disappeared. Another EMU coed, nineteen-year-old Lois D'Orazio from Livonia notified police after seeing the composite drawing of the alleged murderer and reported she had dated Collins. D'Orazio said Collins noticed her ears were pierced and told her he did not like them. Mulholland told the hushed courtroom five of the seven murdered girls over the past twenty-two months had pierced ears. In a statement read to the court by Mulholland, D'Orazio explained how Collins showed her how he strangled cats by putting his hands around her throat.

Reacting to this allegation, John Collins looked up sharply at the stand and shook his head saying "No!" His mother Loretta Collins said from the gallery loudly with disgust, "This is ridiculous!" Judge Conlin ignored the outburst and adjourned the hearing until Thursday.

Afterward, the court spokesperson Michael Devine responded to defense complaints of the hearsay testimony which apparently was not an issue for Ryan when his defense witness Joe Patton had his statement read to the court in absentia. Devine explained to the press, "Officer Mulholland's testimony consisted of hearsay and was admitted only on the basis of the pretrial hearing. Such testimony would be inadmissible in a court trial. The witnesses will be recalled if their testimony is relevant to this case."

At Thursday's hearing, Richard Ryan filed the names of ten persons he said could vouch for the whereabouts of John Norman Collins from shortly after noon to 3:00 p.m. on the day Karen Sue Beineman disappeared. Three Eastern Michigan coeds, five employees from J & J Cycle, and two other witnesses—owner and operator of Roy's Squeeze Inn and his part-time employee.

Now it was the prosecution's turn to bolster its case. William Delhey filed a document with the court listing certain items found in a search of Collins's room and the

Oldsmobile Cutlass registered in his mother's name. John was in full possession of the car since its purchase.

- A partially used spray can of black enamel paint
- A fabric dustcover in Collins's room with "stains"
- A rubberized rain jacket with "stains"
- 175 rounds of .22-caliber long-rifle ammunition
- Blood on the front seat of the car
- Hair on the tire iron, in the trunk, and inside the car
- A pair of gloves with hair on them, and
- A bobby pin from the trunk fender well

Defense Attorney Ryan finally made his expected change of venue motion. He suggested either Lansing or Kalamazoo to the court. The judge said he would review the motion and adjourned the hearing.

People most familiar with this case were surprised at the release of this information to the press after Judge Conlin's court order prohibiting any statement outside the official courtroom proceeding. These documents—though filed— were not read into the court record. When Judge Conlin was asked why he did not invoke the court order regarding leaks to the press, he explained the gag order applied to the defense attorneys, the prosecution team, law enforcement officers, and court personnel—everyone except for the official Michigan Supreme Court– appointed spokesperson for this case, Michael Devine. Devine was the source of the information.

At the October 29 hearing, Richard Ryan added fifteen exhibits to his original motion for a change of venue. They were clippings from Ann Arbor, Detroit, and New York newspapers. One exhibit was a detective magazine from London. Judge Conlin expressed his view he would be able to sit an impartial jury. He thought the extensive publicity was essentially fair. The judge did not dismiss the motion— only delayed it.

It was announced the trial date would be determined by December 8. The reason for the delay was that Judge Conlin had to preside over another case, the trial of Ernest R. Bishop Jr. (28) who was accused of shooting Margaret Ann Phillips, a twenty-five-year-old graduate student at the University of Michigan. Because of the Bishop trial and the upcoming holiday season, Judge Conlin scheduled the Collins trial for after the first of the year.

—15—

Michigan's Perry Mason

THE *DETROIT NEWS* REPORTED on November 25, 1969, that prominent Detroit criminal defense attorney Joseph W. Louisell had agreed to defend John Norman Collins on his murder-one charge. Louisell and his junior partner—thirty-year-old Neil Fink—conferred privately with Loretta Collins over the previous two weeks. The firm of Louisell and Barris accepted the case and was expected to take over on Monday, December 1. After that date, public defender Richard Ryan and his defense team would be officially removed from the case despite being fired by Loretta Collins weeks before.

Fifty-three-year-old Joseph W. Louisell was one of seven children—five boys and two girls—born to Medor Ewing Louisell and Mary Tallon. He grew up Catholic in Duluth, Minnesota, and developed a deep appreciation for the works of Shakespeare from his father who held literature and law degrees from the University of Michigan.

Louisell earned his law degree from the University of Detroit and made a career of defending some of Michigan's most notorious defendants. Known for his defense of reputed Detroit mafia figures, his clients included Pete Licavoli, Anthony and Vito Giacalone, and Matthew "Mike" Rubino, all identified as Detroit mafia figures in testimony before the United States Senate Rackets Committee in 1963, led by Senator John L. McClellan. The hearings were also known as the Joseph Valachi hearings. Louisell defended Jimmy Hoffa and other top teamster officials during the hearings where he received nationwide media exposure.

Prominent victories for Louisell included the acquittal of Carl E. Bolton and Carl B. Renda, both charged with the 1948 shooting of United Auto Workers president Walter Reuther. Louisell also won an acquittal for the beautiful, blonde former model Nelle Lassiter, who was charged with conspiring with her lover to murder her husband—used-car dealer Parvin "Bill" Lassiter in 1959.

At a Detroit press conference announcing he would take the Collins case, reporters asked Louisell about his courtroom theatrics. "All trial lawyers are ham actors at heart," he explained. "Especially me, I guess. Normally, sixty-five percent of my practice is civil and corporate law. That's where the money is. But criminal law has some kicks. That's for fun." When asked how Mrs. Collins would pay for their services in November when she could not afford her Ann Arbor attorneys in August, he answered, "No comment."

On November 26, the *Detroit Free Press* reported that Loretta Collins received a pledge from a national magazine for a large sum of money in exchange for exclusive rights to her son's story. The claim was never confirmed. Another source close to Mrs. Collins said she took out a second mortgage on her home to pay for her son's legal fees. That explanation seems more plausible. Whatever her source of funds, Loretta Collins had retained the state's most expen-

sive and notorious attorney—called by the *Detroit News,*
"Michigan's Perry Mason."

Joseph Louisell's son, John C. Louisell, was a legal aide
in his father's office and did the books for him during the
Collins trial. He remembers his father's partner Ivan Barris
having lunch one afternoon at Greenfield's Restaurant in
Southfield, Michigan, where Loretta Collins worked as a
waitress. "She approached him about defending her son.
Ivan brushed her off and said 'call Louisell.' Mrs. Collins
came into the office, and my father apologized but told her
the firm was too busy to take her son's case.

"Junior partner Neil Fink heard about this and went to
work on my father. Fink promised to do the background
research, try the case, and perform all the heavy lifting pro
bono. Neil wanted to take a gamble. If he won, he would go
from being a fifty dollar per hour lawyer to a five hundred
dollar per hour lawyer. The firm of Louisell and Barris
did not make a dime on this case. It cost them a hundred
thousand dollars."

The trial was not expected to begin until sometime the
following year. It was already being called the most famous
trial in Michigan state history. Louisell and Fink were
expected to make new motions for their client delaying the
trial for another three months. On December 12, Collins's
lawyers asked the judge for a five-week adjournment "to
meet with their client and prepare motions in the case."
By this time, Collins had spent almost four months in his
Washtenaw County jail cell.

The judge asked Collins if he objected to further delay.
He answered, "No, Sir." These were the first words he had
uttered in the courtroom in a dozen hearings since his arrest.
The pretrial hearing was postponed until January 21, 1970.

The *Detroit News* wrote on December 17 that John Collins told an unnamed sheriff's deputy: "I'll do anything my mother thinks best." His jailer said confinement had become a way of life for Collins, "He seems fairly well-adjusted and is sometimes in good spirits." "Stoic resignation" was the phrase used to describe Collins's demeanor in his triple-locked, maximum-security cell.

The sheriff's deputy attributed Collins's adjustment to jail life to his mother Loretta. "She seems to have taken over the case," he said. "Collins's appetite has improved, and he is eating regular prison food. Deputies count the knives and forks when his food tray is picked up, and once a day he is taken from his cell for a shower." It was also learned the prisoner was allowed to shave with an electric shaver kept for him by deputies. The *Detroit News* reporter was informed, "Collins's cell is spot-checked randomly—sometimes several times an hour—while other maximum-security prisoners are checked hourly." The last thing the county sheriff's office wanted was a suicide—though there was no indication Collins had a self-destructive impulse.

Neil Fink bristled when he read the *Detroit News* jail article entitled "Stoic Collins Accepts New Life Behind Bars." Had not Judge Conlin issued a news blackout regarding this case? To strengthen their change-of-venue motion, Fink entered the article as further evidence their client could not get a fair trial in Washtenaw County. He complained bitterly to the judge.

Fink made a motion that the judge write a letter to *Detroit News* reporter John F. Nehman "to protest the inaccuracies" about the story. The judge, glancing at the article, quickly turned down the motion. Judge Conlin was not going to allow this thirty-year-old, out-of-town attorney to manipulate him and add to his already overcrowded workload. Fink asked for a delay in the pretrial hearing until January 21. He stated once again the defense needed "more time to meet with their client to prepare motions in the case."

After the delay motion, Prosecutor Delhey dryly replied to Judge Conlin, "The state is ready, Your Honor."

Conlin asked the defendant if he had any objection to a further delay. Collins answered, "No, Sir, I don't." When the judge informed him the trial might not start until later that spring, Collins was agreeable.

—16—

In Related News

THE *DETROIT NEWS* REPORTED for the first time in December the extent of the scientific evidence the prosecution hoped to present at the trial. The announcement was made in Ann Arbor that human hair clippings found in the Karen Sue Beineman investigation were placed in a reactor and bombarded with neutrons at a California laboratory in search of scientific evidence. Dr. Howard Schlesinger—a forensic chemist with Gulf General Atomic Division of Gulf Oil in San Diego—was brought in to help bolster the prosecution's case.

At the first preliminary examination on August 14, state police experts from the Plymouth crime lab testified short, clipped hairs were discovered on the underpants of Karen Sue Beineman. Michigan State Police crime lab experts believed hair clippings of similar length were found on the basement floor under the clothes dryer at the Leik house.

In a family tragedy of Shakespearean proportions, Uncle Dave rang the alarm bell on his nephew John. The Collins family fell in ruins from this blood-soaked drama. Corporal

193

David Leik testified that his basement was used as a family barbershop where his wife cut his hair and the hair of his three sons. He testified about irregularities like the missing items from his basement utility room and the black spray-paint blotches on the basement floor not there when his family left on vacation.

Dr. Walter Holtz from the Michigan Health Department lab testified that he conducted a microscopic examination and comparison of the clippings from the underpants and those clippings found under the clothes dryer. Dr. Holtz found them to be "of common origin because of similar length, coloration, diameter, and structure." Under cross-examination by defense attorney Neil Fink, Dr. Holtz admitted it was impossible to make a positive identification from hair like it was from fingerprints.

Dr. Schlesinger was brought to Ann Arbor on December 18 to testify at the pretrial hearing. An expert in thermal neutron activation analysis, he explained that this technique was developed in 1961 for use with "hard to identify materials." Schlesinger said it was possible to count and measure the energies of gamma rays to make comparisons. If elements in the two compared samples differ, they do not belong to the same person.

When pressed by the defense, the chemist admitted, "This technique cannot establish positively that two hairs came from the same person. All you can say is there is a certain probability they likely came from the same source." The neutron analysis expert did not reveal his findings at the hearing. It was a day of mixed results for both the prosecution and the defense.

At the close of witness testimony, Neil Fink filed a defense motion for a change of venue. Joseph Louisell was not present, but junior partner Fink insisted Collins could not get a fair trial in Washtenaw County because "Sheriff Douglas J. Harvey and his deputies will be in charge of the jury." Fink believed this was clearly a conflict of interest for Collins. Fink filed for full disclosure of everything found in the police search of Collins's room and his car. Additionally, he wanted the testimony of Diane Joan Goshe suppressed. Neil Fink argued the state used "pre-identification procedures calculated to prejudice the defendant."

Collins was bound over but no date was set for the trial. Judge Conlin would schedule and hear motions following the holiday season. He wished everyone happy holidays and adjourned the proceedings.

On Christmas Eve—as the last decade of the sixties came to an end—the Associated Press Broadcasters and Newspaper Editors of Michigan announced that the Washtenaw County murders and the arrest of John Norman Collins was the top news story of 1969. Based on a system of ten points for the top story and one point for the tenth-place story, the Collins case received 438 points. Governor Milliken's education reform bill came in a distant second with 376 points.

—17—

A New Year but the Same Old Stuff

THE PRETRIAL HEARINGS RESUMED at 3:00 p.m. on Friday, January 2, 1970. A secret session was held in Judge Conlin's chambers at the judge's request. Only the lawyers, the defendant, and a court reporter were present. The prosecution went on record as being opposed to the closed-door proceeding.

The first defense motion discussed was the change of venue the Judge Conlin had postponed from an earlier hearing but now agreed to hear. Rather than focus on the adverse publicity Collins received in the press as court-appointed attorney Richard Ryan had done, Neil Fink made the dramatic pronouncement to the judge that he would "make a record of misconduct that will shock your judicial conscience." The reason Fink gave, "the jury will be placed in charge of Sheriff Harvey and his deputies during

9104839

8728573

the trial." Fink said Harvey and his men "are principals in the prosecution's case against Collins." He argued there was a clear conflict of interest, and his client could not get a fair trial in Washtenaw County.

Neil Fink claimed Sheriff Harvey's "misconduct" included but was not limited to:

- Questioning Collins in jail without his lawyer present
- Permitting an ex-con and former mental patient claiming to be a bishop of an obscure religious cult to visit Collins in jail
- Mistreating Collins during the initial lineup with four Arm of Honor fraternity members
- Being the official who signed the murder complaint against Collins.

Fink went on to say, "If any officer symbolizes the people's case, Sheriff Harvey does."

The second motion made by Neil Fink was to force police to reveal everything they found in their searches of Collins's room and his car. Collins was arrested at the Plymouth crime center the evening before in what the defense claimed was an illegal arrest. This motion was quickly resolved. The prosecution pledged to return all property belonging to Collins that was out of the scope of the Beineman case.

The third defense motion was to suppress the testimony of Diane Joan Goshe.

Not to be outdone, the prosecution moved to endorse twelve new prosecution witnesses, including Andrew J. Manuel. All of the witnesses had addresses listed on the motion except Manuel. Chief Assistant Prosecutor Williams told the judge Manuel moved away and left no forwarding address. This was an awkward moment for Williams, who had vouched for Manuel at the close of his burglary and fraud trial.

Another secret hearing in the judge's chamber was scheduled for January 28 on the misconduct charge against the county sheriff, and another on February 4 to discuss whether Diane Joan Goshe's testimony should be suppressed. The court ultimately rejected both motions. The judge was getting impatient at the slow pace of the trial and urged the defense to move its case forward.

Speaking for Joseph Louisell, Neil Fink explained to Judge Conlin that Louisell was scheduled to appear in a federal trial in Detroit beginning in mid-March. That trial was expected to last until the end of April. Then, the defense would need a minimum of two weeks to prepare for trial. Looking at his docket, Judge Conlin set a firm date of Monday, June 1, 1970, for the trial to begin with jury selection predicted to take several days.

Attorneys for both sides were cautioned not to make any public statements regarding the matters under discussion at these closed-door proceedings. With that, the ninety-minute session was over. Guarded by county sheriff's deputies, Collins was escorted from the courtroom while his family looked on from the gallery.

—18—

Unexpected Developments

On Wednesday, February 11, Judge Conlin announced that a spokesperson for the legal office of Louisell and Barris contacted him with the news that Joseph Louisell had suffered a heart attack on February 2 and was in an intensive care ward at a Detroit hospital. The law firm's official spokesperson said his doctors might allow him to return to work as early as April 1 but not before.

"The trial date," said Judge Conlin, "now is up to the defendant. If he wants only Louisell to defend him, there could be a delay in the June 1 (trial) date. But if one of Louisell's partners is agreeable to Collins, the trial can go on as scheduled."

In the two months since Louisell and Barris had taken over the case, other than Louisell's meeting with Collins in jail a couple of times, junior partner Neil Fink handled all of the motions and court appearances. It was understood Louisell would handle the courtroom defense. The public was restless, and the judge was not anxious for an open-ended delay of this case. Conlin postponed setting dates for future hearings until March 6. Because of Judge Conlin's news blackout, information about the case hung in limbo. That left too many reporters chasing too little news.

———•———

William Schmidt of the *Detroit Free Press* calculated in the year since Jane Mixer's body was found last March, the murder investigations cost the taxpayers well over a million dollars. Michigan State Police paid out over $800,000 in salaries and overtime on this case. The state of Michigan paid out another $100,000 for telecommunications and state vehicles. Ann Arbor police chief Walter Krasne tallied up his department's cost at $80,000 in overtime and equipment costs.

"At its peak last summer," Krasne said, "more than sixty detectives from five different police agencies were working on these cases." The Washtenaw County Sheriff's Department, the Ypsilanti police, and the Eastern Michigan University police spent heavily also. Now, the trial looked like it would stretch on indefinitely and so would the price tag.

———•———

John Norman Collins was indicted by the Monterey, California Superior Court for the sex slaying of seventeen-year-old high school senior Roxie Ann Phillips, a Milwaukie, Oregon, resident who was visiting Salinas, California, for the summer. In an unprecedented move, Michigan and California judges both agreed to a news blackout regarding the Collins case. Monterey County Superior Court Judge Gordon Campbell issued a gag order in an effort to provide a fair trial for Collins. Legal authorities in California could not recall courts in two states ever banning publicity about a single defendant simultaneously.

Fourteen people testified for three hours before a Monterey, California, grand jury on April 15. Michigan officials, including Sergeant Kennard Christensen—head of the Michigan State Police crime lab—provided valuable evidence that the judge described as "the most crucial part of California's case against Collins."

On the following Tuesday, just before the Collins hearings resumed, Neil Fink was asked outside the court-room about the California murder indictment and what effect it would have on his client's case. Fink told report-ers "a lawyer acting on John Collins's behalf in California attempted to have the Monterey County murder indictment quashed pending the outcome of the Michigan case. He failed to do that, but he did get details of the charges sup-pressed until after the Michigan trial." Fink considered this a personal victory.

After the hearing began, Neil Fink complained to the judge, "My client has received more adverse pretrial public-ity than any defendant in Michigan history." Fink produced several newspapers with the latest story about the Califor-nia murder indictment as further evidence to support his change-of-venue motion. Fink's claim that John Collins could not get a fair trial in Washtenaw County set the stage for another in-chambers closed-door session.

After Prosecutor Delhey made a vigorous objection culminating in "society has a right to know," Judge Conlin ruled with the defense saying, "the court does not wish to take any chances on testimony which might not later be admitted at the trial." The lawyers settled into their barrister chairs to discuss Diane Joan Goshe as a tainted witness and whether or not her testimony should be suppressed. The change of venue motion was hashed over again.

Fink wanted the judge to bar Goshe's identification of Collins in a lineup because she was shown a photograph of Collins on the day after he was arrested. Then she was asked to identify the person she saw with Karen Sue Beineman before a lineup of EMU fraternity members. At the first hearing months before, Goshe said she could not and would not identify anyone on the basis of a photograph. "I don't trust pictures," she testified. But when she saw Collins in the lineup, she picked him out instantly.

While the lawyers were in the judge's chambers, the press and spectators waited for the closed-door session to end. As usual, the Collins family waited in the front row of the gallery while John Collins was in the holding area adjacent to the courtroom, also waiting for the judge to enter the courtroom. Collins's older brother Jerry motioned to Sheriff Harvey, and he came over. Jerry Collins asked the sheriff if he would bring John's income tax check to him in his detention cell so he could sign it. Then they could deposit it in John's account. Sheriff Harvey complied.

Ironically, Washtenaw County sheriff Harvey was getting heavily criticized behind the closed doors. After enumerating the reasons for a change of venue, heavily punctuated with the word *misconduct*, Fink argued there was "a pattern of deep and bitter prejudice" against his client and "Sheriff Harvey was more popular in Washtenaw County than President Nixon or Governor Milliken." The defense attorney also moved that the California indictment of his client be inadmissible in the Washtenaw County trial. For the first time, Judge Conlin confided to the attorneys that he was "seriously concerned about empaneling an impartial jury."

Judge Conlin vowed to rule on the change-of-venue motion and on Diane Joan Goshe's fitness as a witness within the week. Much to Neil Fink's chagrin, Judge Conlin refused to suppress Goshe's testimony and denied the change-of-venue motion. The judge was determined to seat a jury.

This opened the door for an appeal by the defense. Fink filed an emergency application with the Michigan State Court of Appeals on May 7. The appeal claimed, "Cowardly law enforcement officers have issued statements prejudicial to the defendant and charged him with every unsolved crime of the century." Once again, Neil Fink displayed his talent for hyperbolic rhetoric.

The prosecutor had until May 20 to file a response brief which William Delhey did. Then on May 28, the defense's change-of-venue appeal was denied by the Michigan appellate court "without prejudice." Judge Conlin announced the trial would finally begin in five days on Tuesday, June 2.

———

Awaiting the trial and something new to report, the press wrote articles about the jury selection process, security precautions at the courthouse, and profiles about the battling attorneys. Seating a jury of twelve with two alternates was expected to last two weeks with the trial estimated to last four to six weeks.

Prosecutor William Delhey endorsed thirty-six witnesses while Neil Fink lined up twenty-five. For the jury selection process, Louisell and Fink had twenty peremptory (without cause) challenges and Delhey had fifteen. Both sides had an unlimited number of for-cause challenges if a juror could be shown to be unfit for this case. The total panel of 150 persons would be summoned. An initial panel of fifty prospective jurors was summoned for Tuesday. When that panel was exhausted, another fifty would be called, and then the final fifty. If there was a failure to seat a jury, Judge Conlin said he would grant the defense a change of venue.

Because of the national and statewide notoriety this case had received and strong feelings among the public, heavy security precautions were instituted. Uniformed and plainclothes deputies were strategically placed throughout the building. Each day, John Collins was transported to and from court by a heavily guarded police van from the Washtenaw County Jail across the street to the county building where the courtrooms were located on the second floor. Then he was taken to a basement prisoner entrance and directly to an elevator that led to a small detention room adjoining the courtroom.

The courtroom seating capacity was sixty persons, with more than forty of those spots reserved for local and national media. Press passes were assigned by Michael Devine, the Michigan Supreme Court–appointed media spokesperson. Devine consulted with courtroom administrators in the Richard F. Speck murder trial in Peoria, Illinois, and the Sirhan B. Sirhan trial in Los Angeles, California, asking for advice on handling a high-profile case. The decision was made that press passes would be issued daily by Devine and returned at the end of the day without fail. Anyone not returning his or her pass would be prohibited from the courtroom for the duration of the trial.

Two days before the trial was to begin, *Ann Arbor News* reporter Bill Treml wrote an article in the Sunday paper entitled "Two Courtroom Wizards Will Clash at Collins Trial." Joseph W. Louisell was described as a "lawyer's lawyer." He is a "stocky and graying middle-aged grandfather who shows in his face the effects of several heart attacks." Louisell's legal strategy was to "chip away at the circumstantial evidence, undermine it, and then discredit it." His adversary, William F. Delhey, was described as a "prosecutor's prosecutor." He is "cool, unemotional, professional, meticulous, methodical, and calculating." The women in Delhey's office called him "the silver fox" because of his full head of gray hair. Now the stage was set for the long-awaited trial, a courtroom battle that would become the most expensive criminal case in Michigan state history.

—19—

The Reckoning

TRIAL BY A JURY of one's peers is a concept deeply embedded in the American democratic ideal, though most legal cases are not tried by a jury. Some are thrown out of court, some are plea-bargained, and some are heard only by a judge. The jury system is highly touted by the American legal community as the fairest way to arrive at the truth in legal proceedings, but even with a well-presented case, innocent people are sometimes found guilty. That's why jury selection is so important to both the prosecution and the defense. Many cases are won or lost simply because mistakes are made in the jury selection process. Prosecutors and defense attorneys know this, so they take great care when selecting a jury.

For John Norman Collins, the stakes were not life or death as many people wished. Michigan was the first state in the nation to prohibit capital punishment. Collins was fighting for his freedom, and barring that, he was avoiding extradition to Monterey County, California, on a grand-jury indictment for the slaying of Roxie Ann Phillips. The

Golden State had capital punishment on the books, and a guilty Michigan verdict would shield Collins from that.

———

On April 28, Judge Conlin announced the trial would begin on June 2, 1970. Fink made a third request for a change of venue noting the public murder indictment of his client in California. He also cited the United States Supreme Court ruling in the Dr. Sam Shepard case in Texas where Dr. Shepard was freed after his conviction because the court ruled widespread news coverage was prejudicial. Judge Conlin said he would take the matter under advisement.

Finally, June 2 arrived. John Norman Collins's ten months of isolation in a maximum-security cell in the basement of the county jail would be punctuated with trips back and forth to the courthouse. Almost a year after Karen Sue Beineman's murder, the trial was about to begin.

No charges were brought against Collins in the other six unsolved murder cases that the prosecutor's office believed to be his handiwork. This conscious decision did not sit well with the victims' relatives or with Washtenaw County residents. Regardless of the cost, these people wanted answers.

Cris Bronson, a secretary in Prosecutor William Delhey's office during the trial, remembers Delhey's decision this way:

> Charging Collins with only Beineman's murder was Prosecutor Delhey's adamant decision. It was directly the result of having another killer freed when the State of Michigan changed its laws with respect to those defendants previously found guilty by reason of insanity and housed in state mental

hospitals. All of those defendants were released to the public. This killer had been previously charged with all of the murders he committed. Because of double jeopardy protection, Prosecutor Delhey was unable to prevent the killer from being released. Thus, when John Norman Collins was accused of killing a number of young women, Delhey held back all but one case knowing he had enough evidence on each of the others to file charges and prevent any future release of Collins. This was not done as some might have inferred because of lack of evidence, nor was it done because the other cases were not as important to Delhey. The death of each victim and the manner of her death was horrific to Delhey.

After recovering from his heart attack in the spring, Joseph Louisell returned to head the defense team. He would be assisted by his junior partner who had handled all the pretrial motions thus far. Washtenaw County prosecutor William F. Delhey would lead the people's case against Collins. Delhey lost the service of his senior assistant prosecutor Booker T. Williams. Williams was maintaining a bedside vigil for his terminally ill wife. Chief Assistant Prosecutor Casper H. Kast would be Delhey's wingman until Williams was back on the job.

The rules of engagement set by Judge Conlin were that each prospective juror would be brought into the courtroom individually and questioned. Because of the nature of this case, it was felt jurors would be more comfortable answering questions without other jurors looking on. Here were Conlin's ground rules:

- The jury would be sequestered for the duration of the trial.
- The names of the jurors were not to be published or announced in the media.
- Everyone attending the proceedings would be searched before entering the courtroom—including the defendant's family.
- No one was allowed to leave the courtroom during the session except during recess or with the judge's permission.
- Photographers were barred from the second floor of the courthouse.
- No pictures could be taken of the exhibits brought into evidence.
- Artists would be allowed in the courtroom to sketch scenes.
- Recording devices were prohibited from the courtroom, except those used by Margaret R. Westfall, the court recorder.
- And reporters would need a special press pass to enter the courtroom which must be returned at the end of the session. Failure to do so would exempt the reporter from further court sessions.

Security was tight. The trial was slated to begin at 8:30 a.m., but by the time the sixty or so spectators were searched, it was after 10:00 a.m. Joseph Louisell arrived an hour late but still arrived before court was called into session. Collins entered the courtroom from the holding cell. He was wearing a dark-gray suit with a white shirt and a red tie.

The county clerk, Betty Tennant, drew from a revolving

drum the first of fourteen slips of paper with jurors' names on them. The jury selection process had begun.

Judge Conlin informed prospective jurors that the trial was expected to last six weeks and the court would be in session from Monday through Friday to expedite this case. The jury would be sequestered in a hotel at Washtenaw County's expense. Supervised visits from family members would be arranged. The judge then began the first round of jury questions with the assembled group.

- Have any of you sat on a criminal or civil case this term?
- Do any members of this panel know Prosecutor William F. Delhey or his assistant Casper H. Kast?
- Do any of you know or have had business dealings with the defense team of Joseph Louisell or Neil Fink?
- Are any of you acquainted with the defendant, John Norman Collins, or any members of his family?
- Are any of you acquainted with the victim Karen Sue Beineman or her family?

This was only the beginning of five weeks of intense bantering and relentless haggling between the prosecution and the defense.

Every nuance of the jury selection process was reported by the Michigan press corps ad infinitum. Every tedious bit of minutia was conveyed and repeated extensively by the assembled press without mention of jurors' names or their places of employment. The news reports made for stultifying reading. As with the previous news blackout, too many reporters were chasing too few reportable facts.

One of the notable points of interest and asides from the proceedings happened on the second day of the trial. A pretty girl with short-cropped blonde hair entered the court-room. This was reported by Cindy Cygan from the *Macomb Daily* whose articles would prominently feature the Collins family. Cygan knew John's sister Gail from attending high school with her at Saint Clement's.

Ms. Cygan reported, "The young woman sat at the back of the spectators' section watching Collins, who was seated facing the jury box. Turning his face to the right, he finally saw her smiling at him and he smiled back, a smile of recognition," Cygan wrote. Throughout the afternoon proceedings, the reporter noticed that each time he looked over at her, the young woman smiled and he smiled back.

At the end of the afternoon session, the young woman identified herself as Ann with no last name given. She stopped to talk to John's mother, Loretta Collins, and John's brother and sister. It was apparent they knew her. She had school books under her arm, but it would have been better if she had an airtight alibi for the defendant.

———

It was reported after Wednesday's proceedings that Mrs. Collins called out to her son to lighten the moment as he was being led away. "Why don't you come home with us tonight?" she said.

"I'll see you tomorrow at nine," John said, deflating his mother's attempt to lighten the moment.

One of the officers guarding her son turned to Mrs. Collins and said, "Don't worry. We'll take good care of him."

It is doubtful Mrs. Collins took much comfort from the officer's assurance.

———

At the Thursday session of the first week, lead defense attorney Louisell began what became a mantra for him during the jury selection process: the impugning of Washtenaw County's highest-ranking law enforcement officer, Sheriff Douglas Harvey. "Would you give more weight or believe him (Harvey) more because he was sheriff?" Louisell asked each prospective juror, implying the sheriff was not to be believed or trusted.

At the end of Thursday's session, Mrs. Collins tried to hand a note to her son as he was being led from the courtroom. She called out his name, but he was hustled out in an instant. The note was an apology for not being able to write John because she was so tired with the trial. Loretta Collins made the ninety-mile round-trip from Center Line to Ann Arbor every week since her son's arrest. Now that the trial was underway, she was making the trip daily. Sometimes Mrs. Collins was accompanied by her two adult children, but occasionally she was accompanied by two young women, one from Eastern Michigan University and the other from Center Line. Their names were never revealed.

After Thursday's session, Mrs. Collins met with reporters in the hallway. She told them she was confident her son would be acquitted. "I know he is going to come home. I just know the people on the jury will know he is innocent and let him come home with me. God will make it right. I don't think the jury will convict him of something they know he is innocent of."

Macomb Daily reporter Cindy Cygan asked Mrs. Collins if her son John was confident he would be acquitted. She answered defensively. "I am! My son didn't have to tell me he was innocent, I knew." Attending court with their mother that day were Jerry and Gail. They stood mute.

———

When court resumed on Monday, Fink asked Judge Conlin for a court order to allow an investigator for the defense to enter the Leik house, the alleged scene of the crime. The defense wanted to inspect and gather additional hair-fiber evidence from the basement. The evidence would be flown to Boston for Dr. Samuel Golub, their fiber specialist, to examine. Sergeant Leik gave his approval without a court order, which Judge Conlin was grateful for.

———

After a week of observation, *Ann Arbor News* reporter Bill Treml noticed an emerging pattern of blue collar versus white collar in the selection of the jurors. Joseph Louisell was seeking a college-educated, more liberal-minded jury who would be better equipped to understand and appreciate technical testimony, whereas Delhey was attempting to seat as few intellectuals as possible. The prosecution wanted a working-class jury for whom issues of proof and motive were less exacting and decisions tended to be based on common knowledge and gut reactions.

———

After Wednesday's session, Cindy Cygan wrote another human interest story on the Collins family. Loretta was accompanied to court by yet another petite young lady, wearing a light-blue dress and matching shoes. The blonde-haired girl was seen frequently exchanging smiles with Collins. At the recess, the young woman said she was a friend of John's but would not identify herself further. The defense may have hoped the image of attractive, young women in the Collins camp might help mitigate the jurors' feelings about the defendant and the crime he was accused of committing. It was a clumsy attempt to sway the jury selection process.

———

By the end of the second week, Judge Conlin was beginning to show the strain. He was overheard to say, "The seating of a jury looks hopeless." The jury process was mired down with motions and objections and the mechanics of the law. Neil Fink saw to that. Despite a difficult two weeks, the atmosphere of the courtroom was relaxed at the intermission. John's older sister Gail was to remarry over the weekend. The juxtaposition of the murder trial and wedding talk made for a strange day in the courtroom.

———

Bill Treml reported in the Sunday edition of the *Ann Arbor News* that Washtenaw County Clerk Robert Harrison feared the jury selection could be the longest and most expensive jury drawing process in county history. Harrison estimated the weekly costs to be $3,500. Once the jury was chosen, the housing and feeding costs for the fourteen people could run as high as $700 a day. The county clerk noted, "The $83,000 circuit court general fund for jurors, witness fees, and mileage was virtually exhausted with the Collins jury drawing certain to empty the fund in a short time."

———

To ease the minds of the prospective jurors, Judge Conlin announced repeatedly "arrangements would be made to permit jurors to visit with their families under sheriff's deputy and policewoman supervision." But Sheriff Harvey expressed concern over the visitation agreement. He told the judge in a brief bench conference he feared his road patrol unit would be stripped of officers in order to escort jurors home. The judge amended his remarks and agreed the sheriff could use auxiliary deputies who are unpaid civilian volunteers for the escort duty.

Not to let Sheriff Harvey bask in his minor victory, Neil Fink questioned a prospective juror, "Do you believe Sheriff Harvey would willfully lie under oath?" Delhey objected to the hypothetical question and it was sustained by Judge Conlin, who seated the woman despite objections by Neil Fink. Once again, the defense attempted to undermine the county sheriff and make him an issue. But the prosecution won a small victory and beat Collins's lawyers at their own game. So the day would not be a total loss for them, the defense disclosed a second expert witness in hair-fiber identification, Dr. R. E. Jervis, a professor of radioactive chemistry at the University of Toronto.

The day's session ended. Reporter Cindy Cygan sent in another Collins family–centered story for the *Macomb Daily*. The defendant's mother, Loretta Collins, talked with one of the deputies in hopes she would be allowed to bring a birthday cake the next day and give her son a present on his twenty-third birthday.

Sheriff Harvey handled the request personally. He informed Mrs. Collins "the rules prohibit prisoners from receiving food except that which is served or can be purchased at the county jail. Prisoners may receive some

packages subject to inspection and approval by jail officials." Loretta Collins appealed again, asking if the sheriff
could make an exception. "I have eighty prisoners in this jail
and they all have birthdays. I cannot permit eighty birthday
parties in this institution," he said.

As a minor concession, the sheriff allowed Mrs. Collins
to present her son with a shirt and tie set after county sheriff's detectives Roy Couch and Arthur Preston—on permanent assignment as Collins's guards—watched her wrap
them. Cindy Cygan reported that Mrs. Collins was permitted to give the wrapped birthday present to her son in the
waiting room lockup—just outside the courtroom.

———

Monday, June 22, marked the beginning of the fourth
week of jury selection. Cindy Cygan wrote another Collins
family human interest piece for the *Macomb Daily*. A second
mysterious blonde spectator appeared at the trial. The
young woman spoke with an unmistakable Swedish accent
as she explained her interest in the trial selection process.
"As a little girl, I would often sit in my father's courtroom
in Sweden...trial by jury was rare. Most cases are tried by
a panel of three judges." This young woman, who remained
unidentified, was one of several regular spectators at the
trial.

———

Thursday, June 25, marked the last of five attempts to
seek a change of venue in this case. The previous motion was
summarily dismissed by the Michigan Court of Appeals, so
it was an easy matter for Judge Conlin to dismiss this latest
request.

The judge became so hoarse from conducting the many interviews that he had to constantly clear his throat and strain to avoid looking bored. The torturous process was wearing on everyone. To show his determination to seat a jury, the judge ordered County Clerk Robert Harrison to draw another 399 names to fill the fifth panel of prospective jurors. It was clear to everyone that the county and the state did not want to bear the double expense of a change of venue.

———

Then on July 9, defense attorney Joseph Louisell startled Judge Conlin when he announced, "I think we have a jury." After five contentious weeks, suddenly it was over. In addition to the judge and the prosecution, Betty Tennant, the court clerk, was as surprised and unprepared as anyone. She searched through her desk to find the notebook containing the medieval oath that binds the jury to be fair and impartial. When Tennant was ready, the seven men and seven women stood and raised their right hands.

"Do you solemnly swear that you will well and truly try and true deliverance make between the People of the State of Michigan and the prisoner at the bar, who you shall have in charge, according to the law and the evidence given you in open court, so help you God?"

At that, five weeks of jury selection came to an end. Judge Conlin had examined 294 people. The defense had three peremptory challenges left and appeared to outsmart the prosecution who had seven. The prosecution wanted to remove some college graduates from the panel. Once the defense indicated they were happy with the jury, it was impaneled. That was state law. Commenting to the press on this self-congratulatory court session, Neil Fink said, "This is the best-educated jury I've ever seen." Fink could not resist gloating before the prosecution, but it was still too early for a victory lap.

Of the fourteen jurors, nine were known to be college graduates and two others had some college background. After all the evidence was heard and jury instructions were given, two jurors would be omitted by lottery from the deliberations to act as alternates after hearing testimony. All fourteen were instructed to return a week later on July 20 at 8:45 a.m. During that week, jurors were to make the necessary arrangements for sequestration.

Judge Conlin told the jury some night sessions and weekend sessions might be held to accommodate witnesses. Conlin cautioned jurors not to read about this case, watch television newscasts, or listen to radio accounts. They were ordered not to discuss the case among themselves or with anyone else.

Mary Terese Fleszar
December 4, 1947–July 9, 1967

Joan Elspeth Schell
December 14, 1947–July 1, 1968

Maralynn Skelton
March 4, 1953–March 25, 1969

Dawn Louise Basom
November 28, 1955–April 15, 1969

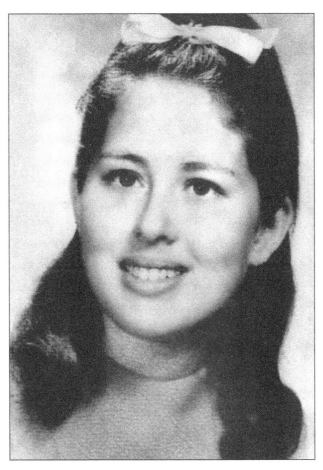

Alice Elizabeth Kalom
December 25, 1947–June 7, 1969

Roxie Ann Phillips
March 21, 1952–June 30, 1969

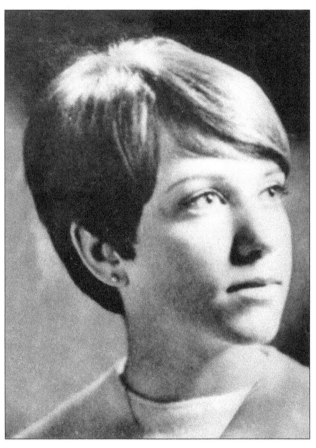

Karen Sue Beineman
February 10, 1951–July 23, 1969

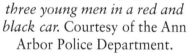

The first composite drawing based on a description by Joan Schell's roommate. She witnessed Joan driving off with three young men in a red and black car. Courtesy of the Ann Arbor Police Department.

This 1969 composite was drawn from a description by two wig shop ladies who saw Karen Sue Beineman drive off with a young man on a motorcycle. Courtesy of the Ypsilanti Police Department.

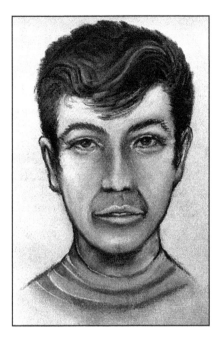

Released on the day before John Norman Collins was arrested. This detailed composite drawing had no impact on his arrest. Courtesy of the Michigan State Police.

John Norman Collins

Michigan State Police securing 619 Emmet Street—the boarding house where Collins rented a second story room overlooking College Place Street. Joan Schell, the second victim, lived in an apartment across College Place Street.

John Collins leaving the Ypsilanti Courthouse on the day of his arraignment.

John Collins and Arnie Davis pose in 1967 for an EMU ski club photo. They were Theta Chi fraternity brothers and lived in the same boarding house until Collins' arrest on July 31, 1969.

After a nationwide FBI manhunt, Andrew Julian Manuel (25) was arrested in Phoenix, Arizona. Manuel rented a room in the same boarding house as Collins and traveled to Salinas, California in a fraudulently rented house trailer with him.

John Collins appeared in the September 1969 issue of Tomorrow's Man, a pocket-sized bodybuilding magazine, when he was twenty-one years old.

The magazine used a pseudonym for Collins. The caption read, "Bill Kenyon displays a fine arm in this pose. Here is a teenage bodybuilder who is a future great."

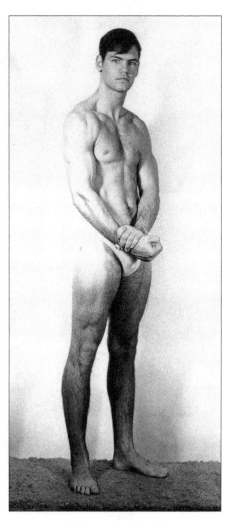

Photo credit: Metecue Associates.

*John Collins'
biological father
Richard Chapman
seated on a
motorcycle. He was
an explosives and
demolition officer
in His Majesty's
Canadian Services
during World War II.*

*In 1944, Chapman
lost his left leg
fighting the Nazis in
Europe.*

*John's mother Loretta Marjorie Collins
conferring with a priest in the parking lot outside
the courtroom in Ann Arbor.*

Washtenaw County Prosecutor William F. Delhey being interviewed by Detroit Channel 7 news anchor Bill Bonds. The women in Delhey's office called him the silver fox. He was known for being a meticulous prosecutor in the courtroom.

Assistant Prosecutor Booker T. Williams handled the complicated scientific testimony in the Collins case.

Lead defense attorney Joseph W. Louisell and junior partner Neil H. Fink walking on Main Street in Ann Arbor. Louisell was nearing the end of his career and Fink was hoping to catapult his.

Washtenaw County Sheriff Douglas Harvey brought the original complaint warrant leading to Collins' arrest. He became a focal point in the defense case.

Dutch Psychic Peter Hurkos caught by the press leaving the Ypsilanti District Courthouse during Collins' initial preliminary hearing.

Now I Lay Me Down To Sleep *was to be a film loosely based on the unsolved murders and the cat-and-mouse game between Collins and law enforcement.*

—20—

The Corpus Delecti

THE TRIAL BEGAN ON Monday, July 20 much like the jury selection process had ended with more motions presented by the defense. Neil Fink moved that the testimony of Diane Joan Goshe and Patricia Spaulding be suppressed as tainted witnesses. They were shown photographs of Collins twice by police before the lineup where they identified Collins. Fink believed showing the wig shop ladies the photographs clearly violated his defendant's right to counsel.

When Spaulding was asked if the defendant's attorney was present at the lineup, she said no. A defense motion attacking the legality of the lineup was denied by Judge Conlin who said, "The lineup was conducted in accordance with the law."

During the previous week's hearing, John Collins's first attorney Robert Francis—no longer representing Collins—told the judge he was at the police station and saw the witnesses going to the lineup viewing window. He also saw the lineup forming outside the room. Francis said he was aware of the lineup but never officially informed it was about to start. The judge overruled the defense objection.

The third defense motion was to suppress scientific testimony concerning the identification of human hair found on Beineman's body that she may have obtained at the alleged murder site. Judge Conlin denied the motion.

In a defense attempt to undermine the police early in the case, Neil Fink complained to Judge Conlin about two instances of police interference. Ann Arbor police sergeant William Canada was accused of pulling defense witness Donald Kaufman out of a bar, putting him in the back of a squad car, and threatening him with perjury if he falsely testified in this case. Then, Neil Fink told the judge that state police sergeant David Leik—John Collins's uncle by marriage—has been "an obstructionist in this case from the very beginning." Fink wanted to depict Sergeant Leik as a hostile witness. He wanted it to appear in the court record that Leik refused the defense access to the alleged scene of the crime—the Leik basement—and he refused to tell the defense the blood type groupings of his family. What Fink did not mention in court was that Leik did allow a defense investigator into the basement to collect forensic samples for their expert in Boston. Once Fink finished, the judge called for a midmorning recess.

When the trial resumed, the courtroom was crowded with news personnel from all over the country. Finally, the moment arrived when Prosecutor William Delhey would begin his opening statement and address the jury. In a strong baritone voice, Delhey told the jury the county would "prove without a reasonable doubt that John Norman Collins is guilty of the murder of Karen Sue Beineman on

July 23, 1969." After a description of the crime, he continued by saying the prosecution would show John Norman
Collins was in the area at the same time Beineman disappeared, he was the driver of the motorcycle on which the
Grand Rapids girl was last seen, and Karen Sue Beineman
"was slain in the house of state policeman David Leik, who
gave access to his home to his nephew John Norman Collins
while Officer Leik and his family were on vacation."

Neil Fink handled the opening remarks for the defense.
Addressing the jury, he agreed with the prosecution that
Beineman's body "was degraded to a point almost beyond
human comprehension. But the prosecution has forged a
chain of circumstantial evidence, and as such, this case is
no stronger than its weakest link." Fink told the jury two
prosecution witnesses would testify they saw Beineman ride
off with Collins, but "both ladies wear corrective glasses
and neither was wearing them at the time." Neil Fink was
attempting to impugn testimony not yet given, but he was
permitted to press on.

Fink added, "The defense will produce witnesses who
will provide an alibi for Collins during the critical three-
hour window from Miss Beineman's disappearance until
her digestive tract shut down. We will also present expert
scientific witnesses to refute the hair fiber neutron analysis
evidence we expect the prosecution to present. After listening to the testimony in this case, you will have serious
doubt, and with the fidelity of your oaths, you will return a
verdict of not guilty."

———

Delhey called the first witness for the prosecution,
Washtenaw County's deputy chief medical examiner, Dr.

Craig R. Barlow. Dr. Barlow began by showing and describing color photographs of Beineman's battered body, including close-up photos of her face, her broken tooth, strangulation marks around her neck, chemical burns on her chest area, and abrasion marks on her wrists and ankles. These exhibits made for grim viewing for the jury, especially the women. The photo exhibits were entered into evidence.

Dr. Barlow testified he arrived at the body drop location on Riverside Drive in Ann Arbor Township at 6:30 p.m. on Saturday, July 26. He said it was "obvious the body had been there for some time due to the decomposition that had already begun. There are definite ligature marks on her wrist, ankles, and neck, plus blows to the head and chest with marks on her breasts and arms."

On cross-examination, the medical examiner told Joseph Louisell he found no fibers on the neck, wrists, or ankles to indicate what was used to beat the young woman, but in his medical opinion, "the body could have been in another location prior to being found on Riverside Drive at least twenty-four hours—maybe longer."

The rest of the session was taken up by court business and settling the jury into their hotel accommodations at the Campus Inn, which was only several short blocks from the Washtenaw County Courthouse. An entire upper floor was dedicated to their sequestration until the end of the trial. Three county deputies were stationed as around-the-clock security, one at the elevator door and the others at each end of the floor guarding the stairwells. The jurors were provided with room-service privileges and a fully stocked bar with hotel staff on call—all courtesy of the taxpayers of Washtenaw County.

On Tuesday, August 21, Judge Conlin's ban on photographs taken on the second floor of the courthouse was broken by an *Ypsilanti Press* staff photographer. Sheriff Harvey was caught on camera wheeling himself into the courtroom with his left leg in a hip-to-toe plaster cast propped up on a wheelchair leg rest. Sheriff Harvey and his son were in a motorcycle accident on Interstate 94 the month before when he ran his new Harley into the back wheels of a semi-truck. The second-floor courtroom photograph made it into the evening edition of the *Ypsilanti Press* despite the judge's ban.

On the second day of the trial, the prosecution called only four witnesses and direct testimony lasted three and a half hours. The first two witnesses were Beineman's Downing Hall roommates, Sherrie Green and Kay Ann Knowles. They were separately called to testify. They shared room 302 with Karen Sue for the summer session at Eastern Michigan. Both girls gave an account of the last time they saw Karen that was virtually identical. The young coeds told how they went to lunch at the dining commons at about noon on July 23, 1969. Green said she had swapped her lunch of a hot dog and watermelon with Beineman, who had ordered a salad. Karen also ate a few corn chips and an ice cream bar and drank an orange drink. This testimony laid the groundwork for the medical examiner to determine the time of Beineman's death from the contents of Karen's stomach.

Knowles testified the three roommates returned to room 302 when Karen said she had plans to go downtown to pick up a wiglet she had ordered the day before. "Karen asked if I would walk with her, but I had an afternoon class and had to study for a test, so Karen left Downing on foot at about twelve thirty."

Delhey asked each girl individually, "When did you see her again?"

Both young women gave the identical response, "I didn't."

Upon cross-examination, Joseph Louisell asked each of the coeds if they were shown underclothing of the victim by investigating police officers. They both answered no. Louisell asked where Beineman washed her undergarments. They responded that she washed them by hand in the bathroom sink and hung them on a drying rack in their room.

The crafty lawyer asked if Beineman used an electric shaver on her legs in their room. Neither coed knew if Karen owned an electric shaver or used it to shave her legs. Knowles did say she knew Karen trimmed her bangs in their room. Not wanting to appear unsympathetic to the uncomfortable witness, Louisell thanked Knowles and told the judge, "No further questions, Your Honor."

———

The next prosecution witness called was Dr. Conrad Mason, a University of Michigan physicist in aerospace engineering. He told Prosecutor Delhey under direct examination that he and his wife were walking along Riverside Drive in Ann Arbor Township to retrieve their mail. He glanced down a shallow wooded ravine and saw the naked body of a female lying face down. That was about 4:00 p.m. on Saturday, July 26.

"The body had only a pair of sandals on her feet," Dr. Mason testified. "I said to my wife, 'Oh, my God. Look!'" Then they ran up the street to their home at 3640 East Huron River Drive and called the county sheriff's office.

The first officer on the scene was Sheriff Douglas Harvey. Soon the Mason home became a beehive of law enforcement activity. In addition to county police, also arriving on the scene were the Ann Arbor police, the state police, and the prosecutor with his chief assistant prosecutor.

Under cross-examination by Joseph Louisell, Dr. Mason said he was asked by police not to disclose to anyone the finding of the unidentified body. Dr. Mason told of the plan to replace the body with a mannequin that prosecutors Delhey and Williams borrowed from J. C. Penney at the Arborland mall. Dr. Mason testified he was told officers would be hidden strategically around the area during the night.

And of course, it rained terribly that evening. Dr. Mason told the court the police used his screened-in porch as a field headquarters. At about 2:00 a.m., two sheriff's deputies knocked on the door and asked to use the phone. One of the officers told Dr. Mason their walkie-talkies were not working. The other officer called the task force at the Holy Ghost Fathers' Seminary barely a mile away. "We've had a contact," Dr. Mason heard the officer say.

———

The fourth and final witness scheduled for the day was Washtenaw County sheriff Douglas J. Harvey. He had signed the original criminal complaint against John Collins. Wheelchair bound, Sheriff Harvey was helped to the stand by one of Collins's guards, Sheriff's Deputy Roy Crouch.

Sheriff Harvey told the court that after the call came in from Dr. Mason, he rushed out to Riverside Drive and was the first person on the scene. He viewed the body from the road above the gully and asked to use Dr. Mason's home phone. The sheriff did not want a report of this to go out on police-band radio that some snot-nosed reporter could pick up. John Cobb of the *Ypsilanti Press* had a police-band radio in his car and often showed up at the crime scenes ahead of the police. Harvey's first call was to the Michigan State Police crime lab in Plymouth. Next, he notified Prosecutors Delhey and Williams. Finally, he called the deputy medical examiner, Dr. Craig Barlow. By then, sheriff's deputies had secured the secluded area.

After the crime laboratory team made their preliminary inspection of the body, Sheriff Harvey explained to the court how he and the prosecutors walked down the steep incline to the body just as it was being turned over. He said Beineman's head was "beaten in." The next time he saw the body was during the autopsy the following day performed by medical examiner Dr. Robert Hendrix at University of Michigan's medical center morgue.

Dr. Hendrix was vacationing on Beaver Island on northern Lake Michigan when Karen Sue Beineman's body was found. He was summoned back to Ann Arbor in a chartered plane to perform the autopsy. He had performed the autopsies on all of the young women in the unsolved Washtenaw County murders of the last two years.

Judge Conlin adjourned the day's proceedings until 9:00 a.m. Tuesday.

———

Police witnesses were scheduled to testify for Tuesday's court session. The cross-examination of Sheriff Harvey began the morning's testimony. Because of the sheriff's hip-to-toe plaster cast, the defense did not want to keep him on the stand any longer than possible, afraid the sheriff might evoke sympathy from members of the jury.

On cross-examination, Louisell asked the sheriff if anyone had ever located the murder weapon. Harvey answered, "We never found the blunt instrument, and no footprints were found because of the heavy rain."

Louisell continued, "Whose decision was it to replace Miss Beineman's body with a mannequin?"

This was a sore point for the sheriff because of the *Detroit Free Press* article a year earlier when reporter Walter Lundy used the label *Keystone Kops* to describe the seemingly random and chaotic stakeout. The defense wanted to exploit this incident by embarrassing the county sheriff and undermining the investigation.

After fifteen minutes of cross-examination, Harvey said he did conceive the original plan but had no part in placing the dummy there. The sheriff told the court he heard the prosecutor's staff discussing it, but he did not know who ordered it. After the stakeout debacle, Harvey said he received several verbal reports but claimed he never received a written report.

At this point, Louisell went to his briefcase files and pulled a copy of the report the sheriff claimed he had never seen. Louisell decided to leave the jury with the impression Sheriff Harvey was being dishonest with them. The sheriff was dismissed as a witness and returned to the gallery.

———

Next, Eastern Michigan University campus patrolman Larry Joseph Mathewson was called to the stand. He was the first witness to testify that he saw John Norman Collins around the campus that day. Mathewson said Collins was "astride a very shiny motorcycle at about 12:30 p.m. on July 23, 1969." The patrolman saw Collins stop and wait for EMU student Lorraine Kellogg to cross the street bordering Eastern's campus.

In cross-examination, Joseph Louisell brought out that Mathewson testified at the preliminary hearing that he passed Collins sometime after noon, but he did not specify an exact time. The defense made what they could of the ambiguity of Mathewson's report. They considered it a minor victory. Judge Conlin called for a midmorning recess.

———

When the trial resumed, forensic pathologist Dr. Robert M. Hendrix was called to the stand. The silver-haired doctor had worked at the University of Michigan for twenty-two years. He conducted the autopsy on Karen Sue Beineman's body and concluded she "had been beaten savagely on the head which caused extensive brain damage, but strangulation caused her death." When Delhey asked Dr. Hendrix what could have been used to strike her, he answered, "A club, a blackjack, a bottle, a fist, a boot—just about anything hard can be a blunt instrument."

The doctor continued his description of her body. "Stuffed deep in her throat was a coarse yellow cloth. Her wrists and ankles had been bound, and small bits of skin were removed from her body. There was discoloration on her neck, shoulders, and breasts that looked like a track made by some sort of fluid flowing over them, some corrosive or tissue-destroying chemical." He suggested a household cleaner or ammonia might have caused the discoloration. Hendrix surmised the killer may have tried to revive her with it. The victim's underwear was found stuffed into her vagina. The pathologist implied she had been raped but did not conduct blood-type testing because he did not think he would get any results. Dr. Hendrix testified that Beineman died between 1:00 p.m. and 3:00 p.m. on the day of her disappearance. "Her digestive process stopped between one-half hour and three hours from her last meal which was at 12:15 p.m."

On cross-examination, Louisell asked about the blow to the right side of Karen's head. Hendrix said it probably rendered her unconscious. He added, "Medical authorities have estimated in strangulation cases that death occurs from seven to fifteen minutes after air is cut off from the throat." Then, the defense counsel asked if there were any cuts on the body. The doctor reported, "While the body had numerous abrasions, there were no cuts found during the autopsy."

When Louisell pressed the prosecution's witness on the exact time of death and the day of her death, Hendrix admitted he was unable to fix an exact time.

"Could it have been the twenty-fourth?" Louisell asked in an exaggerated manner.

"Yes, Sir," Dr. Hendrix answered.

"Or the twenty-fifth?"

"Yes, Sir."

But before the defense attorney could continue, Dr. Hendrix added, "However, the extent of putrefaction, the extent of insect activity on her body, and the warm and rainy weather at the time, make me think she died about three days before I performed the autopsy."

Joseph Louisell could not shake the experienced pathologist from his position. "Were there any fibers around the wrists or ankles of the victim?"

The physician answered, "No."

"No further questions, Your Honor."

After a lunch recess, the prosecution called Eugene Weiler, a Michigan state police detective, to the stand. He lifted Beineman's fingerprints from two of her notebooks and matched them to the body. Next to testify was forensic dentist, Dr. J. Phillip Sapp, from the university hospital. He told the court the young woman had a front tooth broken above the gum line. "It takes a pretty severe blow to fracture a tooth. If the victim had been alive when it occurred," he said, "it would have caused great pain."

Last to testify was Dr. Robert E. Hire, Karen's family dentist from Grand Rapids. He matched Beineman's dental records with her remains at the morgue. With their testimony, the second day of the trial ended.

In the evening edition of the *Ann Arbor News*, William Treml wrote about the day's session. "Karen Sue Beineman met a cruel and lingering death at the hands of a sadistic killer." Treml reported the first phase of the prosecution's case was over—the positive identification of Miss Beineman. Tomorrow, the prosecution would move into the second phase of their case, placing John Norman Collins in the area at the time of Karen Sue Beineman's disappearance.

—21—

Pinning Down the Suspect

SEVEN YOUNG YPSILANTI WOMEN, most of them EMU coeds, were scheduled to appear as prosecution witnesses Wednesday, the third day of the trial. They all told police separately that John Collins had approached them on his motorcycle between 11:30 a.m. and 12:30 p.m. in the vicinity where Karen Sue Beineman was last seen getting on the back of his motorcycle.

Before the day's proceedings began, one of the bailiffs politely offered the defendant's mother two soft green pillows to sit on. Loretta Collins joked with reporters that she had some with spikes for them to sit on. She used one of the pillows to soften the pew-like oak gallery bench she was sitting on. She lent the other pillow to her friend. The Collins entourage included his mother, his sister Gail and her new husband, and another unidentified young woman who predictably smiled at Collins throughout the proceeding.

The first coed to be called to the stand was mentioned in the previous day's testimony by EMU patrolman Larry Mathewson. Linda Campbell was an EMU graduate who worked part-time as a waitress at the Inn America on Washt-enaw Avenue. She told Prosecutor Delhey that she dated Collins in late 1968 and early 1969. Campbell testified that "on the time and date in question, I talked with John for about twenty minutes on Lowell Street between Jarvis and Forest Avenues. John had just returned from California, and we talked about it," Campbell said.

Any mention of Collins's trip to California was not good for their client. Neil Fink objected immediately and wanted the reference to California struck from the record and the jury instructed to disregard it. The judge sustained the objection and purged the remark from the record but not from the minds of the jury.

Linda Campbell described how Collins was dressed: "Blue jeans and a blue and yellow striped T-shirt." She added, "The motorcycle he was riding had a lot of chrome."

Prosecutor Delhey asked Campbell to walk over to a floor stand holding a map exhibit of the area under discussion. "Please place a red pin on the exact location where you encountered Mr. Collins." Each of the girls to testify the rest of the day would be asked to mark a location. The map made a compelling courtroom exhibit that was used seven times to drive home the prosecution's point that Collins was cruising the area.

The next witness was Judy Lawnizack, a seventeen-year-old Ypsilanti High School student. She testified she'd dated John about ten times in the fall of 1968. She saw Collins riding a motorcycle on West Cross Street near Perrin Street. "He was wearing a green and yellow striped T-shirt." Judy also placed a pin on the prosecution's map exhibit.

One of the girls thought the shirt had green stripes and the other said they were blue. It is likely the true color was in between, most likely teal, which was a popular color in the late sixties. The shirt was never produced in evidence. This was a minor discrepancy in their testimony that the defense left unexplored.

The third young woman to testify she saw Collins that afternoon was Lorraine Kellogg. She spoke with Collins for about twenty minutes outside her apartment at Forest and Ballard Streets. She placed the time at just after noon because she was returning from a class dismissed at 11:50 a.m. Prosecutor Delhey had now established a firm time and definite place for Lorraine's encounter with Collins.

"Miss Kellogg, do you remember what Mr. Collins was driving that day?"

"Yes, a flashy blue motorcycle."

"Could you by any chance describe what the defendant was wearing that day?"

"He was wearing Levis and a green and yellow striped shirt."

"What else can you tell me about your encounter that afternoon?"

"We talked for about twenty minutes or so."

"Was there anyone else present?" Prosecutor Delhey asked.

"Yes, Joe Westmore, a resident of my apartment building. He had just driven up in his car, and John moved his bike over so Joe could park."

"How long was Joe there with you and John Collins?"

"For about ten minutes. Then he went inside and made us lunch."

"What did you talk about with the defendant?"

"We made some small talk. I never formally met him, but I knew who he was."

"How did you know Mr. Collins?"

"My roommate dated him."

"Fair enough. Do you remember what you and John Collins talked about?"

Lorraine Kellogg thought for a brief moment. "We talked about motorcycles and mutual friends. He asked me if I would like to take a motorcycle ride with him sometime."

"How did you react?"

"I said, 'Sorry. I'm going steady with someone.'"

"How did he react?"

"He said, 'Maybe some other time.'"

"I want you to remember carefully," Delhey said. "Did you observe a young woman matching the description of Karen Sue Beineman pass by you that afternoon a year ago?"

"A young woman passed by us and walked on."

"Did you take a look at her?"

"No."

"Why do you think a woman passed by you when you didn't see her?"

"My back was to the sidewalk, but John was on his motorcycle facing the sidewalk. I noticed him glance at someone who walked past and he said hello, smiling. I didn't want to turn around to take a look because I didn't care who it was."

"What happened next?"

"Not long after, Joe came out and said lunch was ready. I excused myself and went inside."

"What did John Collins do?"

"Said good-bye and drove up Ballard Street."

"What do you mean by 'up Ballard Street,' Miss Kellogg?"

"Toward downtown—away from campus."

The prosecution wanted to leave the jury with the impression that it was Beineman who passed by that afternoon while Kellogg was talking with Collins.

Under cross-examination by Neil Fink, Kellogg did not remember telling prosecutors she could not remember the color of the shirt in her original statement to police. She also made a statement that Joe Westmore joined the conversation for twenty minutes or so, but Fink pointed out again that her pretrial statement indicated Westmore talked with her and his client for only ten minutes.

"I don't remember saying that," she said.

"Your memory is very selective, Miss Kellogg," Fink said.

"Objection, Your Honor."

"Sustained."

Without missing a beat, Fink continued, "What else do you not remember from that day?"

"That's about it."

"When my client asked you out, how did he make you feel?"

"What do you mean?"

"Did he make you feel uncomfortable or threatened?"

"No."

"Would you have accepted his invitation, if you weren't going steady with someone?"

"Probably not."

"Why not?"

"Because he asked my roommate on a date to his room to watch color TV one night. He spent the entire evening trying to get her into bed."

That was not the answer Fink hoped for. "No further questions, Your Honor."

Judge Conlin called a recess to allow the defense team to listen to a tape recording of Kellogg's police statement the previous October. While on recess, some of the jury complained to the bailiff they were having trouble hearing because some of the spectators were talking while testimony was being given. When court resumed, Judge Conlin admonished the gallery and warned that any spectators who talked during the testimony or disrupted the court while in session would be removed and banned from the courtroom for the remainder of the case.

Next up to testify was twenty-two-year-old Susan Bonner.

"Miss Bonner, on Wednesday, July 23, did you see John Collins?"

"Yes."

"Would you tell the court where and when, please?"

"On Ballard Street—at about twelve thirty or one o'clock in the afternoon."

That broad time frame was not good for the prosecution's case. "How certain are you of the time?" asked Delhey.

"Pretty close. I left my class at noon and went to Ned's Bookstore for about half an hour. Then walking home, I saw John Collins."

"One moment before you continue, Miss Bonner, don't ten a.m. classes typically end at eleven fifty and not twelve?"

"Yes, I guess they do."

"Did you stay longer after class for some reason?"

"No, I just rounded the time off."

"Could you have been less than thirty minutes at the bookstore?"

"Maybe, I was in no rush to be anywhere, so I took my time."

"But thirty minutes is only a rough estimate?"

"Yes."

"Miss Bonner, is it possible you passed by Mr. Collins earlier than twelve thirty p.m."

"It was closer to twelve thirty p.m."

"What did you see?"

"John sitting on his motorcycle talking to a young woman."

"So you recognized John Collins?"

"Yes, we knew each other on a social basis. He was in a fraternity and some of my sorority sisters dated him. The girl standing on the sidewalk had her back to me, but John and I smiled at one another."

"Did you know the young woman he was talking with?"

"No, she didn't turn around, but I could tell I didn't know her."

"Is this the person John Collins was speaking to?" Prosecutor Delhey asked handing her a photograph of Karen Sue Beineman.

"No. The girl he was talking to had long brown hair."

The prosecution hoped Bonner could identify the woman talking to Collins as Karen Sue Beineman. Now it was certain she saw Lorraine Kellogg talking with Collins. Still, they were able to have Bonner verify the time she saw Collins and place another stickpin on the prosecution's map exhibit showing where she encountered Collins.

When it was the defense's turn to cross-examine Susan Bonner, she was asked what her opinion of John Collins was.

"He is a very nice guy."

"What did your sorority sisters say about Mr. Collins?"

"Objection, Your Honor. Defense counsel is asking for hearsay testimony."

"Sustained."

"No further questions for this witness, Your Honor." Louisell was pleased with her testimony.

Next up to testify was Sarah Herrera, a teenaged bride who said Collins tried to pick her up while she was waiting for her mother outside Ypsilanti High School on Adams and West Cross Streets. Like the other girls who testified they saw Collins, she rose from the stand and placed a red pin on the map exhibit. Returning to the stand, she said a man in a striped, blue-green shirt rode up to her on a motorcycle at around 11:30 a.m.

Louisell asked the high school girl how she could be certain of the date. She explained, "Well, I ordinarily wouldn't remember when someone tried to pick me up (a common occurrence in a college town), but there was something in the paper," Herrera said.

Louisell wanted to crush that line of testimony and did not follow up on the point. The observant young woman also added she noticed the motorcycle had a square-shaped rearview mirror on the left side of the handlebars. This was testimony that did not please the defense. They dismissed Sarah Herrera as quickly as possible.

Another EMU coed, Eileen Gale, testified that at about 11: 25 a.m. on the date in question, a motorcyclist stopped her as she was walking alone on Perrin near Forest Street. Another red pin went on the map. She remembered the motorcycle had a blue tank and the driver was neatly dressed. "He had on a knit shirt with a large amount of green and yellow in it," Eileen Gale said. "I only spoke with him for a minute or two. Then I ran down the street to my girlfriend's apartment."

"Why did you run down the street?" the prosecutor asked.

"Something didn't feel right. With all the murders, I felt a little paranoid."

The defense declined to cross-examine Eileen Gale and the judge dismissed her.

The final witness to testify she saw John Collins in the area was twenty-two-year-old Mary M. Thompson, an EMU senior. She said the defendant drove up to her sometime before noon on July 23 as she was walking up College Place between Forest and Cross Streets. She said Collins was "wearing a green-striped shirt and driving a shiny motorcycle." Thompson explained she spoke to him for only thirty seconds to a minute.

All seven girls who testified placed pins on the map exhibit to show where they crossed paths with Collins. All contacts were within several blocks of each other near the EMU campus and within blocks of where John Collins lived.

Wednesday's final witness was Michigan State Police trooper Donald Collins, no relation to the accused. He had drawn a diagram of the street outside Wigs by Joan on North Washington Street in downtown Ypsilanti. William Delhey wanted the scaled diagram entered as a courtroom exhibit and indicated another diagram would be entered into evidence later in the day, a diagram of the basement of Sergeant David A. Leik, the alleged scene of the murder. With the judge's approval, both drawings were entered into evidence.

On the one-year anniversary of Karen Sue Beineman's death, her sister Barbara attended the trial for the first time. She sat in the back row of the small courtroom and on the opposite side of the aisle from Loretta Collins, who appeared every day at the trial including the five weeks of jury selection.

Karen Naylor, a young woman described in all the papers as John Collins's former girlfriend, began the day's testimony. William Treml reported in the *Ann Arbor News* that "The tall, long-haired blonde wept quietly as she identified Collins in the courtroom." He smiled back at her. She composed herself and explained that a year ago she was a student at Washtenaw County Community College, just northwest of Eastern Michigan University where she was currently enrolled.

Naylor explained she met Collins while she was washing her car outside her apartment house named the Huron Hills on LeForge Road where she lived. "This handsome, well-built guy was visiting some fraternity brothers who lived in the same building as me. After a couple of minutes, he discovered I was into motorcycles and had my own Yamaha. Then, several days later when I was out riding my bike, he pulled up alongside me and asked if I wanted to go riding with him."

"Is that how he phrased it?" the prosecutor asked.

"Yes. After he said it, I thought most people would ask 'Do you mind if I ride with you?' But he made it sound like it was a great privilege to ride with him. I was struck by his self-confidence."

"Is that all you were struck by?"

"Well, no."

"What else?"

"John had on a tight T-shirt and shorts. I remember thinking how well-toned his body was."

"Are you John Collins's girlfriend as the newspapers describe you?"

Naylor answered, "We dated through March, April, May, and July of last year."

"Not June? Why not June?"

"Most of June, he…"

"Objection," Louisell bellowed. "That question is not within the scope of this case and is inadmissible as part of Your Honor's earlier ruling."

"Sustained," Conlin ruled. "Mr. Delhey, stay within the parameters of this case."

"My apologies to the court, Your Honor. It won't happen again." The prosecutor did some backpedaling. "Miss Naylor, were you and Collins ever engaged?"

"Objection! The prosecution is leading the witness."

"Overruled, Mr. Louisell. The court is interested in the witness's answer."

"No, Sir. We weren't. We hung out and went off-roading quite a bit on one of several bikes he owned. He had two Bultaco dirt bikes we rode around the backcountry. We would go on romantic picnics along the Huron River, but never anything very serious. We always had a good time together."

"What other motorcycles did he have at his disposal?"

"John had a green Triumph 450 with high handlebars and a big blue Triumph 650 with a square rearview mirror on the left handlebar."

Naylor told the court that the Saturday before Beineman disappeared, Collins made a date to take her to the beach on Wednesday. It wasn't like him to not show up or not make a phone call. He stood me up."

"Would you explain what you just said in more detail?"

"John never showed up. The next morning, I went to his

apartment and he wasn't there. Then I looked for him inside the garage. He wasn't there either but both Triumphs were. But there was no sign of the square mirror. However, on the blue Triumph, there was a crushed and bent round mirror."

"How did Mr. Collins take care of his motorcycles?"

"He was meticulous. He didn't like to go out in the rain and mud with them."

"Would John Collins ever put a defective part on one of his motorcycles?"

"Objection, Your Honor. The answer calls for an opinion and assumes facts not in evidence."

"Sustained, Mr. Fink."

At this juncture, Fink interrupted Naylor's testimony and requested the Triumph motorcycles be brought into the courtroom for examination before the jury. Prosecutor Delhey conferred briefly with Sheriff Harvey who was in a wheelchair at the rear of the courtroom. Delhey approached the bench and told the judge the motorcycles were being stored at an undisclosed location. They would need to be trucked in which could take some time.

"Perhaps Sheriff Harvey could ride them in?" Judge Conlin smirked, in a rare light moment in the courtroom. The county sheriff had recently crashed his own motorcycle and smiled at the prospect of driving each of those bikes up the stairwells and roaring into the courtroom in front of John Collins. While the spectators enjoyed a bit of comic relief at the judge's remark, Conlin adjourned the proceedings for the lunch recess while the motorcycle exhibits were retrieved. As her son was led back to his jail cell, Mrs. Collins waved and smiled at him as bravely as she could.

When court resumed, the two Triumph motorcycles were wheeled into the courtroom. John Norman Collins reached out in a rare show of emotion and touched the handle grip on one of the bikes and grinned as he made his way to the defense table.

It was time for the rest of Karen Naylor's testimony. She identified the motorcycles as belonging to Collins. Then Delhey asked her to testify about the square mirror and which of the bikes she saw it on last. "The blue one," she testified. "John had a minor accident with the green bike and transferred the cycle's handlebars with the square mirror to the blue Triumph."

When Joseph Louisell cross-examined Naylor, he asked her to point out the damage on the green cycle. She walked over to the exhibit and pointed to a small dent on the gas tank. She told the court Collins had a square mirror on the green cycle at the time of the accident.

"If I told you the handlebars on the blue bike were purchased in July, would you change your testimony?" said the wily attorney.

"No, because they weren't." answered Naylor.

Naylor testified Collins had a square rearview mirror on his motorcycle like the one she had on her motorcycle.

"Didn't you pay six dollars for yours, and didn't John tell you it was no good?" Louisell probed.

"No! That's not true. We never talked about that," Naylor answered defensively.

Joseph Louisell was going nowhere with his line of questioning and simply gave up. "No further questions, Your Honor." The defense would vent their frustration on the next witness, Diane Joan Goshe, owner of Wigs by Joan.

The Wig-Shop Ladies

ALL THE NEWSPAPERS DESCRIBED Diane Joan Goshe, the prosecution's key witness, as "a tall, slender woman with silver-blonde hair piled high on her head." Because of the gravity of Goshe's testimony at the pretrial hearing, the defense asked that the jury be excused while the wig-shop owner was questioned by the prosecution about the conversation she had with Beineman. The judge complied with the defense request.

Ten minutes later, Goshe testified Beineman told her, "I'm the bravest customer you've had today. I bought a hairpiece, which is something I've always wanted, and I accepted a ride from a stranger on a motorcycle."

Judge Conlin ruled the testimony inadmissible about Beineman accepting the ride because it was a past action and hearsay. The statement Beineman made about purchasing the wig was irrelevant. Goshe would be allowed to testify the girl told her the motorcyclist said he would take her back to her dormitory.

"After the conversation, what did you do?"

Goshe said, "I went outside my shop to get a better look at him."

"Did you see his face?"

"I saw a three-quarter profile of him. I looked at him for more than a minute at a distance of thirty feet."

"What was he doing?"

"He was sitting on his motorcycle. The motorcycle came within fifteen feet of me as they drove off."

When asked to describe the clothing the young man was wearing, she answered, "A horizontally stripped yellow and green T-shirt."

The description matched descriptions given from the previous day's testimony. Goshe was asked if she could point out the person in the courtroom. She pointed to John Collins as the person she saw on a motorcycle with Karen Sue Beineman that afternoon.

"What happened after that?" Delhey asked.

"They drove off and turned right onto Michigan Avenue."

When Judge Conlin called the jury back to the courtroom, Goshe repeated the same testimony in their presence without the prejudicial remarks the judge ruled inadmissible.

Thursday afternoon's proceedings were adjourned until Monday morning at nine o'clock when cross-examination of Goshe would begin. The rest of the afternoon, Judge Conlin researched opinions and ruled on a variety of issues brought by the defense. He told the jury and the attorneys he fully intended to conduct a Monday-through-Friday court schedule, but he had other court business to take care of this Friday.

When court reconvened on Monday, July 27, Neil Fink moved to strike the testimony given the previous Thursday by Karen Naylor—John Collins's former girlfriend. "Miss Naylor contradicted herself about the testimony concerning the square mirror. Her testimony is highly prejudicial and not based on fact."

Judge Conlin said dryly, "I will review the woman's testimony before making a decision."

Today's cross-examination of Goshe was also going to be handled by Neil Fink. This would be a punishing two hours on the stand as the defense attorney attempted to attack her character and truthfulness. So far, the women who testified were handled with care, but Fink changed tactics now.

"Mrs. Goshe, you told this court Miss Beineman came into your shop between noon and twelve thirty p.m. Did you not?"

"Yes."

"But didn't you first tell police it was at twelve fifteen p.m.?"

"I'm not certain."

"Not to worry. It's written down right here on the police statement you made and signed." He held a clipboard with the report and showed it to her. "Then during the pretrial hearing, you testified under oath that Miss Beineman arrived at your store between twelve thirty and one. So when was it? twelve, twelve fifteen, twelve thirty, one p.m.?"

"I don't have a definite time period when Miss Beineman arrived. It was sometime after noon and before one p.m."

"Are you sure?"

"Objection," Delhey interjected. "Defense counsel is badgering the witness. Mrs. Goshe answered his question."

"Sustained."

Neil Fink continued, "Mrs. Goshe, you originally described in your police report that the motorcyclist had dark, curly hair and medium sideburns, correct?"

"Yes, Sir."

"But Mr. Collins has straight hair and short sideburns. Were you shown any photographs of Mr. Collins prior to giving the police your description of the person on the motorcycle?"

"No, Sir. I gave the description to the police. Officer Mathewson showed me a grainy photo of John Collins standing by a Christmas tree. I told the officer I wasn't certain and didn't want to make any identification from a photograph."

"Were you shown any other photographs of the defendant?"

"Yes."

"And what was the result of that?"

"I was unable to identify Collins from three photographs I was shown by Sheriff Harvey. One of the photos looked like him, but I also told the sheriff I wasn't comfortable making a positive identification from a photograph."

"What was Sheriff Harvey's reaction?"

"Disappointment."

"What did he say?"

"Thank you and he left."

"Do you wear corrective lenses, Mrs. Goshe?"

"I wear glasses when it is bright and for long distance."

"Were you wearing them on the day you allegedly saw John Collins in front of your shop?"

"No. He was not that far away or difficult to see."

"Does your employee, Mrs. Spaulding, wear glasses?"

"Sometimes."

"Was she wearing them the day she claimed she saw John Collins on the motorcycle parked outside your shop?"

"I don't remember."

"I'd say there is a lot you don't remember. Do you remember ever marrying your husband?"

"What?" Goshe said.

"Objection," interjected Delhey. "This line of inquiry is irrelevant and immaterial to the facts of this case."

"Your Honor, this speaks to the integrity and truthfulness of this witness."

"Objection overruled. Continue, Mr. Fink."

"Come on now, Mrs. Goshe," Fink probed, "It's an easy question. Do you remember marrying your husband?"

When pressed further, Goshe admitted she lied twice under oath when she said she was married to a man named Whitting with whom she was living.

"That was a lie, wasn't it?"

"Yes," she said.

Fink asked Goshe to walk over to the motorcycles and examine them. When she returned to the stand, she said she could not connect either motorcycle to the man seated before her. "I'm not that familiar with motorcycles."

Fink continued to undermine Goshe's judgment. He asked her about a former male companion who he claimed was a convicted rapist. "Aren't you afraid for your son's safety or to be seen in public with this man?"

"No. I don't turn my back on my friends."

Fink suddenly took another tack. "What about the reward?"

"What reward?"

"The seventy-four thousand dollars you were bickering over with your employee Patricia Spaulding about who should claim the reward?"

Prosecutor Delhey objected strongly saying the defense was muckraking.

"No further questions at this time, Your Honor," Fink said.

"The jury will disregard the remarks about the reward money, and the court recorder will strike them from the record," Conlin instructed.

On redirect, Prosecutor Delhey made an attempt to reestablish the credibility of his star witness. "Mrs. Goshe, would you explain to this court the circumstances behind your first marriage?"

"When I was fifteen years old, I ran away from home with my boyfriend to St. Louis, Missouri, in an attempt to get married. When I returned home with my male companion some time later, we claimed we were married and lived together for eight years as husband and wife and purchased a home. I lied under oath because I wanted to protect my eleven-year-old son who has to grow up in this town. I made the mistake. He shouldn't have to suffer for it."

After two hours of interrogation, Goshe never wavered in her testimony that it was John Norman Collins who drove Karen Sue Beineman away from her wig shop one year before.

The second prosecution witness of the day was Carol Wieczerza, an EMU coed and an employee of Jacobson's women's clothing store in Arborland. The previous year, she worked at the Chocolate Shoppe next door to Wigs by Joan. The twenty-one-year-old clerk testified the shop was empty of customers, so she was gazing out the front window. "I saw a young man and a woman pull up on a flashy motorcycle and park in front of the shop. It was around twelve thirty or so when they rode up."

"What happened next?"

"The girl got off and walked down the street toward the wig shop. About fifteen minutes later, the girl came back and got on the motorcycle. She got off again, talked with the man, and got back on. Then they rode off."

"Can you identify that man?"

"The man resembled John Collins, but I can't be sure."

Unlike the ladies in the wig shop, Wieczerca could not positively identify Collins as the motorcyclist that day, but she could identify what he was wearing—a green and yellow striped T-shirt and blue jeans.

"Do you have any recollection of the motorcycle, Miss Wieczerca?"

The young clerk was a bike enthusiast and rider herself and easily recognized the big blue bike with all the gingerbread chrome detail. "It was a blue Triumph 650. That one over there." The defense could not get Carol Wieczerza off the stand quickly enough!

—————

Now, it was Patricia Spaulding's turn. She would be the second witness to place Collins and Beineman together on the motorcycle that fateful afternoon. Spaulding had shown Beineman how to wear her new wiglet in her hair.

After Spaulding identified who she was and where she worked, Prosecutor Delhey began his questioning. "Mrs. Spaulding, would you tell the court what you witnessed on Wednesday afternoon, July 23, 1969?"

"Miss Beineman came into the shop at about twelve thirty p.m. to pick up a hairpiece called a fall she ordered it the day before."

"How long was she in the wig shop?" he asked.

"For only fifteen minutes maybe."

"Did you have any direct contact with her?"

"Yes."

"Would you describe your interaction with Miss Beineman?"

"I showed her how to store the hairpiece and how to style her hair using the hairpiece."

"Tell the court what happened next, please."

"Well, I went outside the shop with Mrs. Goshe and looked toward the Chocolate Shoppe and saw a man waiting on a motorcycle for the young woman. I took a look at him and went back into the shop and watched them out the window as they headed toward Michigan Avenue. Miss Beineman was wearing her hairpiece when she left."

"Is the driver of that motorcycle in this courtroom today?"

Patricia Spaulding pointed at Collins.

"Have the record show Mrs. Spaulding pointed at the defendant," said the judge.

"Can you describe the motorcycle he was riding?"

"It was dark blue, shiny, and well-kept with a square rearview mirror on the left side of the handlebars."

"Is that motorcycle in this courtroom?"

"I couldn't say for sure. My husband rides a motorcycle, but I couldn't identify a particular bike. I was focused on the driver—not the motorcycle."

"Thank you, Mrs. Spaulding. No further questions,

Your Honor," Delhey said, walking to the prosecution table satisfied he had made his case.

Diane Joan Goshe and Patricia Spaulding placed Collins and Beineman together on the motorcycle, and another credible witness, Carol Wieczerza, was able to identity the motorcycle and the make—a Triumph 650. This witness was not sure about the rider since it was the motorcycle that caught her eye.

Just before the lunch recess, Judge Conlin interrupted Spaulding's testimony to rule on a defense motion made the previous Thursday. The judge said he would strike evidence given by Karen Naylor regarding her conflicting testimony about Collins switching the square mirror on his motorcycles. Later in her testimony, Naylor said she saw only a picture of the square mirror on the blue bike, but no such photograph was in evidence. The jury was instructed to disregard that portion of her testimony. This was by no means a victory for the defense. Several other witnesses testified about the square mirror, so the prosecution won their point.

Returning from the lunch recess, Spaulding came under intense cross-examination from Joseph Louisell about her lunch break with Goshe. "Did you or Mrs. Goshe discuss your testimony at lunch?"

"We didn't," she answered.

"What did you discuss? The reward money and who would claim it?"

"Objection! Defense counsel is putting words in the mouth of the witness."

"Sustained, Mr. Delhey."

"Allow me to rephrase that. Did you talk about the reward money at lunch?"

"Mrs. Goshe said she was thinking about claiming the

reward if Collins was convicted, but we didn't discuss that at lunch today."

When Louisell pressed Spaulding about her original police statement, she said she never gave the type of motorcycle, and she did not identify Collins from the three photographs Sheriff Harvey showed her. She did say, however, that the motorcycle had a square mirror on the left side. The wig stylist also admitted she made no attempt to get the license plate number of the motorcycle as it passed in front of the wig shop.

Spaulding added she was not satisfied with the composite drawing made by Ypsilanti police sergeant William Stenning. The sideburns on the drawing were longer than on the man she witnessed that day. "His sideburns came more to the middle of the ear." Patricia Spaulding added little to the testimony already given by her employer. In the end, both women stood their ground.

—23—

The Worm Turns

ARNOLD DAVIS, SELF-DESCRIBED "BEST of friends" with John Norman Collins, roomed in the same boarding-house across the second-floor landing from Collins. A year had passed since Davis graduated from Eastern Michigan. He was currently working as an operations supervisor at LaGuardia Airport in New York City.

"When Davis arrived in court, Collins stared intently into the witness's eyes for at least five minutes," John Cobb of the *Ypsilanti Press* reported. "Both Davis and Collins bear a remarkable resemblance. Both are of the same build and have square jaws with sharp features. Their hair is worn in the same style with a wave over the right side of the forehead. Davis differs from Collins by having longer sideburns."

Arnie Davis began his testimony Tuesday morning without the jury present. Judge Conlin ruled that to protect the record, it would be best to take the testimony first in their absence. The judge and the prosecution feared a mistrial could be called if information related to any of

the other murders connected with Collins came out during
Davis's testimony.

Arnie Davis was dressed in a pink shirt, a red and gray
tie, and a gray suit. He began his testimony in a relaxed and
thoughtful manner. Prosecutor Delhey questioned him about
Sunday evening, July 27, 1969.

"Two police detectives came to our house at around
eleven at night. John went out on the porch and talked
with them for about fifteen minutes before agreeing to leave
with them. He returned home between one and one thirty
Monday morning," Davis told Delhey.

"Did he talk to you about the incident with the police?"

"Yes, he said the cops suspected him of the Beineman
murder and asked him to return later that day for more
questioning. I laughed and said, 'They're suspecting a lot of
people.'"

"What happened next, Mr. Davis?"

"John called home and told his mother he was in trouble."

"Can you tell the court what happened the next evening
at about eleven p.m.?"

"John and I returned home after feeding a dog belonging to his uncle. The family was away on vacation. When
we returned home, John took a knife wrapped in a shop rag
from under the seat of one of his motorcycles."

"What did he do with the knife?"

"He took it upstairs."

"A short time later, I carried a dark green or blue blanket
from the trunk of John's car, while he carried a cardboard
box to his room," Davis testified.

"Did you notice anything in the box?"

"I glanced and saw a pair of women's shoes, some rags
or clothing, and a burlap handbag."

"Do you know what he did with those items?"

"Fifteen minutes later, John left the rooming house with the blanket and the box. Within half an hour, he returned home empty-handed."

"Did you ask him about the items?"

"I asked him about the blanket.'"

"And what was his answer?"

"He got rid of it."

"Did Mr. Collins give you anything that night?"

"Yes, he did."

"Would you tell the court what he gave you?"

"John brought a hunting knife to my room and asked me to keep it for him."

"Did you?"

"Sort of."

"What do you mean, 'sort of'?"

"I told him to put it someplace, and he placed it in my dresser drawer."

The defense team objected strenuously to Davis's testimony regarding the contents of the box and the hunting knife.

Ruling on the admissibility of the testimony, Judge Conlin said, "it has not been shown Miss Beineman was wearing a pair of dress shoes (her corpse was wearing sandals), and there isn't sufficient identification of the handbag to indicate it was similar to hers or that either are connected to Miss Beineman in any way. As regards the testimony about the knife, there has been no claim by the prosecution of any knife wounds on Miss Beineman's body and only her underpants were with a sharp instrument."

The judge ruled "certain parts of Davis' testimony were ruled inadmissible and could not be brought before the jury. The knife did not enter into the cause of death and the contents of the box are irrelevant to the disposition of this case."

The defense won a major victory against the aggressive prosecution.

The jury was brought into the courtroom at 10:10 a.m. to hear the admissible parts of Arnie Davis's testimony. William Delhey carefully led Davis through his twenty minutes on the stand.

"How long have you known the defendant, Mr. Davis?"

"Just over two years. We pledged the same fraternity in the spring of 1967 and common association led to friendship."

"And which fraternity was that?"

"Theta Chi...on West Cross Street."

"What kind of car did Mr. Collins drive when you met him?"

"A blue and gray 1958 DeSoto. After that, he drove a silver, 1968 Olds Cutlass."

Davis testified he and Collins lived in a rooming house on Emmet Street from the summer of 1968 until August of 1969. Arnie Davis said of his relationship with Collins, "We were good friends...best of friends."

Prosecutor Delhey asked Arnie Davis to carefully trace his contacts with Collins from Tuesday, the day before Beineman disappeared, to the following Sunday, July 27.

"On Tuesday night, we ate dinner at the Ponderosa Steakhouse in Ann Arbor. Then, we went to the home of Collins's uncle to feed his German shepherd while the family was away. I stayed in the car while John went through the garage door to feed the dog."

"What about July twenty-third, the day Karen Sue Beineman went missing?"

"I went to work at J. C. Penney in Arborland from nine a.m. until twelve forty-five p.m. When I arrived home afterward, Collins wasn't there, so I started working on a project for the store. After about thirty minutes, Andy Manuel and I went to Grant's in the Gault Village Shopping Center. We stayed there between three forty-five p.m. and four fifteen p.m. when we went home. Fifteen minutes later, John walked into the house. He said he was at Joe's motorcycle shop getting parts for his bike."

"Would you identify who Andrew Manuel is for the court?"

"Andy was a work friend of John's who recently moved into our house."

"After John Collins got home that evening, what did the three of you do, Mr. Davis?"

"We watched television in John's room. John went out to work on his bike. He stayed in the garage for a couple of hours. When he returned, we watched TV until eleven thirty p.m. Then, he remembered he had to feed his uncle's dog. John went to his uncle's house and was gone for over an hour. When he returned, the James Cagney movie Andy and I were watching was nearly over. After the movie finished at one, Manuel left to get some pop, and Collins went to wash his car at the quarter car wash."

"What did you do, Mr. Davis?"

"I went to sleep."

"When did you next see John Collins?" Delhey prodded.

"On Thursday afternoon, I saw John in the garage working on his motorcycle and talking to an EMU campus policeman. I just returned from the Secretary of State's office with a license plate for one of..."

Louisell interrupted Davis. "Objection, Your Honor. This line of inquiry is irrelevant and immaterial."

"Sustained, Mr. Louisell."

Arnie Davis testified the next time he saw Collins was on Sunday, July 27, just before 11:00 p.m. Davis asked Collins if he had a good time on his date. Just then, the doorbell rang and Arnie asked Collins to answer the door. It was the police again. They asked John to go to the crime center for some questioning. He returned home after 1:00 a.m. The next day Collins was arrested.

At the finish of Arnie Davis's testimony for the prosecution, the defense team objected strongly to his testimony saying it was "tainted by illegal police misconduct during questioning." This made an issue of the voluntary nature of Davis's testimony. "All his testimony comes from mental torture, and we object to everything he testifies to. It's all tainted. We want that on the record," said Joseph Louisell.

At 4:15 p.m., Judge Conlin ruled, "It's almost quitting time. We'll adjourn now and give the defense time to interview the witness (Davis). We don't want to get into grounds for a mistrial."

———

The defense got their chance to cross-examine Arnie Davis on Tuesday morning. During Monday's session, Davis gave key prosecution testimony about their client's movements at the time of the Beineman murder. The defense chose to ignore Davis's testimony, awaiting a ruling by Judge Conlin to strike it from the record. Joseph Louisell chose to focus on Davis's treatment by police, which virtually overshadowed the testimony of his friend's comings and goings. When Louisell should have pressed this witness, he decided to go easy on him instead.

"Would you tell the court, Mr. Davis, about your trip to Kentucky with Mr. Collins in 1968?" the seasoned attorney began.

Davis described how "Collins swerved his car to avoid hitting a cat in the road, but the vehicle struck and killed it."

"And didn't John stop the car and go over to the animal?"

"Yes, Sir, he did."

The vignette the defense attorney painted for the jury did not touch on the question of why he stopped or what he thought he could have done about it. Did Collins pray over the animal? Did he bury it? Did he place it on the shoulder of the road? Did he grieve over the cat's carcass? Or did he have a morbid curiosity and watch this mangled and torn creature twitch in its death throes? The prosecution was puzzled where the defense was going with this line of questioning, but for the present, they let it continue.

"Was your friend working his way through college?" Louisell asked.

"Yes, he was."

"Where did he work?"

"John worked part-time at Motor Wheel Corporation on Norris Street in Ypsilanti," Davis said.

"Is it true you and Mr. Collins often talked about Vietnam and the draft?"

"Objection," said Delhey. "This line of testimony is irrelevant and immaterial to the matter before this court."

Louisell appealed to Judge Conlin. "My question is meant to bring out Collins's peaceful and law-abiding self."

"Objection sustained."

"Mr. Davis, would you tell the court about the arrest of your friend?"

"Yes, Sir. The police came to the house looking for John on Saturday morning, July twenty-sixth."

"Where was he?"

"He was in Center Line at his mother's house."

"Did you tell the police officers that?"

"I did but they still staked out the house. At one point, I went up to their unmarked police car and invited them in for a cup of coffee."

"Did the police avail themselves of your hospitality?"

"They said, 'No, thanks' and left."

"When did John get home?"

"About eleven p.m. Sunday night."

"Anything out of the ordinary happen?"

"The doorbell rang and I asked John to answer it."

"Did you know who was at the door?"

"I had a pretty good idea. I mentioned to John the police were at the house looking for him over the weekend."

"Who was at the door?"

"Two police detectives."

"Then what happened?"

"John went out on the porch and talked with them for about ten minutes and left with them."

"Where did they take him?"

"When John returned home at two o'clock Monday morning, he said the police took him to the crime center on Washtenaw Avenue."

Using a police report as a hand prop, Joseph Louisell led the witness. "Didn't John describe his interview with police that night as horrible?"

"Yes."

"And didn't he tell you," Louisell said, reading from the police report. "'I want to help them. I want to, I want to. I want to help them solve this crime, but gosh, it was horrible. They let the real killer get away, and now they are harassing me.'"

Arnie Davis agreed those were the words Collins used. In a roundabout way, the defense was able to get some hearsay testimony of their client into the record, despite muzzling Collins from testifying in his own defense. The "They let the real killer get away" remark was engineered to enter into testimony the abortive mannequin fiasco at the Beineman stakeout.

Arnie Davis said he was at McKenny Union on the EMU campus when he heard his friend had been arrested. "I hurried home and there were police and newsmen at the house. A crowd had formed outside. The police wouldn't allow me into the house and took me to the crime center for questioning."

"You mean the Holy Ghost Fathers' Seminary where the task force was headquartered."

"Yes, Sir. I was questioned there until three or four in the morning."

"Mr. Davis, do you remember the names of any of the officers who questioned you?"

"Morrison, Little, Canada, and sometimes a prosecutor..."

"Did they all question you at the same time?"

"No, in relay teams."

"Did they threaten you at all, Mr. Davis?"

"I was told I could be arrested for suspicion of the Beineman murder if I didn't cooperate."

"Did they accuse you of lying?"

"Yes."

"Did they use loud voices?"

"Yes."

"What happened next?"

"The questioning finally ended at three or four Saturday morning. The police took me to the Inn America with a detective who told me I could 'get up and leave' if I wanted."

"But were you left with the impression if you chose to leave, you would be arrested?"

"Objection, Your Honor," Prosecutor Delhey interrupted. "Defense counsel has been leading the witness all afternoon. Whatever Mr. Davis's impression may be is not a fact in this case or subject to the rules of evidence."

"Objection sustained."

Louisell made no mention to the jury that the boardinghouse on Emmet Street was a secured crime scene and nobody could go inside the house without police authorization. Apparently, Arnie had no place else to go, so he was taken to one of the nicest hotels in the greater Ann Arbor area, the Inn America, for free lodgings with room service, all paid for by the county.

As his testimony stretched on, Davis continued to cast aspersions on the police at Louisell's promptings. "The police picked me up later the next day on Saturday and interviewed me most of the day until about one o'clock Sunday morning."

"Did they ask you the same questions?"

"Over and over again, but this time they threatened to implicate my twin brother in the murder case. I was questioned by police for four or five hours almost every day at the crime center."

"At one point, didn't you tell the police they could write down whatever they wanted and you would sign it?"

"Something like that. They kept asking me about a square rearview mirror. I told them 'I don't recall such a mirror!' They seemed mad."

"Objection! The question doesn't require the witness to draw a conclusion based on his answer."

"Sustained, Mr. Delhey."

"Once you graduated from Eastern Michigan and moved to New York, did police interest in you continue?"

"State police detective Max Little kept calling me at my place of employment in New York City. I finally told him I wouldn't cooperate with him anymore if he continued to harass me."

"Were you ever offered counsel during these interview sessions?"

"I was never represented by counsel during numerous police interviews and was not always told my statements were being recorded. State police Lieutenant Morrison told me it was to my advantage not to have a lawyer present during questioning."

"Were you told by your interrogators, 'If you are innocent, you won't need a lawyer'?"

"Yes. Morrison told me he could get a warrant for my arrest, but he was holding back."

"So Lieutenant Morrison gave you legal advice?"

"Yes, I suppose so."

Before the prosecution could lodge an objection, Louisell said, "I'd like to withdraw that question, Your Honor."

"Did Morrison speak with you about the reward money?"

"He told me he couldn't offer me any inducement or reward, but it was his understanding that rewards were available in the Beineman case."

"No further questions for this witness, Your Honor."

On redirect, Prosecutor Delhey did not respond to Davis's charges against the police. "Do you remember, Mr. Davis, what you told investigators John Collins said to you on the night of Sunday, July twenty-seventh, after the discovery of Miss Beineman's body was reported?"

"I'm not sure. The police questioned me about many things," he hedged.

"Yes. We just heard your sworn testimony, Mr. Davis." An uncomfortable silence ensued while Delhey carefully scanned a police report. "Mr. Davis, let me read to you from the police report taken that day. Collins asked you 'If anybody asks, remember what time we went riding on Wednesday. It was early afternoon. Right!' Does that ring a bell with you, Mr. Davis?"

"Vaguely."

"What time did you tell the police investigators you had your motorcycle driving lesson with Collins on Wednesday?"

"Around four p.m. until seven p.m."

"Was the lesson three hours long?"

"More like two hours. We took the long way through the back country to our house, about two or three hours all together."

"You testified he drove you to the parking lot on Eastern's North Campus."

"Yes."

"Who drove back?"

"He did. I was on the back of John's motorcycle."

"Do you remember the route you took?"

"The scenic route: Huron River Drive to Superior Road, Superior to Geddes Road, Geddes to Prospect Street, and Prospect to West Cross Street. Then we turned left on College Place and went up a block to our house on the corner of Emmet Street."

"You remember the directions home pretty well," Delhey remarked. "Do you remember now what John told you the day Karen Sue Beineman disappeared?" Delhey asked, putting on his glasses and bringing the police report within reading distance.

Reluctantly, Arnie said, "John told me he wanted me to say the lesson was earlier in the afternoon."

"Is that all he told you, Mr. Davis?"

Squirming a bit, Arnie said, "And not to 'fuck him up!'"

"No further questions, Your Honor."

———

Assistant Prosecutor Booker T. Williams was back on active duty after his family leave. His wife passed away after a long illness. The next witness was Collins's other rooming-house friend Andrew Manuel, who was brought over to the courthouse from the county jail across the street. He was serving a sixty-day sentence for a parole violation from two other Fourteenth Circuit Court cases, which not coincidently involved his Motor Wheel work buddy John Collins. Any mention of these cases could result in a mistrial, so Williams was cautious with his questioning.

A mistrial in the Collins case would mean that the entire process would have to begin anew. At this point, the prosecution did not want this case to slip away and cost the taxpayers an endless amount of money. The defense did not want a mistrial because if Michigan Governor William Milliken decided to honor California Governor Ronald Reagan's extradition request, Collins could be tried in California. Further upping the stakes was the death penalty. California had capital punishment on the books and Michigan did not.

Andrew Manuel's testimony roughly followed what Davis said earlier. Manuel agreed Collins returned to the rooming house between 4:00 p.m. and 4:30 p.m. on Wednesday, July 23. Manuel testified, "Collins and Davis left to get something to eat." Here was where his testimony varied from Davis's account. Davis claimed Collins was giving him motorcycle driving lessons during the same time frame.

When Arnie and John returned, Andrew Manuel testified they ate their evening meal at the W.T. Grant store in the Gault Village Shopping Center off of South Grove Road in Ypsilanti Township.

"Mr. Manuel, didn't you just testify Mr. Collins and Mr. Davis left earlier to get something to eat?"

"That's what I thought, but I don't know what they were doing. I wasn't there," he wisely answered.

"What did you do after your evening meal together?" Chief Assistant Prosecutor Williams asked.

"We went to the Emmet Street house at about nine or ten p.m. and watched television."

"Do you remember what you watched?"

"Arnie and I watched a James Cagney movie but Collins left for a time. I think he was in the garage working on his bike."

"What did you do when the movie ended, Mr. Manuel?"

"Following the movie, I went to a gas station to wash my car. Collins arrived there a while afterward."

"Isn't that kind of late to be washing your car?"

"Not when you're used to working midnights."

"While John was waxing his car, I left. The next time I saw him was in his room Tuesday. The three of us went out for supper and stopped at John's uncle's house to feed the dog," Manuel said. "Arnie and I stayed in the car while John went inside for fifteen or twenty minutes."

"Inside where? The house or the garage?"

"Maybe both, I wasn't paying attention."

"Did you see Collins over the weekend?"

"No, John was at his mother's house."

"Do you know who fed the dog while John was out of town?"

"No, Sir, I don't."

"No further questions, Your Honor," said Assistant Prosecutor Williams.

When Judge Conlin asked Neil Fink how long he expected his cross-examination of Andrew Manuel to last, Fink said about an hour. The judge announced the afternoon recess. However, when court reconvened, Fink stood up and simply said, "We have no questions for Mr. Manuel." The defense felt there was little to be gained by placing Andrew Manuel back on the stand and lots to lose if he messed up in redirect examination by the prosecution. To the informed eyes in the courtroom, it was difficult to discern who wanted Andrew Manuel off the stand more, the prosecution or the defense.

—24—

Family: Ties That Bind Sometimes Strangle

MICHIGAN STATE POLICE SERGEANT David A. Leik was called to the stand to testify for the prosecution against his nephew on Tuesday, July 28. One year earlier, suspected blood spots shrouded by blotches of black spray paint on his basement floor led the then Corporal Leik to report his nephew's suspected activity.

Testifying for the prosecution, Sergeant Leik explained how he and his family had just returned home from an eleven-day vacation to visit his brother in Madison, Wisconsin, with a side trip to Beaver Island in Lake Michigan.

"Can you give the court a time and date when you arrived home?" Prosecutor Delhey asked.

"Tuesday, July twenty-ninth at eleven thirty p.m."

"Did you notice anything unusual when you got home?"

"My wife noticed scuff marks on her clean kitchen floor, apparently made by rubber heels."

"Can you describe the scuff marks in more detail?"

"They were of varying lengths and looked like skid marks. Sandra mopped the floor before we went to bed."

"Would you tell the court, Sergeant Leik, what you discovered the next morning?"

"At eight thirty, my wife called me down to the basement. I could tell by her tone something wasn't right. She wanted to know if I had spray-painted anything on the basement floor."

"Had you?"

"No. That's when I first saw six or seven spots of black spray paint on the laundry room floor. The spots started at a door opening in the middle of the basement leading to the laundry room. They trailed to the dryer in the southwest corner of the basement. There was some black paint near the ladder too."

"What ladder?"

"The night before leaving on vacation, I painted the hall ceiling and afterward placed a homemade ladder on its side in the basement laundry room next to the oil storage tank. I finished around ten p.m. Then my wife washed clothes and cut the boys' hair."

"Did she cut your hair that evening?"

"No, Sir."

"Where does your wife normally cut hair?"

"In the basement under the staircase landing across from the clothes dryer."

"Tell us more about the spots of black spray paint. What size were they?"

"They varied in shape and size. I didn't measure them."

"Was there a black aerosol spray-paint can in your basement before you left on vacation?" Prosecutor Delhey asked.

"Yes, Sir, there was."

"Where did you keep it?"

"In a storage cabinet on the east wall of the laundry room."

"Did you find the spray can there when you returned from vacation?"

"I looked but couldn't find it."

"Anything else out of the ordinary happen that day, Sergeant Leik?"

"Yes. I was due back at the state police post on Thursday, but I got a call from Corporal Brown telling me I should come down there [the Ypsilanti state police post]. I was briefed by Captain Walter Stevens in his office and told my nephew was the prime suspect in the Beineman murder case. Afterward, I mentioned the black paint on my basement floor."

With the Collins family glaring at David Leik from the first row of the gallery, he continued his testimony. "When I got home, I didn't know how to tell my wife her nephew was a suspect in the Beineman case. We tried to call John all day with no success to hear if he had a reasonable explanation for the paint. Sandra called her sister Loretta to see if John might be at his mother's house."

"What time was that?"

"About eight thirty at night," Officer Leik testified. "Loretta told us John was out, but she would have him call when he got in. John called an hour later. After some small talk, I asked him about the scuff marks on the kitchen floor.

He said he knew nothing about them. Then I asked John if he spray-painted anything in the basement while we were gone."

"What was his reaction and response?"

"After a brief hesitation, John said, 'What paint, Uncle Dave?' I told him a can of black spray paint was missing."

"What was his answer?"

"He said, 'I didn't enter the house, Uncle Dave. I had no reason to.'"

"I asked John if someone could have gotten into the house while we were gone on vacation. John said he didn't notice anything unusual. He only watered and fed our dog in the garage. I told him I would have to report a suspected breaking and entering and the spray-paint blotches to my post commander. John replied, 'Let me know what they find out.'"

After his nephew's denial, Sergeant Leik said he and a detective friend scraped under the paint and placed samples in evidence envelopes to have them tested. Leik did not reveal the results of the tests and was not asked to do so.

"Please describe for the court what happened the following day."

"I made my report to Sergeant Christian Walker, assistant commander of the state police post, and returned to my home with Staff Sergeant Carl Freeborn, post commander, to wait for the crime lab to arrive."

When asked if the defendant had a key to his home, Officer Leik testified that John had a key to the front door since 1967, but Collins told him he did not know where it was. "I placed a key to the side door under the doormat, so John could feed our family dog while we were away."

"Did Mr. Collins ever return the key?"

"Yes."

"No further questions at this time, Your Honor."

Judge Conlin dismissed Sergeant Leik but asked that he return the next morning to begin his cross-examination by the defense.

The last witness of the day was State Trooper Donald L. Collins—no relation to the defendant. He entered into evidence a scale drawing of the Leik basement. The state trooper said he made the drawing on September 25, 1969. He presented the prosecution exhibit with a plastic overlay showing black spots representing the blotches of spray paint. There was no defense objection or motion to suppress the exhibit. Judge Conlin adjourned court until eight thirty the next morning.

———

When court resumed, Sergeant Leik's cross-examination was delayed to allow the prosecution to enter more exhibits into evidence. Ten color slides and eight photographs of the Leik house on Roosevelt Street were introduced into evidence by Michigan State Police detective Thomas J. Nasser. The jury was not present to give the defense a chance to view the items first.

When the jury was settled in, Sergeant Leik was recalled to validate the new photographic evidence entered into court. Leik said all of the exhibits were true representations of his house and basement when he returned home from vacation—except for one slide showing an area where he had scraped some paint. All but that exhibit were entered into evidence.

Now, it was Joseph Louisell's turn to cross-examine Officer Leik. The defense attorney asked the state trooper if his nephew John ever showed any interest in joining the Michigan State Police.

"We discussed things like salary, benefits, and retirement pay."

"What did you tell him?"

"I told him to contact a district recruiter but advised him to stay in school and complete his education."

"On the day the crime lab investigators were gathering evidence in your basement, what were you doing?"

"I was upstairs trying to console my wife."

"What was your involvement on the day your nephew was arrested?"

As if matters were not already bad enough between the Leik and the Collins families, this testimony spelled out the critical moment of family betrayal and John's last day of freedom.

"On the thirty-first of July, I went with Captain Walker Stevens to John's rooming house in Ypsilanti. We took John to the state police crime lab in Plymouth. Captain Stevens contacted Robert Francis, an Ann Arbor attorney who was John's lawyer at the time."

"What happened next, Sergeant Leik?"

"At the crime lab, John was questioned by Captain Stevens. When Robert Francis got there, he denied police permission to fingerprint or photograph his client."

"Was John fingerprinted?" Louisell asked.

"Captain Stevens and Mr. Francis got into a heated argument and voices were raised. Then John and his lawyer stepped outside to confer."

"What were you and Captain Stevens doing in the meantime?"

"Captain Stevens called Prosecutor Williams. Afterward, Stevens asked John to reenter the crime lab where County Sheriff Captain Mulholland arrested him for the murder of Miss Beineman."

"Then you were instrumental in the arrest of your nephew, were you not?"

"I was present and a witness to it."

Joseph Louisell made a dramatic pause. The courtroom was bereft of sound as the portly defense attorney lumbered to his next point. "When your nephew was arrested in the middle of the night on July thirty-first, you were a corporal then?"

"Objection, Your Honor. David Leik's promotion is irrelevant to these proceedings and is calculated to discredit the witness."

"Would both attorneys approach the bench," the judge directed.

"Mr. Louisell, what are you driving at?"

"I want to establish a quid pro quo relationship that speaks to the fitness of this witness's testimony."

"Judge Conlin, Sergeant Leik is already in a difficult position having to testify against his nephew with his in-laws glaring at him from the gallery. This line of questioning is irrelevant and misleading and should be struck from the record."

"That's all well and good, Mr. Delhey. But the issue is floating out there. If it isn't handled in court, the press will run with it. It may be best to get it out in the open and be done with it."

The prosecutor reluctantly agreed and returned to his table.

"Proceed with your line of questioning, Mr. Louisell."

"Officer Leik, I will ask you again. Was your promotion in any way connected with your testimony here today?"

"Absolutely not!"

"Then how do you explain the timing?"

"I was up for promotion before this situation with my nephew developed. One thing has nothing to do with the other." Leik was able to squelch Louisell's leading question and contain any collateral damage.

"Fair enough, Sergeant Leik. You have testified a can of black spray paint was missing from your storage cabinet, did you not?"

"Yes."

"Do you remember where you purchased the paint?"

"Yes, I do."

"Do you remember when?"

"Yes."

"Would you enlighten the court please?"

"I bought the spray paint at a hardware store in Flushing, Michigan, when I was stationed at the Flint post in 1967."

"Had you ever used it?"

"Yes."

"After using it, couldn't you have thrown it away?"

"Most of the paint was still in the can. I remember holding it upside down and clearing the nozzle, then placing it on a shelf in the storage cabinet."

"Doesn't your garage have an electronically operated garage door, Officer Leik?"

"Yes."

"Is it not true that when a button is pushed, the door opens and the light automatically goes on?"

"Yes. But much of the time I unscrew the light, so it doesn't go on."

"Was the door left ajar over your trip?"

"The door was up about eighteen inches from the driveway to give the dog some ventilation."

"Where was the dog food kept?"

"In the garage."

"So there was no reason for your nephew to enter the house to feed the dog."

"None."

"Wasn't there a note on the fuse box left undisturbed when you returned from your vacation?"

"Yes."

"You have previously testified your wife cuts your sons' hair in the laundry room. Does she cut your hair as well?"

"Usually."

"In the same place?"

"Yes."

"At the same time?"

"Not this time. My wife cut my hair a couple of days before."

"Does she ever cut more than three-eighths of an inch when cutting your hair or the children's?"

"She may have. I don't know."

This was an important point for the defense. Joseph Louisell was expected to claim the hairs found in Karen Sue Beineman's underpants could not have come from the Leik basement, as some were longer than three-eighths of an inch.

At this point, Louisell asked Judge Conlin if he and Neil Fink could view the Leik basement and kitchen areas under discussion. Conlin asked Officer Leik if he would agree. He nodded yes. The judge called for an early noon recess, so Prosecutor Booker T. Williams could personally escort both defense attorneys on a tour of the Leik basement and kitchen area.

Upon resumption of the trial, Louisell attacked Officer Leik's refusal to allow the defense access to his home earlier in the investigation as "obstructionist."

"Isn't it true Officer Leik that you have been hostile to the defense in this case from the beginning?"

"No, Sir."

"Didn't you refuse defense attorneys admittance to your home previously?"

"No. I wouldn't let you both come in at the same time with all of your investigators. Today wasn't your first opportunity to see the basement."

Sergeant Leik denied categorically he had refused the defense entrance to his home.

"In point of fact, Officer Leik, didn't you in the presence of another officer tell my investigators to 'Go to hell!'?"

"No, Sir! There was no profanity used."

"No further questions at this time, Your Honor."

The oppressive atmosphere in the courtroom was aggravated by a July heat wave escalating the tension. Sandra Leik was up next on the prosecution's list of witnesses. On her way to the stand, she looked at neither her sister nor her nephew. She was a woman torn between her sense of duty and justice toward her community and her conflicted blood ties to her relatives. It was evident the prolonged stress had taken its toll. Mrs. Leik was a tortured witness on the stand.

Sandra Leik began testifying about when her family got home from vacation. She immediately noticed some fresh heel scuff marks on her kitchen floor, some as long as six inches, in front of the refrigerator near the stairwell leading to the basement.

"Are you certain they were not there before you went on vacation?"

"Yes."

"Are you positive?"

"Yes, I mopped the floor just before we left. I don't like coming home to a messy house after a vacation. The floor was clean."

"What happened to the scuff marks?

"I mopped the floor clean before I went to bed."

"Did you notice anything else unusual after you arrived home?"

"The following morning, I went into the basement to wash the children's clothing and noticed their toys were moved, and there was black spray paint on the laundry room floor. Then, I did a load of laundry and reached for the ammonia container and it was gone. Also missing were an empty Bold detergent box and an empty bleach bottle I placed on the washing machine before we left on vacation. David was supposed to throw them out, but he didn't."

"Anything else?"

"There was a wet rag hanging on the edge of the laundry tub that was dirty and had hair on it."

"Was the wet rag there when you left?"

"We were gone two weeks. It would have been dry by then."

A slight chuckle went through the tense courtroom to the mild embarrassment of the prosecutor. "Of course, Mrs. Leik, what was I thinking? Let me rephrase the question. Was the soiled rag hanging on the laundry tub before the family left on vacation?"

"No. It was clean and folded in the laundry room cupboard."

"What happened to the rag?"

"It was soiled, so I threw it away."

Mrs. Leik admitted she unknowingly destroyed some evidence in this case. To contain the damage, Prosecutor Delhey asked Mrs. Leik if she threw the rag out before or after she discovered her nephew was under suspicion for murder?"

"Before," she said.

"Let's move on. Your basement is divided into a family room and a utility room separated by a thin wall," the prosecutor said, pointing to the diagram exhibit. "Is it not?"

"Yes, a family room and a laundry room."

"Where do you cut your sons' hair?"

"In the laundry room across from the clothes dryer."

"When was the last time you cut your children's hair?"

"The day before we left on vacation. When I finished, I swept up the floor quickly because I needed to make some final preparations for the trip."

"Did your husband have any explanation for the paint marks?"

"I asked David if he remembered painting anything before we left on vacation."

"Had he?"

"He said no."

"What happened next?"

"After trying all day to reach John in Ypsilanti, we called my sister in Center Line at about eight thirty to see if he was home visiting his mother."

"Was he?" Delhey asked.

"Yes, but he was out, and my sister said she would have John call me when he returned."

It was painfully uncomfortable for Sandra Leik to speak about her sister in the third person with Loretta sitting in the front row riveted to her every word.

"Did he ever call back?"

"About an hour later, my husband and I talked to John and his mother in a four-way conversation."

"What did you talk about?"

"I asked John how everything had gone while we were away. He said 'Just fine.' I asked him what he had been up to in our basement. He said, 'What do you mean?' Then, we asked if he had painted anything in the basement. He answered, 'No, I didn't.'"

"No further questions, Your Honor."

Under cross-examination, Joseph Louisell asked Mrs. Leik, "When did you first begin to suspect your nephew?"

"The next day when David came home early from work and told me John was a suspect, and the crime lab was on the way over to our house."

"How did you react to the news?"

"With shock."

"Were you at home when the crime lab team arrived?"

"I was weeping in bed much of the day."

"Where were your children?"

"David sent them out to play baseball with the neighbor kids."

"When did you tell your husband about the missing items?"

"The next day."

"Mrs. Leik, this is what you wrote in October to review and summarize the items missing or found different in your laundry room. This is your handwriting, is it not?" Louisell handed the court document to Sandra Leik.

"Yes. My husband asked me to write a summary of everything I remembered different from how we left it. I didn't write it with suspicion of him [Collins] being involved, but it was an essay of what I noticed missing in my house."

"Did you write it in October because you were more composed by then?"

"I haven't been composed for a year," she snapped back.

"Of course not. Would you take a moment to read this copy of your October twelfth essay?"

A brief moment passed before she looked up from her summary.

"Is there a word in that report about a missing ammonia bottle?"

"No."

"Is there a word in there about a missing soap box?"

"No."

"Is there a word in there about a missing bleach bottle?"

"No."

"Is there a word in that report about a wet rag?"

"No."

"Mrs. Leik, before you left on vacation, did you leave a note for your nephew on the kitchen table telling him there was a watermelon in the basement refrigerator?"

"Yes."

"Had the note been moved from where you placed it?"

"No, the note was still on the kitchen table?"

"Was the watermelon ever eaten?"

"No, the watermelon was untouched when we returned home."

"No further question for this witness, Your Honor," Louisell said sounding disappointed in the witness.

Court was adjourned for the day. Mrs. Leik, escorted by state police sergeant Earl James, walked briskly past Loretta Collins, who stared forward in benumbed silence. On Sandra Leik's way out of the courthouse with her husband by her side, she collapsed from the ordeal and the withering heat. David Leik carried his wife to their car and drove her to nearby St. Joseph's Hospital. Tensions were running high all day. It was grueling on the stand for the Leiks and a devastating day for the Collins family.

—25—

Science Enters the Scene of the Crime

ON THURSDAY MORNING, DR. Marjorie Barnes was given her moment on the stand. She was a surprise witness for the prosecution. "Would you identify yourself to the court and give your address, please?" Prosecutor Delhey asked.

"I'm Dr. Marjorie R. Barnes, a science education consultant. I live at 615 Cornell Drive in Ypsilanti."

"Dr. Barnes, would you please describe your day on Wednesday, July twenty-third, 1969, for the court?"

"I was out of town between eleven thirty a.m. and three p.m. but returned home to finish cleaning my house in preparation for a dinner party."

"Can you see the Leik house from your house?"

"Yes, I have a clear view of the west side of the Leik house."

"Have you observed any unusual activity around the Leik house?"

"I knew the Leiks were on vacation because once a day I noticed somebody coming by to take care of their dog. After July twenty-third, I noticed the same person was at the house several times."

"Did you see him each time?"

"No, usually I just saw his motorcycle parked on Cornell."

"Did you notice anything else?"

"On the twenty-fourth or twenty-fifth, I saw this same person leave on his motorcycle with a large Bold detergent box."

"Where did he go?"

"He drove north on Cornell."

"Can you identify the person you saw on the motor-cycle that day?"

"He was not as tall as you but approximately the same build. Maybe not as tall—but as big."

Delhey was over six feet tall. Collins was five foot eleven inches.

"Do you see that person in the courtroom today, Dr. Barnes?"

She looked directly at the defendant and said, "I can't be certain."

"Thank you, Dr. Barnes. No further questions."

In his cross-examination of Barnes, Joseph Louisell asked if she told the police or the prosecution she could identify the person she saw going in and out of the Leik house.

"I said I could not recognize the person as an individual, just his general stature and coloring."

"Where is your house in relation to the Leik house, Barnes?"

"Across the street."

"But not facing each other?"

"That is correct. My house..."

Louisell cut her answer short. "That's good, Dr. Barnes. You answered my question." What the defense attorney did not want Barnes to say was she literally had a picture-window view of the side door of the Leik house directly across the street.

"When did you give your statement to state police detective Gordon Hurley?"

"On August first. All the neighbors were being questioned door to door. The detective asked if I had seen anything unusual within the last week or so. That's when he took the report."

"Did you discuss the incident with anyone else?

"No."

"What about the Leiks?"

"Never."

"Wasn't there some confusion in your original statement to the police about the date you saw someone leave the Leik house with the detergent box?"

"Yes, I had to reconstruct my week, but I was able to narrow it down to two days—either that Thursday or Friday."

Barnes produced several pages of notes on a small yellow pad and handed them to Louisell. He read them before handing her notes back. Louisell tried but could not shake her from her testimony.

"How can you be certain the box you saw was a Bold detergent box?"

"I had just received a free sample in the mail, so I recognized the packaging."

"Were you wearing your glasses at the time of this sighting, Dr. Barnes?"

"Of course, I always wear my glasses."

"Dr. Barnes, isn't it true you refused to speak with defense investigators about this case?"

"People other than police tried to question me, but I declined to discuss the matter with them."

"Why didn't you tell them what you knew?"

"I decided not to talk to reporters or anyone. That's my right!"

"Dr. Barnes, were you instructed by the prosecution not to cooperate with the defense in this case?"

"No. The decision was mine and mine alone. I wasn't instructed by anyone to remain silent."

"Forget the reporters. These persons identified themselves as working on behalf of John Norman Collins. Why did you refuse to talk to them?"

"I just didn't want to talk about it."

"I have no further questions, Your Honor," Louisell said.

During redirect examination by Delhey, Barnes insisted there was no doubt in her mind she saw a man leaving the Leik house carrying a Bold detergent box on either Thursday or Friday—a day or two after Karen Sue Beineman went missing.

———

Assistant Prosecutor Booker T. Williams was slated to handle the scientific portion of the testimony. The prosecution strategy now shifted into the third stage of the people's case, the critical hair and blood evidence that marked the beginning of the scientific testimony. The prosecution needed to establish Karen Sue Beineman was in the Leik family basement the day she was raped and murdered.

First up to testify on the physical evidence was the commanding officer of the state police crime lab Staff Sergeant Kennard Christensen. He told the court, "There were fingerprints found in the Leik basement which contained too few points of identification and could have belonged to either Mr. Collins or Miss Beineman. They were unidentifiable."

"Did you find any identifiable fingerprints?"

"Of the one hundred or so prints we lifted, all belonged to the Leik family as far as I know. I didn't personally lift the prints—other detectives did."

"What part did you play early on in the investigation of the Leik basement?"

"Officer Leik and I did an initial investigation. I got down on the concrete floor and used a spotlight to inspect the laundry-room floor for evidence."

"Did you discover anything?"

"Yes. I saw hair clippings and what looked like blood near the clothes dryer. At that point, I called for additional expert help."

"Did you test the possible blood spots covered by the black paint?"

"Yes, I did."

"And what did you discover?"

"Only one showed evidence of blood being present. Another detective tested another area on the floor and the wall."

"What were the results of those tests?"

"I don't know," the Michigan State Police crime lab commander said.

"The autopsy reports a blow was struck to the face of Miss Beineman with a blunt instrument with enough force to break one of her front teeth above the gum line. Did you ever locate the weapon?"

"I examined tools in a cabinet and a length of two-by-four. Neither showed traces of blood or hair."

"Officer Christensen, we have a photo of a baseball bat leaning against the basement wall. Could that have been the murder weapon?"

"No!"

"Why not?"

"Because it was a Wiffle-Ball bat made of a light plastic that couldn't cause the injuries Miss Beineman sustained."

"Was any other evidence removed from the basement and brought to the crime lab for further analysis?" Williams asked.

"Yes, there was. We took the bottom front of the clothes dryer, a children's shirt hanging in the laundry room, several pillow cases, samples from the floor, sweepings from a vacuum cleaner bag, and many fingerprints."

"Was the garage checked for fingerprints?" Williams asked as an afterthought.

"Yes."

"What did you find?"

"We didn't find any of Collins fingerprints in there either."

"Not even on the dog's food or water bowl?"

"None."

"Your Honor, the prosecution would like to enter into evidence five jars given to Detective Sergeant Christensen immediately after Karen Sue Beineman's autopsy was performed."

Judge Conlin looked over at the defense bench but no

objection was forthcoming. The exhibits were entered into evidence. Prosecutor Williams questioned the state police detective about the contents of each.

"The first jar contains a yellow cloth taken from the throat of Karen Sue Beineman. There were no chemical tests performed, but the cloth was examined under a microscope by me and then given to another detective to examine," Christensen said.

"The second jar contains blood drawn from Miss Beineman's body. The third and the fourth jars contain hair samples pulled and not clipped from Miss Beineman's head by Dr. Robert Hendrix when he performed the autopsy. The final jar contains Miss Beineman's underpants which were lodged in her vagina."

"What was the chain of custody for this evidence?"

"The jars were taken by me immediately to the Plymouth crime lab, catalogued, and placed in a refrigerated vault. They were later taken to Lansing for further study."

"You saw the body in the location where it was discovered, did you not?"

"Yes, we saw it together."

"For the record, would you tell this court what you saw that morning?"

"Miss Beineman's body was found lying on its stomach in a wooded gully. Her right arm was extended over her head and her left arm was tucked under her body. Her feet were crossed. The only clothing she had were her leather sandals."

"Was there the presence of hair or blood evidence on the sandals?"

No. We examined them carefully. The only piece of physical evidence found was the body."

"Were there any footprints found?"

"Some at the edge of the road, but we determined they were made by our initial investigators."

"Were plaster casts made?"

"No, Sir. It was raining."

Sergeant Christensen's lengthy report to the Washtenaw County Prosecutor's Office was handed over to Louisell, who asked for some time to read it before cross-examining Christensen. Judge Conlin complied and called an early lunch recess with the cross-examination to begin at two p.m.

When the court was called back to order, it became apparent Christensen and Louisell had known one another for a long time. Louisell's folksy interrogation of the state police commander was more like a conversation between neighbors across a fence than adversaries in a notorious murder case.

"How would you characterize the investigation of the Leik basement?"

"It was a slow, methodical, meticulous search for evidence."

"Did any fingerprint man find prints of the defendant or the deceased in the upstairs section of the house?"

"Not to my knowledge," Christensen replied.

"And no fingerprint man has ever indicated to you that the fingerprints of the defendant or the deceased were found in that basement?"

"That's right. My men did find prints in the house, but they contained too few common points for a positive identification of either party."

"Officer Christensen, were you involved in the mannequin incident?"

"We discussed the possibility of substituting a mannequin for Miss Beineman's body and staking out the area in an attempt to catch the killer."

"We? Who exactly?"

"The prosecutors seemed to be taking the lead."

"Wasn't County Sheriff Doug Harvey a party to this plan?"

"Not to my knowledge, Sir."

Joseph Louisell was clearly disappointed. Earlier in the trial, he hammered away on the county sheriff hoping Harvey perjured himself on the stand by denying direct involvement in the plan. But Christensen closed ranks and backed up Sheriff Harvey's testimony.

"Did you help implement the plan, Officer Christensen?"

"No, but I heard about it later."

"Then your testimony is hearsay, isn't it?"

"Objection! The defense is asking the witness to draw a conclusion about his testimony."

"Sustained, Mr. Williams."

———

Much of the afternoon testimony focused on hair and blood evidence. Officer Christensen told Louisell, "I don't feel legally qualified to be an expert witness on hair." Still, he testified that several hundred hairs were taken from Beineman's head and "many things can be determined from a strain of hair."

"Did you examine the hair fibers yourself?"

"No, Dr. Walter Holtz from the Michigan Department of Health crime laboratory took the samples and ran tests."

"Why was the yellow cloth found in Miss Beineman's throat only examined under the microscope for stains and not given any other treatments?"

Christensen replied, "You will have to ask Dr. Holtz that question, counselor."

"Were you able to determine the origin of the cloth?"

"I had no way of determining where the cloth was made. It did have a seam in it similar to a manufactured garment. It may have been a shop rag."

"But you don't know for sure, do you?"

"No, Sir."

Before Christensen completed his testimony, the detective was instructed to walk to the scale drawing of the Leik basement and mark where he made his tests for the presence of blood evidence. The defense had no further questions for Commander Christensen.

Sergeant Leik—who had spent two hours on the witness stand the previous day—was recalled by Prosecutor Delhey to testify about clippings of his and his sons' hair cut by Mrs. Leik. "Samples from each of us were placed in separate evidence envelopes, sealed, labeled, and turned over to state police Lieutenant Harold Morrison," Sergeant Leik said.

"Did you volunteer these samples or were they requested?"

"Lieutenant Morrison requested the samples."

"Did you require him to have a court order?"

"No, Sir."

"No further questions, Your Honor."

Late in the day, the prosecution called state police Lieutenant Harold Morrison. He became the thirty-third witness to take the stand. He testified he received four envelopes containing the Leik family hair clippings and turned them over to Dr. Walter Holtz at the State Department of Health in Lansing.

In his brief cross-examination of Lieutenant Morrison,

Louisell asked about an incident at the Leik house on June 10, 1970, when Louisell and Fink appeared to inspect the basement.

"Was I refused admittance to the house?"

"No, Sir. You were invited in twice." Lieutenant Morrison contradicted the defense attorney.

"Didn't Sergeant Leik say I couldn't go in if Fink did?"

"Yes," Morrison replied.

"Wasn't there considerable profanity by you and Leik?"

"No, Sir."

"Is it not true you conducted the same tests Neil Fink and our aide ran in the basement when they appeared there on June tenth?"

"Yes. I felt it would be a good idea to have the same type of samples you had for whatever value they might prove."

"The defense has no further questions for this witness, Your Honor."

Next up to testify for the state was a forensic investigator from the Michigan Health Department, Dr. Curtis Fluker, who did much of the forensic lab work. Under direct examination by Assistant Prosecutor Williams, Dr. Fluker testified the hair clippings found in Karen Sue Beineman's underwear ranged in color from brown to blonde and all were under an inch in length.

When Louisell cross-examined Dr. Fluker, he disputed the hair evidence. "Isn't it true that brown to blond hairs can be found on any head of hair which is called brown?"

"No, that's not true," the lab expert replied.

"Isn't mounting hair on a dry slide as you have done a disapproved method of analysis?"

"I don't know of anyone who has disapproved it," Fluker said.

"Isn't it true there are not enough differences in hair to determine a source?"

"No."

"If I were to tell you the statement came from the FBI, would you still disagree?"

"I've disagreed with the FBI before, and I would disagree on this point."

Louisell produced a copy of an FBI law enforcement bulletin, which he handed to Dr. Fluker to examine. He looked at it for a brief moment and replied, "Mr. Louisell, this bulletin is dated August fifteenth, 1952. That was eighteen years ago. Forensic science has come a long way since then."

"Would you describe for the court how you made your comparison?"

"With a high-powered compound microscope, I examined hairs taken from the victim's underpants and determined they were all head hair, ranged in color from blonde to brown. The ends were cut and probably came from a person with short hair. I can't conclude the hair clippings all came from the same person though."

All of Officer Leik's sons had hair color ranging from brown to almost blonde and each wore his hair close cropped, as did their father. Dr. Curtis Fluker's testimony strengthened the state's evidence and the prosecution's case. So ended Thursday's testimony.

———

Friday, before the morning session, Judge Conlin granted three of four defense motions raised by Louisell. The defense wanted county sheriff Captain William M. Mullholland to appear to answer questions about the photos he showed

Patricia Spaulding, the wig stylist who pointed at Collins in the courtroom the previous week. The defense attorney also wanted any witnesses who were involved in the mannequin incident to be called to testify. Louisell was determined to get the embarrassing episode into the court record. The third motion Conlin granted called for the handing over of all blood-typing documents from the murder victim not attached to the original autopsy report.

Judge Conlin denied a motion to force the prosecution to call four alibi witnesses who were already scheduled to testify for the defense. The judge remarked, "This goes beyond that which is required of a prosecutor. The court does not think the prosecution should be required to provide a character witness for the defense."

———

With the jury called and settled into the box, Dr. Walter L. Holtz became the thirty-fifth state witness. He identified himself and outlined his scientific training and background for the court. For the last five years, he has served as chief of the Michigan Department of Health Criminalistics Division in Lansing. He was called to investigate the Leik basement, the alleged scene of the assault and murder.

Williams handled the scientific portion of the people's case. "Would you tell the court how you went about your investigation and what you discovered, Dr. Holtz?"

"I got down to eye level on the basement floor with a special ultraviolet light. I discovered some rust-colored spots near the clothes dryer which were proven in the lab to be human blood."

"Dr. Holtz, is there anything else you could tell from the spots on the floor?"

"The drops were tear shaped which indicated they came from the direction to the left of the clothes dryer and perpendicular to the wall."

"Were these drops covered with black paint?"

"No. But I also ran tests on those spots under the paint."

"And..."

"Only one of those spots tested positive for blood. The rest were varnish stains."

"Were you able to test for blood type?"

"Yes. It was type A."

"Did you find other blood evidence in the basement?"

"I saw a red-brown stain on a boy's blue and white striped shirt which was hanging over a barbering gown [Sandra Leik's dental hygienist tunic] and two moist rags found in a potato sack between the clothes dryer and the west wall."

"Were these items tested in the lab?"

"Yes. The shirt tested positive for blood."

"Dr. Holtz, did you transport any evidence to Dr. Samuel Golub in Dedham, Massachusetts?"

"Yes, I did. I took underclothing removed from Miss Beineman's body at the autopsy and segments of clipped hair found on the clothing."

"Did you take any other evidence to an out-of-state agency for examination?"

"Yes. I went to Gulf General Atomic Laboratories in San Diego, California."

"What was the nature of that trip?"

"I brought hair clippings found in the Leik basement and four envelopes with samples of clippings from the three Leik boys and Sergeant Leik for examination."

"How large was your sampling of hair clippings?" Williams asked.

"More than five hundred segments of hair were removed from Miss Beineman's undergarment, and a greater number were recovered by investigators from the floor of the Leik home."

Over mild objections by the defense, Judge Conlin admitted into evidence Beineman's underclothing and three separate lots of hair evidence: the clippings taken from Karen's underwear, clippings recovered from the Leik basement floor, and clippings collected from the heads of the four Leik males and placed in separate envelopes.

Dr. Holtz testified he examined the hair found on the underwear and the hair taken from the Leik basement floor and found them to be similar in all respects. All the hairs were Caucasian, all were from the head, all ranged in color from blonde to dark brown, all were less than an inch in length, all matched according to the three hair segments—the two outer layers and the core—and all had been cut with electric clippers.

"Dr. Holtz, how did you reach the conclusion the hair was cut by electric clippers?"

"I'm convinced for three reasons. Both ends of the hair were cleanly cut, the hair was cut very short, and there were partial cut marks on some hairs, as if the clippers brushed the hair but not cut it. Had scissors been used, there would be partial cutting marks on both sides of the hair." He produced an envelope containing material found in front of the clothes dryer, three slide mounts of hair found on the floor by the clothes dryer, and four mounts of hair taken from the underwear which the prosecution entered into evidence.

Under cross-examination, Joseph Louisell attempted to discredit the scientific testimony of the prosecution's criminology expert. "Dr. Holtz, isn't it true that after your visit to our defense expert witness Dr. Samuel Golub in Dedham, Massachusetts, last May, you discarded the comparison base of the hair?"

"No."

"Didn't you advise the prosecution, 'We'd better forget about the angle business,' after Dr. Golub showed you how to measure the angles of hair correctly?"

"Absolutely not!" In open court, the criminalistics chief restated his scientific conclusion. "The hair segments found in the underclothing of the victim are the same as the hair clippings found on the basement floor of Sergeant Leik's house."

After three days on the stand being pounded by Louisell, Dr. Walter L. Holtz was excused. His unyielding testimony considerably strengthened the prosecution's case.

With a surprise defense motion toward the end of the day's session, Judge Conlin recessed court early so the jury of seven women and seven men could view the alleged scene of the crime firsthand. In addition to the fourteen jurors, defense attorney Fink and two sheriff deputies arrived at Officer Leik's home just before four o'clock. They inspected the basement laundry room the prosecution contended was the murder site. What the defense hoped to accomplish was unclear. All of the evidence was removed almost a year earlier. With the exception of the close quarters and placement of the utility room fixtures, the only possible evidence to see was several black spots sprayed on the concrete basement floor.

—26—

The Mannequin Debacle

TUESDAY'S TESTIMONY CENTERED ON the failed mannequin stakeout. This was the first public account of the incident since it happened the night of July 26, 1969. An *Ann Arbor News* account of the "running man" the previous year claimed someone approached the mannequin, bent down, looked at it, and then fled through the woods. The newspaper report also said shots were fired at the fleeing man. Prosecutor Delhey denied the report at the time, but for over a year, the public wondered if the mysterious running man was Karen Sue Beineman's killer. Had he slipped through the police dragnet?

Prosecutor Delhey did not list any of the stakeout duty officers as prosecution witnesses because he knew their testimony was irrelevant to their case. The defense would portray the debacle as evidence of police incompetence. A *Detroit Free Press* article at the time labeled the stakeout a "Keystone Kops" operation. The prosecution did not want the incident brought up in open court. It was embarrassing and could result in a mistrial if not handled properly.

The defense believed the mannequin trap provided an alibi for their client. Based on the belief that only the killer would know where the body was dumped, this unknown runner must have been the guilty man. The defense contended their client was in Ortonville, Michigan, sixty miles away riding dirt bikes with friends. They were prepared to call six witnesses to testify about John Collins's whereabouts the night of the stakeout.

Four of nine officers on the stakeout reported seeing the runner. They each were called to testify: John E. Markwell with EMU campus police, Washtenaw County sheriff's deputy Basil Baysinger, EMU campus police officer Paul De Fresne, and Sheriff's Deputy Eugene Alli.

Delhey was irked the defense insisted on calling the stakeout team. Because Judge Conlin granted their motion, Delhey added them to his master list of witnesses. All he could do was point out to the jury that the police were being called only at the behest of the defense lawyers and under a court order by Judge Conlin.

Each officer in turn told of being assigned to the stakeout in the area where the body was discovered. The stakeout team was aware a mannequin was substituted for Beineman's body in the gully. Assistant Prosecutor Williams instructed the men to apprehend and identify anyone who approached the body drop site. The officers were cautioned not to fire their service revolvers. The team was told to show up in SWAT uniforms and bring plenty of mosquito repellant.

The officers were deployed around the site at 10:00 p.m. Three of the men were positioned across Riverside Drive—the dirt road across from the gully. They were hidden behind trees and brush. All of the officers said it rained steadily most of the night. Two unmarked police cars, each with two officers, were hidden strategically nearby. And two officers were stationed at Dr. Mason's house, which served as their impromptu command center.

Sergeant Markwell stated in his testimony that he was briefed by Lieutenant Bordine and Prosecutor Williams at the crime center on Washtenaw Avenue.

"What was the reasoning behind the stakeout?" Louisell probed.

"The decoy was planted," said Markwell, "because in two previous area murders, we [police] had evidence indicating someone returned to either the murder scene or where the body was dumped. The man I saw appeared for a split second but the road turns and he disappeared behind the hill where we were stationed."

The testimony referring to "previous area murders" was allowed into the record. The defense could not object because Louisell opened the door with his inquiry.

"Where were you positioned, Officer Markwell?"

"I was paired up with Sheriff's Deputy Baysinger, hidden among the trees and rough brush on a rising across Riverside Drive, opposite the decoy. We were positioned about seventy-five feet away in a shallow gully."

"What time did you see this phantom runner?"

"Sometime after midnight, I spotted a man running full out on Huron River Drive."

"Did you call out to him?"

"No, it happened so fast. I held a slight conversation with Deputy Baysinger whether it was justifiable to take action. We tried to call our commander on the handheld radio, but it wasn't working. By the time the scout car was contacted, the running man was gone."

"Would you be able to identify this running man if you saw him again?"

"No, Sir."

"Did anything else noteworthy happen that evening, Sergeant Markwell?"

"About forty-five minutes after the sighting, a tracking dog was brought in and he picked up a scent. It led the canine officer and a couple of deputies to a house party in full swing half a mile down the road."

"Is it possible the suspect slipped into the party?"

"Possible but unlikely. We didn't check because we didn't want to draw the attention of the partygoers to our investigation."

"Is there anything else you can tell the court about that night?"

"As the night wore on, a car passed the area four times and was stopped by sheriff's deputies and released. While we repositioned ourselves taking the natural cover on Huron River Drive, another car went past and stopped around the bend. It sounded its horn three times—then it took off again. When I tried to radio a police interceptor to chase down the vehicle, the radio failed to work."

"Didn't another car come by which aroused suspicion that night?" the defense attorney led the witness.

"Yes, a third car came by with people screaming and yelling out the windows."

"Were they stopped and questioned?"

"Yes."

"Who were they?

"People from the party."

The gallery laughed.

Sergeant Markwell was dismissed, and Sheriff's Deputy Basil Baysinger uncomfortably approached the stand. Neil

Fink took over for Louisell and questioned Baysinger. The sheriff's deputy told of seeing a running man after midnight going in a southerly direction. "He appeared to be wearing light clothing. I saw him for a fraction of a second. No one shouted and no shots were fired."

"Did you see his face, Deputy Baysinger?"

"No, Sir."

"Was there any physical evidence this runner left?" Fink asked.

"I found what appeared to be a footprint in the mud near a string of mailboxes on Huron River Drive. I carefully placed my coat over it."

"Did you tell your commanding officer?"

"Yes."

"Was a plaster cast made of the print?"

"No."

"Were any photographs taken of the footprint?"

"No."

"Why not?" continued Fink.

"The officer in charge said it was an investigator's footprint and dismissed it."

"What happened next?"

"We tried to make radio contact with a police car but our radio phone wasn't working. We made contact about four minutes after we saw the runner, but he had disappeared by then. I went up to the house where our field headquarters was on Dr. Mason's front porch.

"Did you hear any of the officers tell Dr. Mason 'we've made a contact'?"

"We had not made a contact."

"Why didn't you shout out to the running man, Deputy Baysinger?"

"I felt it might be someone running to get in from the rain, and if it wasn't the person we were looking for, I didn't want to give away our position."

It was now EMU patrolman Paul DeFresne's turn to testify. He told Louisell he had only been a policeman for two months with no formal police training when he was volunteered for the stakeout.

"It was pretty rough that night wasn't it?"

"The rain was bad enough but the mosquitoes were worse."

"Where were you stationed?"

"Closest to the mannequin, about sixty feet away."

"Did you see the running man?"

"Yes, running southeast across Riverside Drive where it comes out at Huron River Drive. I only saw him for a second."

"Did he hesitate or look down toward the gully?"

"No, he was jogging."

"Were there any shouts or shots fired?"

"No, Sir. Prosecutor Williams instructed us not to shoot our service revolvers."

"Did you make out a written report of the incident?"

"No, but I made a verbal report to state police detective Max Little."

"How long did you remain on duty in the area?"

"Throughout the night and until one p.m. the following day," the rookie officer said.

"No further questions for this witness, Your Honor."

The fourth and last officer from the stakeout team was Sheriff's Deputy Eugene Alli. Prosecutor Delhey asked him to point out on a rough sketch made by Dr. Mason the first day of the trial where the various members of the police team were stationed.

Much to the chagrin of Prosecutor Delhey, when it was the defense's turn to cross-examine Officer Alli, Louisell had no questions. After all, it was at Louisell's insistence that Allie and the other policemen were summoned into court. Delhey knew dredging up this incident was a defense diversion to distract the jury from the damning scientific evidence presented by the prosecution.

———

Sheriff's Captain William M. Mulholland was called to the stand for the second time Tuesday—both times at the insistence of the defense. Showing his impatience with defense counsel, Prosecutor Delhey took less than ten seconds for his direct examination.

"What is your name, rank, and length of service with the sheriff's department?"

"Captain William M. Mulholland. I've been with the sheriff's department for fifteen years."

"No further questions for this witness."

Neil Fink handled Mulholland's cross-examination. "You showed Mrs. Patricia Spaulding of Wigs by Joan some photographs on August 1, 1969, did you not?"

"I showed eight photographs to Mrs. Spaulding, three were of Collins and the others were of jail inmates with jail numbers across the bottom."

"What did Mrs. Spaulding say to you after viewing the pictures?"

"She said she wouldn't identify the man on the motor-cycle from a photograph."

"Let me ask you about Sue Bonner. She testified that on the afternoon of the murder, she walked past Collins on Ballard Street while he was talking to a girl she didn't know. Do you remember that testimony, Captain Mullholland?"

"Yes, I do. Miss Bonner was walking on Ballard Street the same day Miss Beineman disappeared."

"Did you state at one time that Sue Bonner, if pressured, would say the girl Collins was talking to was Karen Sue Beineman, but she wouldn't make a good witness in court?"

"I don't recall that wording," Officer Mulholland replied.

Neil Fink demanded to see the report Mulholland filed after his interview with Bonner. The prosecution produced the report, and Fink read from it, "Sue Bonner can't be sure but if pressed would identify the girl as Beineman, but it will do no good in court."

"Captain Mulholland, is this sentence in your report?"

"Yes."

"No further questions, Your Honor."

"No redirect, Your Honor," Delhey said.

—27—

Radioactive Evidence

THE LAST OF THE prosecution's scientific evidence was ready to be presented in open court. Dr. Howard L. Schlesinger, a forensic chemist from the Gulf General Atomic Laboratory in San Diego, California, was flown to Michigan to testify. He outlined his experience and education. When asked to tell the jury what a forensic scientist does, he explained that he dealt with evidence in criminal and civil justice proceedings.

Dr. Schlesinger, the current head of the activation analysis group, explained to the court in layman's terms the process of neutron activation analysis (NAA), the most recently accepted method for comparing hair. "This method of analysis uses the bombardment of atoms with neutrons which converts some atoms into radioactive material and then later detects this material. The process identifies large numbers of chemical elements in a sample and tells how much is present."

The forensic scientist testified he was given several vials of hair samples taken from Beineman's underpants, the basement floor of the Leik home, and known samples from the heads of the four Leik males barbered by Mrs. Leik. After washing the hair to eliminate possible human contamination, Dr. Schlesinger exposed all of the hairs to radiation for one minute, and after initial analysis, exposed the hairs for an additional sixty minutes and tested them again. The floor and panty samples were then exposed for another fifty hours of neutron radiation and more tests. After each bombardment, he counted chemical elements found in the samples.

Dr. Schlesinger said he found twelve elements that all the hairs had in common. Once chromium was eliminated for technical reasons, he found cobalt, manganese, gold, mercury, tin, zinc, selenium, antimony, chlorine, bromine, sodium, and potassium. The last four elements were eliminated for comparison purposes because they could have come from another source, such as the washing of the hair fibers before testing. The first nine elements were part of the internal structure of the hair.

When Assistant Prosecutor Williams asked about the accuracy of his data, Schlesinger declined to quote mathematical probabilities regarding how many other people might have hair with the same chemical composition. He testified, "It's difficult to come up with straightforward figures...it's difficult to say...the percentages could be twenty-five or thirty-five percent different either way."

During cross-examination, Fink asked, "Dr. Schlesinger, are your forensic observations objective and scientifically certifiable?"

The scientist answered, "In many cases, subjective evaluation is based on our own previous experience when making a conclusion...I know what the prosecution hoped would be the results. But there has been more than one occasion where I have testified opposite to what my client had hoped for."

"So what is your conclusion on the hair evidence in this case?"

"As a result of my analysis, my conclusion is that with a high level of probability, the hairs taken from the victim's panties came from the same source as the hair from the basement floor of the house where police believe Miss Beineman was killed."

Maybe for spite or because Neil Fink wanted to jab Prosecutor Williams, Fink ended his cross-examination with this question, "Did you know, Dr. Schlesinger, that the prosecution tried to get Dr. Jervis—our defense expert—to be a witness for them?"

Prosecutor Williams rose from his chair and objected. "That's absolutely not true." Before the judge could rule on it, Fink said, "I withdraw the question, Your Honor. No further questions for this witness."

The final prosecution witness was Dr. Schlesinger's former supervisor, Dr. Vincent P. Guinn, currently a professor of radiochemistry at the University of California, who had been flown in at the people's expense. Dr. Guinn testified, "The panty hair samples were remarkably similar to the other samples…it is definitely very feasible to state the panty hairs had the same origin as the hairs from the floor and the heads of the Leik males. We use charts for each of the elements to calculate the probability of our conclusions with straightforward, simple arithmetic."

He categorized eight hundred hair clippings into smaller groups until he reached four groups, the same number of male members in the Leik household. During his calculations, he came up with the following conclusion, "A conservative conclusion…an unbiased calculation allowing for some possible correlation of accidental match…the chances of it happening again are six times ten to the seventh power. In other words, if you took all two hundred million people in the United States, there might be thirty groups of four people in the country with the same percentage of the same elements in their hair."

"Have you ever testified in a court of law before using neutron activation analysis as evidence, Dr. Guinn?" Fink inquired.

"No. The Collins trial is the first I know of in North America to have NAA entered into testimony in such a crucial manner."

"Then Mr. Collins is being used as a guinea pig?"

"Objection, Your Honor," Prosecutor Williams jumped out from his seat. "The use of the word *guinea pig* is prejudicial."

"Sustained. Strike the remark and the question from the record," Judge Conlin instructed the court reporter while raising an eyebrow at the defense attorney.

Neil Fink continued undeterred, "Dr. Guinn, have you ever been asked to compare samples from four possible sources before?"

"This is my first experience comparing samples from four unknown samples, but I believe my calculations are sound, and I'm willing to defend them."

"No further questions for this witness at this time, Your Honor."

Williams asked that the hair evidence and lab report results be entered into the record. Over the vocal objections of the defense team, the prosecution rested its case with a flourish. Now it was up to Joseph Louisell and Neil Fink to make the best case they could to prove the innocence of their client.

—28—

The Defense Case

SHORTLY AFTER NINE THIRTY-FIVE on Thursday morning, without the jury present, Neil Fink made the first of five motions before calling his first witness. Addressing the judge, Fink asked for a "directed verdict of not guilty. I just can't believe it. It is inherently incredible. To permit this case to go on to the jury would be an injustice. I just do not believe if this were not the Collins case, it would ever go to the jury."

The judge denied the motion saying "the evidence, if believed, places the deceased in the basement through her blood type and hair samples. There is evidence, if believed, which could result in the jury's finding the defendant guilty, and I believe it's enough for this case to go to the jury."

Neil Fink's rationale for a directed verdict lacked specificity, was factless, and sounded hollow to courtroom observers. It was an inauspicious beginning for the defense case. Undeterred, Fink called to strike the testimony of Dr. Walter L. Holtz, which drew the conclusion the hair clippings on the Leik laundry room floor matched the hair clippings found in the victim's underpants.

"I don't think saying the words makes it so," said Fink. "It's making a guinea pig of Collins, which is grossly unfair."

"Objection."

"Sustained, Mr. Williams. Mr. Fink, refrain from referring to your client as a *guinea pig*."

Judge Conlin denied this motion on the same grounds as the first. "The scientist's conclusion is a question of fact for the jury to decide if acceptable, counselor."

Next, Fink asked for a motion to strike the testimony of the prosecution's expert scientific witnesses, Dr. Howard Schlesinger and Dr. Vincent P. Guinn, as "an attempt to validate their research findings using a technique never before used in a court of law. Their figures on neutron activation analysis and statistical probability will overload the jury."

Once again, Judge Conlin denied the motion saying both men were qualified as expert witnesses. "It would be up to the jury to decide how much weight to give their testimony."

Neil Fink's fourth motion was a request that all police statements taken from defense witnesses yet to be called be turned over to the defense immediately. This began an argument between the attorneys that Judge Conlin shouted over to be heard.

Prosecutor Williams argued, "These are defense witnesses. There is no reason why we should provide the defense with our reports. There might be a time when we would ask for their reports."

Neil Fink threatened, "If you ask that in front of the jury, we'll move for a mistrial."

Judge Conlin assured the defense attorneys they would not be asked to provide reports on their witnesses. "The law only applies to prosecution witnesses, so the defense cannot demand prosecution investigative reports on their own witnesses."

Neil Fink was zero for four, but he presented one last motion.

The fifth motion called for the prosecution to produce a receipt for a motorcycle chain ordered by Collins on July 22 and paid for the next afternoon when Karen Sue Beineman was believed murdered. The judge granted the request, and a police officer was sent to the crime center to obtain the receipt. In an offhand remark, Fink was heard to say, "Maybe we'd better have a perpetual motion in this case."

"This perpetual case is a perpetual motion," commented the unamused judge.

———

The first of the defense's five alibi witnesses was Joseph Dudley Patton, owner of J & J Cycle, located just east of the Ypsilanti city limits. Joe Patton testified that John Collins came into the shop between 1:00 p.m. and 1:30 p.m. to pay a motorcycle repair bill.

"I told him I would take his money when I was done eating my lunch."

"Can you fix the time?"

"Me and my crew usually take lunch at the same time every day."

"How did Mr. Collins appear to you when he entered your shop?"

"Nothing unusual, I'd say."

"Would you come over to the blue Triumph and examine the handlebars, Mr. Patton?"

"Sure." The motorcycle shop owner approached the Triumph 650.

"Do you see any marks from a mirror being attached to the handlebars?"

"No. But sometimes people place tape on the chrome to prevent them from being scratched."

"Did you ever see a square mirror on this motorcycle?"

"No, Sir."

When William Delhey took over for cross-examination, he introduced a typewritten statement Joseph Patton admitted signing after he talked to Sergeant William Canada on September 17, 1969.

"The statement you signed has two p.m. written on it, but it was crossed out and one p.m. was inserted as the time Collins was in your shop. Was it not?"

"I recall telling him [Sergeant Canada] he was supposed to make corrections," Joe Patton told Delhey.

Fink objected to admitting the statement into evidence because of stray marks on the document. The judge said he would not admit it into evidence, but it could be used by the prosecution to refresh the witness's memory.

"Is it possible Mr. Collins could have come into the shop as late as two p.m.?" Delhey asked.

"I don't think so. It would take a real emergency for me to eat lunch that late."

"No further questions at this time, Your Honor."

Former J & J mechanic John Lehto, who was now living in Toledo, Ohio, was the second alibi witness called by the defense. Lehto said Collins came into the shop at about 1:15 p.m. and hung around for forty-five minutes to an hour. "I signed the same statement as Joe but changes were made after I signed it." Lehto claimed Collins was in the shop at 2:00 and maybe late as 3:00 p.m.

During Prosecutor Delhey's cross-examination, Lehto said there was a typographical error in the police report regarding when Collins was in the shop.

"What time should it have been, Mr. Lehto?"

"I heard the approximate time he left from another person in the shop."

"Oh, so you're basing Collins's appearance in the motorcycle shop on what someone told you—on hearsay and not firsthand knowledge?"

"Well, yes."

"I move to strike this witness's testimony from the record, Your Honor."

"Sustained."

"No further questions."

The third alibi witness was J & J motorcycle salesman Donald H. Kaufman. The jury was excused for the first part of his testimony to hear charges that he was harassed by Sergeant Canada during his questioning.

Neil Fink began. "Would you explain to the court where and when this happened, Mr. Kaufman?"

"A friend of mine who had just gotten a weekend pass from basic training woke me up at seven thirty a.m. to go drinking with him and some other friends. We went to the Union Bar—the only one we knew was open that early."

"Shortly afterward, Sergeant Canada came in and asked me to talk with him outside. I went out and he told me to get in the squad car. I wasn't too pleased but had cooperated in the past and saw no reason to stop now. I was interviewed numerous times at the shop already, but by that time

I would have gone along with anything they wanted me to say."

"They?" asked Fink. "Who was the other person in the squad car?"

"The other man wasn't introduced to me."

"What did they ask you, Mr. Kaufman?"

"While in the police car, this other person asked if I remembered a person named Patrick Henry in the shop on July twenty-third. I said I didn't. They told me I had to remember because I sold him a bike that day. Officer Canada told me I would be perjuring myself if I didn't remember. He threatened me with perjury."

Fink made a show of directing the judge to protect Donald Kaufman with immunity.

Judge Conlin preferred instead to counsel the witness to tell the truth. "There can't be any perjury if you have no recollection. You have a right to say that. Don't worry about perjury unless you are perjuring yourself, Mr. Kaufman."

An angry flurry broke out between Fink and Delhey over the interview taped in the back of the squad car. "As far as this so-called harassment goes," Delhey said, "we have a taped statement we'd like to play for the jury recorded October twenty-third, 1969."

"I'm going to move for a mistrial if the prosecutor in the presence of the jury again threatens to play a tape about something it is implied the defense doesn't want the jury to hear," Fink threatened. "There are sinister connotations to the jury when Mr. Delhey threatens to play the tape."

"The court is not convinced such a mention has a sinister connotation," Conlin said. "The jury has heard the tapes before. Bailiff, call the jury please."

Kaufman again went through his testimony about the

Union Bar and the squad car interview. He fixed the time Collins was in the motorcycle shop at between 12:30 p.m. and 1:30 p.m. on July 23.

The alibi witnesses did nothing to bolster the defense argument that Collins was at J & J Cycles when Karen Sue Beineman died and therefore could not have killed her. So far, the defense was not connecting with its own witnesses, much less the jury.

Fink decided to take a different approach hoping to discredit the testimony of Dr. Marjorie Barnes, who said earlier she saw a man riding a motorcycle one-handed, leaving the Leik home holding a Bold detergent box. Fink asked the motorcycle salesman, "Is it possible to start up and drive away on a motorcycle one-handed?"

"That would be impossible," Donald Kaufman said.

"Your witness."

Prosecutor Delhey inquired on cross-examination, "Couldn't an experienced rider balance such a box sitting on the gas tank between his outstretched arms and still operate the hand controls of the motorcycle?"

"It might be possible."

"I can assure you it is possible, Mr. Kaufman."

"Objection," Fink blurted out. "Prosecutor Delhey's statement assumes a fact not in evidence."

"Sustained, Mr. Fink.

"Were the police officers who questioned you in or out of uniform?"

"Out of uniform."

"Was the car marked or unmarked?"

"Unmarked."

"So it wasn't a squad car?"

"It was an unmarked police car."

"One more thing, Mr. Kaufman. What was Collins wearing the afternoon he was in the motorcycle shop?"

"Blue Levis and a yellow and green striped T-shirt, I think."

"Were the stripes vertical or horizontal, Mr. Kaufman?"

"Horizontal."

"Are you certain?"

"Positive."

"No further questions, Your Honor."

The fourth employee of the cycle shop to testify for the defense was John McDougall. He testified Collins was in the shop between twelve noon and two p.m. "There was nothing unusual about his behavior. I spoke with him for about half an hour." McDougall also described the T-shirt Collins was wearing that afternoon in the shop. This witness had nothing new to add and was dismissed.

The day's briefest testimony came from the fifth and last alibi witness, Michelle Flanders, a Michigan State University coed. She told the court she was in Ortonville, Michigan, with Collins and several other persons throughout the day and evening of Saturday, July 26, the night of the mannequin stakeout.

Her testimony was calculated to refute the widely held belief that Collins was the running man seen by undercover policemen. If Collins was in Ortonville, the implication was that law enforcement allowed the real murderer to escape. Delhey wanted to ignore the incident completely and had no questions for Flanders.

———

On Friday, August 7, the defense brought in the first of their scientific hair experts to refute the testimony of the prosecution's experts. Dr. Auseklis K. Perkons from the University of Toronto in Ontario identified himself as a self-employed hair-evidence expert. Perkons explained he held a doctorate degree in nuclear chemistry with a neutron activation analysis (NAA) specialty from the University of Toronto. His doctoral thesis was on the comparison of the individual characteristics of human hair using NAA. He wrote the element comparison tables used by prosecution experts in their testimony.

Perkons described himself as a protégé of Dr. Robert L. Jervis, a University of Toronto hair-evidence expert who pioneered the NAA methodology of comparing objects using neutron bombardment. Jervis's method was used by the prosecution's experts.

Both prosecution expert scientific witnesses testified hair clippings on the Leik basement floor, samples taken from each of the Leik males, and hair clippings found in the victim's underpants all came from the same source. Dr. Perkons testified that only four of the eight essential elements for a valid comparison were found on the hair clippings of the underpants when matched with the hair clippings found on the Leik basement floor from the heads of the Leik children. He said two other necessary elements did not match at all.

Armed with Dr. Perkons's conflicting scientific testimony, Fink continued to undermine the testimony of the prosecution's expert witness, Dr. Holtz, chief of the Michigan Department of Public Health Criminalistics Division.

"Dr. Perkons, are you familiar with any authorities who maintain that the microscopic examination of hair is an unreliable method of hair comparison?"

"Yes, Sir, I am. The microscopic analysis of hair is subjective and could be classified as an art, depending to some extent on the experience of the examiner. Neutron activation analysis brings examinations up to the level of science. Microscopic examination of hair was the only method used until ten or fifteen years ago, but it is unreliable."

"Can you provide the court with a list of references supporting your opinion that microscopic analysis of hair is unreliable?"

"Yes," he answered, submitting a prepared list of references cited in his doctoral thesis.

Prosecutor Williams asked for a recess so he could study the reference material. Williams was given the difficult task of questioning the top experts in their field about this highly technical, state-of-the-art scientific process. Both prosecution expert witnesses from San Diego stayed on as scientific consultants to assist him.

After an extended lunch recess consulting with his experts, Prosecutor Williams asked Dr. Perkons in cross-examination if it was true there exist a wide variation in trace analysis of different hair samples. Prosecution and defense experts agreed there was a 32 percent variation in the hair found in the Leik home. When asked to make a "probability calculation" in this case, Dr. Perkons refused saying, "Because of the mixture of hair from four different people, the variables are too great to produce a credible figure."

Next up for the defense was Dr. Robert Jervis, professor of applied chemistry at the University of Toronto and the father of neutron activation analysis. After stating his background and qualifications, Jervis told the court that neutron activation analysis was currently the accepted scientific procedure in the examination of hair when there was a large enough sample for testing.

Fink asked the leading world expert on hair-fiber analysis his opinion on the evidence in this case. Jervis weighed in. "The hair from the Leik home does not have the same sources as the hair found in the underclothing of the victim." Without prompting, the researcher continued to assert, "I do not feel there is scientific support for the comparison of a mixture of hairs in this case. I feel many more samples should have been collected from the basement for analysis."

Under cross-examination by Williams, Jervis admitted there is sometimes a variation of from 10 to 50 percent in elements found in hair from the same person's head.

"Dr. Jervis, would you agree Dr. Vincent Guinn, witness for the prosecution on Wednesday, is among a small number of scientists who are knowledgeable about research projects involving hair analysis?"

"Yes."

"On another matter, in a Canadian murder case, did you and several other University of Toronto scientists analyze hair samples for the Royal Canadian Mounted Police?"

"Yes, we did."

"Is it not true that only two trace elements were found in hair analysis as reported in your publication about this case?"

"No, about seven elements were found in that study," Jervis responded.

"But you used only two elements," Williams quickly followed up.

"These two elements were the easiest to compare," the research scientist conceded.

Under redirect by Fink, Dr. Jervis admitted he did not testify on the case cited, but two of his associates did. "The case was in 1958, the third year of attempts to analyze hair by neutron activation analysis."

Under re-cross-examination by Williams, Jervis admitted he had not personally examined trace elements using NAA protocol since 1964—six years earlier.

With that, Conlin adjourned the trial at noon, so he could meet with the attorneys in closed chambers to discuss arrangements for the Monday appearance of Dr. Samuel Golub of Boston, Massachusetts—an expert witness on hair analysis for the defense. Conlin also granted a prosecution request to have the jury tour the site where Beineman's body was discovered. The jury spent an hour examining the wooded gully just east of the Ann Arbor city limits in the sparsely inhabited area off Huron River Drive.

A spokesperson for the defense team who asked not to be identified told the press that John Norman Collins might take the stand in his own defense next week if an arrangement with the prosecution to restrict the scope of the testimony could be agreed upon. Collins's attorneys were reluctant to let their client take the stand because that would open him up to punishing cross-examination.

Court observers speculated if the cross-examinations were not prolonged, the jury could be given the case and possibly return a verdict by the end of the following week. If a guilty verdict was returned in the Michigan case, the California case of murdered seventeen-year-old Roxie Ann Phillips might never reach the California courts. A guilty verdict in the Michigan case would bring an automatic life sentence.

If Collins was found innocent—or if a mistrial was called—California authorities would petition to extradite Collins to Monterey County to face a grand-jury indict-

ment, where it was believed they had a strong case against
Collins. Delhey had serious concerns if Collins was released
to California to face charges since he could possibly be
acquitted there. Then Collins would be released in California and never formally returned to Michigan. That was a
risk Prosecutor Delhey was unwilling to take.

Cris Bronson, a secretary in Delhey's office during the
Collins case, remembers the California extradition issue this
way: "Prosecutor Delhey's long-term plan was to prosecute
Collins with successive murders one after the other until
Collins was imprisoned permanently in Michigan. William
Delhey had enough evidence on each of the unsolved
Michigan slayings to proffer charges against Collins in the
event his lawyers were able to secure an acquittal or win an
eventual appeal in the Beineman case."

———

Monday, August 10, the fourth week of the trial began.
Dr. Samuel J. Golub, assistant director of the Fabric Research
Laboratory in Dedham, Massachusetts, was the eighth
defense witness called. "Are there any inherent problems
with the comparison of brown hair, Dr. Golub?" Neil Fink
began.

"There are not enough similar characteristics in brown
human hair to say they came from the same source. The
problem with brown hair is a great variety of hair coloring
shades from light to dark and all the characteristics used in
comparison are so variable in one person's head, it is impossible to make a comparison."

Drawing explanatory diagrams on a blackboard as he
spoke, Dr. Golub lectured the jury about the underlying
structure of hair fiber. He believed neither the diameter, the

medullary area, the cortex, the cuticle, the color of the hair, nor the angle at which the hair was cut were conclusive points of comparison. "Microscopic examination of only two hundred hair samples is useless to me," the fiber expert said. "There are more variations in one head of brown hair than there are between two different heads."

Dr. Golub testified he also compared hair found in the underpants of the victim to brown hairs shaved from the legs of two female technicians who worked in his lab. The hair expert testified the hairs were the "same general color and indistinguishable from the hair found on Miss Beineman's underpants and on the basement floor." Williams objected to the introduction of the women's leg hair into evidence but was overruled.

"Mightn't the hairs found on Miss Beineman's panties come from shaving her legs or from washing her panties in a basin where her brown-haired roommate clipped her bangs?"

"Objection, Your Honor. The question is hypothetical and calls for a conclusion by the witness."

"Sustained."

"Can you draw any conclusion concerning the hair evidence?" Fink asked.

"Only negative conclusions can be drawn from such comparisons. The comparison of hair samples can show only they came from different sources. The only conclusions I can draw are the hair was brown and Caucasian."

"Did you find any other trace evidence in the samples you examined?"

"Yes. I found textile fibers and paint particles mixed with the hairs in the samples taken from the Leik basement floor. But this is most surprising: I didn't find any textile fibers or paint particles with the hairs found on Miss Beineman's underpants. I would expect textile fibers to adhere to the underpants just as readily as hair fibers."

Dr. Golub testified for most of the day and was excused until Tuesday's session when the prosecution would cross-examine him. As soon as the witness stepped down, the lawyers assembled in the judge's chambers to discuss the conditions of Collins's possible appearance on the stand. Louisell and Fink wanted Conlin to order the prosecution to exclude certain subjects from their cross-examination of Collins.

- Questions about the two Triumph motorcycles confiscated on July 31, 1969. (Neither one was registered to Collins with the Michigan Secretary of State.)
- The blanket and the Bold detergent box, said by witness Arnie Davis to contain woman's apparel removed from the trunk of Collins's car and disposed of shortly after Collins was questioned by police.
- Mention of a hunting knife given to Arnie Davis by Collins for safekeeping after he removed it from under the hinged seat on one of his motorcycles. (The knife was later surrendered to police by Davis.)
- The contents of the Bold detergent box thought to contain trophies from some of the other murdered girls
- Any reference to attempts Collins may have made to pick up other girls on the same day Beineman disappeared.

If Conlin denied the defense motion, nothing would be lost. If he granted the motion, Collins could be placed on the stand with some level of immunity. There was no legal obligation for Collins to take the stand in his own defense. The decision rested with Collins and his lawyers.

———

When court resumed on Tuesday, the cross-examination of the defense hair expert began when Booker Williams asked Dr. Golub, "Did you personally analyze any evidence for this case?"

"Yes. I examined adhesive tape and panties rubbed on the basement floor of the Leik house."

"Did you personally gather the samples?"

"No. William Menzies gathered the specimens for me at the behest of the defense. Then a Michigan State Police detective brought the samples to my lab."

"Do you know when these samples were collected?"

"Yes, in June of this year."

"Do you know the date when Karen Sue Beineman was allegedly murdered in the Leik basement?"

"No, not exactly."

"July 23, 1969. Your evidence was gathered nearly eleven months after Miss Beineman was murdered. Was it not?"

"I suppose it was."

"Might that account for the differences you noted yesterday regarding paint specks and textile fibers between the two samples?"

"I would expect to see similar fibers in a laundry room eleven months later."

"You would expect?"

Dr. Golub was shown slide evidence of the girl's underpants revealing fiber material he missed in his earlier examination and testimony.

"You testified in this courtroom yesterday that you spent three days examining the evidence with a Michigan State Police crime lab expert. Correct?"

"Yes."

"Were they full eight-hour days?"

"Well, no."

"How much total time would you estimate you spent with the state police expert examining the evidence on those three days?"

"It's tough to say."

"Estimate it."

"About twelve hours."

"You also testified for the defense you found no textile fibers in the panty hair samples you examined. True?"

"Yes."

"But upon closer examination today, you noticed textile fibers you overlooked the first time around. Did you not?"

"Yes, there are more here than I previously testified to."

"Can you explain the discrepancy of your observation?"

"Apparently, I didn't examine the lace-covered waist-band."

"Dr. Golub, how long did you examine the panties?"

"About fifteen to thirty minutes?"

"That's quite a range. Can you be more specific?"

Dr. Golub began to appear confused and indecisive under Williams's pointed questioning. "As long as it took me to observe them under a microscope a quarter-inch at a time," he relented.

After most of the day on the stand, Dr. Golub remarked he was getting fatigued. He wrapped up his testimony by saying an assistant measured the angles of the cut hair segments and attached no significance and no practical use whatsoever in comparison. "The angles ranged from fifteen to ninety degrees—too great a range for comparison," he said.

"Dr. Golub, can you rule out that the two sets of hair came from the same source?"

"All I'm saying is there is reasonable scientific certainty the hair did not come from the same source."

"I'll ask again. Can you rule out the possibility the two sets of hair clippings came from the same source?"

"No."

"No further questions, Your Honor.

—————

The remainder of the day's session included the redirect examination of several prosecution witnesses. First to be recalled was Sandra Leik. She was brought to the stand briefly to testify there was little or no change in the condition of the laundry room in the past year, except she had cut her father's hair in the basement during the winter months.

Following Mrs. Leik on the stand was Lieutenant Harold Morrison of the Michigan State Police. He was called to testify regarding the chain of custody of the gathered basement hair evidence. "I saw former state police investigator, William Menzies, place adhesive tape on the floor in two places and scrub the floor using a new pair of women's panties taken from a plastic bag."

"Did you do anything after Menzies left the house?"

"I duplicated his procedures on the floor and gave the items to the Michigan Department of Health. I thought it wouldn't hurt to have what the defense had."

Last up to testify was John F. Youngblood, an associate of Joseph Louisell. Youngblood testified he took the materials gathered from the Leik basement and flew them to Boston where he gave them personally to Dr. Golub for analysis.

———— • ————

Wednesday, August 12, began with the lawyers meeting in the judge's chambers to discuss the defense motions to limit Collins's testimony if they decided to place him on the stand. Conlin denied all the motions to exclude areas the defense did not want explored, except the one regarding the contents of the Bold detergent box which the judge did grant. The items contained in the box would bring the other Washtenaw County murders into testimony leading to a mistrial motion.

During the last part of a ninety-minute delay in the morning proceedings, Collins's immediate family was allowed to visit him in the judge's chambers with his attorneys present. Court observers wondered if Collins was about to take the stand in his defense. The atmosphere in the courtroom was bristling with anticipation as the press and gallery waited for the start of the day's session.

With the principal parties assembled, Judge Conlin called the courtroom to order. Neil Fink addressed the judge directly. "May it please, Your Honor, it is the sincere and professional opinion of the defense that the people have failed to show their case."

Prosecutor Williams jumped up and said, "I object on the grounds that—"

Before the assistant prosecutor could finish his objection, Fink surprised the packed courtroom by saying, "Then, Your Honor, the defense rests."

So they were not caught off guard, Louisell and Fink

decided against putting their client on the stand. The prosecution wanted to cross-examine Collins, but the defense could not predict how their client would hold up under their withering questioning.

The prosecution had three rebuttal witnesses ready to testify. Eastern Michigan University police sergeant John E. Markwell testified he had driven motorcycles for seventeen years. He ran time and distance comparisons for the police between 1307 Roosevelt Boulevard, the Leik house, and J & J Cycle at 1196 Ecorse Road—the location of Collins's alibi. The tests were run between 12:40 p.m. and 2:00 p.m. to duplicate the traffic congestion and time frame of the Beineman killing. After taking several timed runs, Sergeant Markwell calculated it took between seven and never more than eight and a half minutes to make the trip, depending on the traffic, rather than the fifteen- or twenty-minute trip the defense contended and Joe Patton testified to.

The second rebuttal witness, State Trooper Terry Brenay, was called to refute the testimony of Joe Patton, alibi witness for Collins. Patton insisted under staunch cross-examination that he and his crew ate lunch generally between 1:00 p.m. and 1:30 p.m. every day. "It would take something extraordinary to alter that," Patton had testified.

Officer Brenay told the court he visited the motorcycle shop seven days this June and two days in July. On one day, he said, he did not observe anyone eating lunch, but on the other days, lunch was eaten in the shop as early as 1:33 p.m. and as late as 2:25 p.m. The lunchtime discrepancy left a gaping hole in Collins's story and suggested the start time was moved up to accommodate his alibi.

The third rebuttal witness was prosecution expert Dr. Holz. His microscopic examination of the hair-fiber evidence was roundly criticized by Fink and his defense team of science experts—particularly Dr. Golub and Dr. Jervis—for being inconclusive and obsolete. When Jervis examined mounted slides of the panty hairs, he claimed he found no evidence of textile fibers in them as the Leik basement floor sample had.

Prosecutor Delhey asked Dr. Holz to show photographic slides to the jury of the underpants from the autopsy of Karen Sue Beineman. The head of the Michigan Public Health Criminalistics Division pointed out the presence of numerous textile fibers refuting Dr. Golub's defense testimony.

"The people rest their case, Your Honor."

Suddenly, it was over. Judge Conlin announced that closing arguments would begin at 12:30 p.m. on Thursday and would continue until complete. Jury deliberation would begin on Friday, August 14. After Conlin gave his instructions to the jury, two names of the fourteen jurors would be drawn from a revolving drum, and those individuals would be excused. One year and twenty-two days after the disappearance of Karen Sue Beineman, Michigan's most publicized and expensive murder case went to the jury.

Courtroom observers speculated John Norman Collins did not take the stand because Conlin did not grant the defense motions to gag the prosecution. Outside the courtroom, Fink said the decision not to call Collins to the stand was a hard one, but he would not elaborate. Fink told the press gathered outside the courtroom, "The prosecution's case is riddled with inconsistencies. I feel at this point we have won."

A reporter interjected a quick question on everyone's mind: "Was it just too risky to place Collins on the stand?"

"Listen, we did not want to jeopardize the case on testimony our client may have given under grueling cross-examination. Joseph Louisell and I are confident we made the right decision." A flurry of questions followed as Fink walked away. "No further comment," he said, heading out of the building to the parking lot.

—29—

The Summations and Jury Instructions

IN HIS EIGHTY-MINUTE SUMMATION on Thursday afternoon, Prosecutor Delhey began by telling jurors John Norman Collins tortured, sexually violated, and murdered Karen Sue Beineman on July 23, 1969, in the basement of his aunt and uncle's home while they were away on a family vacation.

"Using common sense—or applying reasonable doubt—is it possible to believe there were two men dressed the same way riding a motorcycle in the same area at the same time who had legal access to a house where barbering was performed and where traces of type A blood were found? It isn't.

"Because of the nature of the crime, the binding of the girl's wrists, and her gagging, which show malice, willfulness, and premeditation, I respectfully submit to you that the People of the State of Michigan have proven beyond all reasonable doubt that John Norman Collins is guilty of murder in the first degree."

William Delhey's summation had five categories:

1. Beineman's activities on July 23, 1969
2. Collins's activities on the same day and time
3. Evidence found at the alleged murder site—the Leik home
4. Expert scientific analysis of that evidence
5. The discrepancies and holes in the defense case

Delhey and Williams made a number of strong points with the jury. Among them was testimony that five women saw Collins riding his motorcycle around the EMU campus between 11:30 a.m. and 12:30 p.m. Their testimony placed Collins in the area where Beineman was picked up by a motorcyclist wearing a green-and-yellow horizontal-striped T-shirt, riding a blue motorcycle.

Three other witnesses testified they saw Collins drive off with Karen Sue Beineman from Wigs by Joan between 12:30 p.m. and 1:00 p.m. on the day she went missing. The wig-shop ladies could identify John Collins as the man on the motorcycle, but they could not identify the motorcycle. A young woman who worked the counter next door at the Chocolate Shoppe testified she saw someone drive off with a girl on a "blue Triumph with lots of gingerbread chrome and a square mirror." She could identify the motorcycle but not its rider.

Testimony from Sandra and David Leik revealed they found black spray paint blotches on their basement floor and several cleaning items missing when they returned from vacation. Their nephew John Collins had a key to enter the house from the side door, but he fed the Leik family dog in the garage. He had no reason to enter the house. Sandra Leik testified she cut the hair of her three sons in front of the clothes dryer in her basement laundry room the night before leaving on vacation.

Dr. Marjorie Barnes lived across Roosevelt Street from the Leik house and testified she saw the person taking care of the Leik dog leave their residence with a large Bold detergent box—one of the missing items from Sandra Leik's basement laundry room. Dr. Barnes said this person rode north on Cornell Street with the box on either July 24 or July 25.

Dr. Robert Hendrix, Washtenaw County coroner, testified that Karen Sue Beineman was either dead or put in mortal fear of her life before 3:00 p.m. on the day she disappeared. There was also testimony about Collins's behavior and whereabouts from two of his roommates and information from a former girlfriend of Collins at the time of Karen Sue Beineman's murder. Collins stood-up Karen Naylor for a date the afternoon Beineman went missing. He had never done that before.

Expert scientific hair and fiber testimony showed the hair clippings and fibers on the basement of the Leik laundry room were similar in all respects to hair clippings and fibers discovered on Karen Sue Beineman's underpants found lodged inside her vagina. This was damning forensic evidence linking Beineman to the Leik basement.

"Isn't it amazing?" Delhey said. "Although John Collins had access to the house and three people have testified he entered through the side door, none of his fingerprints were found in the house or the garage where he fed the dog? Strange, indeed! Pay attention to the little facts."

As Delhey wound down his closing remarks, he suggested Collins paid for his motorcycle bill at J & J on July 23 with money taken from Beineman—the dying young woman. He noted Collins had no cash on July 22, but the following day he paid a $20.03 bill at the motorcycle shop to establish an alibi. "The workers at the motorcycle shop can only account for one hour of his time. What about the two hours before 4:00 p.m. when his roommates Arnie Davis and Andrew Manuel say he returned home?"

Delhey also pointed out "discrepancies in statements by the four alibi witness and the three defense scientific witnesses leave gaping holes in the defense case. The defense has spent a great deal of time trying to throw sand in the jury's eyes, but I don't think you will be misled. While you must be guided by the doctrine of reasonable doubt, you should use common sense when reaching a verdict. Time is important in this case."

———

Despite the apparent strength of the prosecution's case, even Judge Conlin admitted earlier in the week that the people's case was based primarily on circumstantial evidence. This, the defense felt, was their strongest point against conviction. After a short recess, Neil Fink led off for the defense, presenting a twenty-five-minute summation discrediting the testimony of the witnesses who placed Collins with Beineman outside the wig shop.

"It is obvious their testimony is full of inherent incredibilities and obvious inconsistencies. I certainly can't prove John is innocent, and I can't produce the guilty party. But the prosecution simply has not linked our client to the girl's death beyond a reasonable doubt."

Neil Fink warned the jury of the Perry Mason syndrome and lashed out at the prosecution. "The pressure to find somebody bred confusion, and confusion bred a rush to judgment, and that rush to judgment led to the arrest of John Collins. Every right-thinking human being would say the murder of Miss Beineman was monstrous and the work of a vicious dog that should be punished. However, it is just as monstrous to send somebody to prison that is innocent both in truth and fact."

Joseph Louisell took over the summation. "Collins's arrest and the charges against him are merely a rush to judgment against a background in which a nervous community demanded a solution. It wasn't a search for truth and justice—it was a search to justify conclusions already reached by the police."

Louisell attacked the conclusions and the credentials of the prosecution's expert scientific witnesses, implying they did not have the experience to analyze evidence with any degree of scientific certainty. After carefully avoiding the subject throughout the trial, Louisell mentioned the murders of six other young women in the area that hung like a dark cloud over this case. "Against a different background than the background that has prevailed here [Washtenaw County], we'd never be in this court trying this case," the famous defense attorney proclaimed. "The community demanded a solution, and the police manufactured one."

———

Booker T. Williams closed the summations with the prosecution's rebuttal. "The defense has said we are contending that John Norman Collins is a sadist and murderer who borders on near genius. Well, I don't doubt that, but he is a near genius who panicked and did one stupid thing leading to his detection. If he had not sprayed the black paint on the basement floor, the chances are good the Leik family would never have noticed anything missing in their basement when they returned."

Williams chided the defense for bringing out the personal history of Diane Joan Goshe, one of the prosecution's key witnesses. "The only person hurt was a twelve-year-old boy," Williams said referring to Goshe's son.

"It was John Norman Collins who rode off with Karen Sue Beineman that day. The two wig-shop ladies made a positive identification of Mr. Collins driving away with Miss Beineman never to be seen alive again. There is nothing circumstantial about what the other women who saw Collins on the day Beineman disappeared testified to. There is nothing circumstantial about the conditions the Leik family found in the basement of their home.

"Collins made the same mistake his uncle made—he mistook a substance on the basement floor as blood. When he couldn't remove the spots, he panicked. He did the one stupid thing which eventually led to his apprehension. Except for the black spray paint on the basement floor, Sergeant Leik would probably have noticed nothing unusual.

"Then there is the scientific evidence. The defense discounted the use of the microscope in identifying hair segments, then, later approved the use of it. Neutron activation analysis was used by both sides to compare hair clippings in this case.

"The killer of Karen Sue Beineman committed a cold-blooded murder. The prosecution believes we have proved beyond any reasonable doubt that John Norman Collins is guilty of the brutal sex slaying of Karen Sue Beineman. We ask the jury to return a guilty, first-degree murder verdict. Thank you."

The summations lasted over three and a half hours. John Collins sat grim faced listening intently while the jury sat impassively. At the end of the day, Collins appeared cheerful and managed a smile directed at his mother. To her credit, Loretta Collins attended every day of the trial and pretrial hearings for her son, and soon his case would go to the jury.

The four lawyers faced each other across the bar of justice for the last ten weeks. Each side wanted to make its final statements memorable to the jury. The five-hour session was the last time the lawyers could address the jury before they would decide the case. The prosecution called forty-eight witnesses over thirteen days, while the defense called eight witnesses over four days. As William Treml of the *Ann Arbor News* reported, "They all seemed drained and jaded, the battle flame out, the shadows of self-doubt gathering."

Friday marked the day the case went to the jury. Their morning was spent listening to Judge Conlin's opening remarks. "It is not for the attorneys to tell you what the facts are, but for you the jury to decide what the facts are, what testimony is to be believed, and what weight is to be given."

Judge Conlin defined *reasonable doubt* as "a fair doubt growing out of the testimony in this case based on reason and common sense." He reminded the jury, "the law presumes the defendant innocent until you are convinced of his guilt, beyond reasonable doubt."

After defining *murder in the first degree* as "the willful, deliberate, or premeditated taking of a life," Judge Conlin narrowed down the range of verdicts. "The evidence shows Miss Beineman was struck with a blunt instrument and strangled. Since that is the case, there is no room for a lesser offense such as second degree or manslaughter. It is either a verdict of guilty of murder in the first degree or not guilty."

The judge also defined *circumstantial evidence* as "a chain of well-authenticated circumstances."

Judge Conlin advised the jury to give careful attention to the testimony of retained (paid) expert witnesses. "Treat them in the same manner as any other witness. The mere fact that testimony was presented by experts does not give it more weight. Closely review the testimony from police officers who are 'witnesses under pay' and anyone who might lay claim to a reward.

"Because Mr. Collins did not take the stand, there is to be no prejudice against him. He has a right not to take the stand in his own defense.

"This is an important case, important to the People and to John Norman Collins. You will now weigh out and administer justice, and that justice should not be administered with sympathy or vengeance."

After a brief two-minute conference with the lawyers to give them an opportunity to enter any objections about his charge to the jury, Judge Conlin ordered the names of the fourteen jurors be placed into a revolving drum and two chosen to be excused as alternates. A male juror in chair six and a female juror in chair eleven were excused from deliberations, their names withheld due to Judge Conlin's earlier court order protecting their identities. The excused jurors were instructed not to discuss this case with anyone until a verdict has been returned by the remaining twelve sitting jurors.

At 11:35 a.m., the jury retired to the jury room.

With that, defense lawyers Joseph Louisell and Neil Fink went to lunch at the Town Club restaurant at 210 West Washington Street in downtown Ann Arbor. Sheriff Doug Harvey was seated nearby with several people when he overhead Louisell tell Fink he "better win this case or look for another law firm." Louisell headed back to Detroit leaving Fink to await the jury's verdict and wind down the case alone. The next five days would be nerve-wracking for Neil Fink.

—30—

The Jury Deliberates

AT 11:35 A.M. ON Friday morning, Judge Conlin gave the jury their charge: decide the fate of John Norman Collins. The jurors went to an undisclosed Ann Arbor restaurant for lunch and were back in the jury room at 1:10 p.m. to begin their deliberations. They continued until 9:30 p.m.

From behind a locked door, the jury requested several exhibits, including the detailed composite drawing of Collins, as described by Goshe and Spaulding on July 24, 1969—the day after Karen Sue Beineman disappeared. They were the last known people to see her alive except for her killer. At 3:15 p.m., Collins was brought from the nearby jail to the courtroom so the jurors could compare his face with the state police artist's composite sketch. That was an awkward moment for all concerned.

After Collins's appearance in the courtroom, he and the deputies escorting him back to his maximum-security cell noticed a note attached with a postage stamp to one of the stair risers in the county courthouse. Written on the back of an invoice statement from Ann's Flower Shop was a message that read, "John, we're still rooting for you." Apparently, it was from two teenaged girls seen earlier in the hallway outside the courtroom with a box of flowers. They gave the box of black-eyed Susans to the deputies guarding the courtroom door, but the flowers were never delivered to Collins.

At 3:40 p.m., the jurors asked for a rehearing of the testimony of six witnesses. Jurors were not allowed to take notes during the trial, and they felt they needed to refresh their memories on the testimony of Goshe and Spaulding. The jury wanted to review the testimony of Carol Wieczerza, the clerk at the Chocolate Shoppe, and both of John Collins's former roommates, Arnie Davis and Andrew Manuel. The jury wanted to review the testimony of Karen Naylor, Collins's alleged girlfriend who dated him before he was arrested. At the very least, Collins and Naylor spent time together and went riding motorcycles in the backcountry where the bodies of six of the seven unsolved murders were found. But the slaying of Karen Sue Beineman was this jury's singular concern.

They listened for one and a half hours while court reporter Margaret R. Westfall read the testimony of Spaulding and Wieczerza. The jury deliberated for thirty minutes on what they heard before they left for dinner at five o'clock. When they returned, they changed their minds about hearing the testimony of the other witnesses. They deliberated until 9:30 p.m. when they were finally taken to their rooms at the Campus Inn.

The jury was back deliberating Saturday morning at eight twenty-five. It was reported the session was marked by conflict as raised voices could be heard in the corridor by the press outside the jury room. The jurors asked again to rehear the testimony of Patricia Spaulding, Karen Naylor, and Arnie Davis.

The sticking point was testimony about the square mirror on the blue motorcycle. As they listened to the testimony of the three witnesses being read to them, the jury heard Patricia Spalding say she saw Collins driving off with Beineman and noticed a square rearview mirror on the left handlebar of his blue motorcycle. Karen Naylor testified John had a detachable square rearview mirror he used on whichever of his four bikes he was driving. But Arnie Davis, who rented a room across the landing from his best friend John, told the court Collins did not own a square rearview mirror.

Saturday morning, the jurors left the jury room and spent fifteen minutes in the courtroom examining the two motorcycles still parked there. The green Triumph had a broken round mirror on the left handlebar, while the blue Triumph had no mirror at all. When the defense read in the Sunday newspapers about the jury's visit to view the motorcycles, Neil Fink immediately requested the judge have the cycles removed because they were never officially entered into the court record as evidence.

Fifteen minutes before the jury entered the courtroom on Monday, Collins and Neil Fink inspected the motorcycles for one last time. Looking thin and pale, Collins lightly rubbed the handlebars of one of his bikes. When he glanced up at the courtroom door windows, newsmen were peering inside. The motorcycles were removed before the jury entered the courtroom per Neil Fink's request. Both bikes were taken to an undisclosed police storage facility.

A point never pursued by the prosecution or the defense

was the legal ownership of the two Triumph motorcycles. Neither was registered to Collins. Both bikes were stolen property. Delving into this area would open up testimony that the prosecution felt might lead to a mistrial charge. The defense did not want the jury to hear about John Collins's burglary crew (Collins, Davis, Manuel, and others), which would complicate the defense of their client. The opposing lawyers agreed on this point.

After their Saturday lunch break, the jury listened for over two hours to reading from the court transcripts of Dr. Vincent P. Gruinn's scientific testimony about the hair clippings. After they returned from their dinner recess at six thirty, the jury heard the testimony of Dr. Perkons for twenty-five minutes followed by forty more minutes of Dr. Jervis's testimony. The reading of Perkons's and Jervis's testimony went faster than the previous readings because the phonetically coded court transcripts were retyped by Westfall during the long periods of jury deliberation. These were easier to read and listen to.

When the jurors finished their review of the scientific evidence at 7:50 p.m., Judge Conlin offered the jury the option of returning to their hotel rooms until Monday morning or pushing on until 9:00 p.m. One of the male jurors addressed the jury foreman, "Come on, we can do it." The jury attempted to reach a verdict within the hour but were unsuccessful.

Some jurors told Judge Conlin earlier in the day they wished to attend church services on Sunday. Although there was no legal reason they could not meet on Sunday, the judge granted the request. The judge was a practicing Catholic and had just that day attended a holy day service himself. Besides, the jury put in two long, stressful days and needed to rest up for Monday morning's session. As it turned out, the two members of the jury who planned to go to mass received religious dispensation from Monsignor Vincent Howard of Saint Thomas Church in Ann Arbor, releasing them from their weekly obligation to attend mass.

During the final hour of Saturday's deliberation, Mrs. Collins was denied permission to visit her son in the courtroom lockup despite the request being granted by the judge. The deputies charged with guarding Collins would not allow her to visit him for security reasons. Earlier in the day, Mrs. Collins—accompanied by her daughter Gail—went to Saint Thomas Catholic Church to pray for her son. The *Macomb Daily* ran a photograph on the front page of them praying at the communion rail with a quote from Loretta Collins. "We're just sitting with our fingers crossed. We're hoping, we're praying everything is going to work out all right," she said.

Fink appeared depressed and worried as he paced outside the courtroom following the jury's evening meal recess, but he perked up when the jury failed to reach a verdict in their final hour of deliberation Saturday night. After two days and twenty-one hours of deliberations, this jury was about to become the longest seated jury in Washtenaw County judicial history. A verdict was close but just out of their reach. They would resume their civic responsibility on Monday morning at 8:30 a.m.

The Collins jury entered its third day of deliberations. Judge Conlin, responding to growing concerns there might be a hung jury for this case, said he felt it was too early to speculate. "I am not ready to set any time limit on their deliberations. If the jury declares itself hung, a mistrial will be declared. If that happens, the long process of selecting another jury and taking four more weeks to hear the testimony will begin again, but not in Washtenaw County. Where would we get another jury?" he concluded.

In sequestration, the jury reviewed and finished discussing the scientific evidence from Saturday's contentious deliberations. At 10:30 a.m., the jury notified the court they wanted to hear excerpts from the testimony of Arnie Davis concerning the whereabouts and activities of Collins on the day Beineman disappeared.

The jury also requested a photograph of a child's T-shirt Sandra Leik testified she had laundered before the family went on vacation. She found a dark spot not there before they left. The shirt had been hand washed and hung up backward from the way it was before the Leik's left on vacation. The judge granted the request. The jury also wanted to see the note Mrs. Leik wrote listing changes she found in her basement after the family returned from vacation. The judge denied that request because the list was never formally entered into evidence.

Court observers felt the jury was hung up on the validity of the circumstantial evidence key to the prosecution's case. The validity of the scientific hair evidence and the expert testimony from conflicting lab technicians was thought to be a major point of contention among jurors.

Shortly before adjourning, the jury asked Judge Conlin to repeat his instructions on circumstantial evidence and reasonable doubt. Tired newsmen seeing the lights go on in the judge's courtroom thought the jury had come in with a verdict. But they were disappointed. After patiently reviewing his instructions and redefining terms for the jury, Judge

Conlin adjourned deliberations at their request. They went through another long and exhausting day.

———

The jury spent Tuesday struggling with the circumstantial evidence and whether the prosecution had proven beyond a reasonable doubt that Collins willfully committed first-degree murder upon Karen Sue Beineman. Much of the day was spent listening to Westfall reading Arnie Davis's testimony. The jury debated point by point everything Davis testified to. He was difficult for the jury to understand. On the one hand, some of the most devastating circumstantial evidence against John Collins came from him. But in cross-examination, Davis testified in favor of the defense complaining about the police harassing him daily for months. The jury was not sure what to make of his testimony.

Arnie Davis testified he saw Collins leave the boardinghouse with a used detergent box and a blanket removed from the trunk of his car. He could not remember the brand name of the detergent or the color of the blanket. This was shortly after Collins was questioned by police. Davis also testified he and Collins took the green Triumph for a motorcycle driving lesson in the North Campus parking lot of Eastern Michigan University in the early afternoon—several hours earlier than they actually had gone. When Davis asked Collins why, Collins pressured him to agree without an explanation. The jury needed to make sense of it. A young man's life was at stake.

Twice on Tuesday, Judge Conlin asked the jury if they were hopelessly deadlocked on reaching a verdict. Their deliberations began at 8:30 a.m., and after three and a half hours, the judge called them into the courtroom. "Do you feel there is reasonable probability of jury agreement?"

The jury foreman answered yes.

After a short lunch break, the jury was not heard from again until 5:00 p.m. when they filed back into the courtroom. They were poker-faced and gave no clue of an imminent verdict. "You've been deliberating for eight and a half hours today and are going to decide for yourselves about deliberating more tonight or tomorrow," Conlin told them. "Is there still a reasonable probability this jury can arrive at a verdict?"

"Yes, there is a good probability," the foreman replied.

They left the courtroom and sent a note back to the judge ten minutes later. They preferred to return to their hotel rooms and resume their charge tomorrow. After four days of jury deliberations, speculation about a hung jury was over. At this stage of the proceedings, neither side wanted a hung jury. The costs to Washtenaw County for this trial were estimated to be $75,000. The costs of a new trial in another county would be even higher.

Tension was running high outside the courtroom. A reporter from a Detroit radio station almost came to blows with a Detroit newspaper reporter over the use of a pay phone. Michael J. Devine, press liaison for the Collins case, hastily arranged to have most of the phones in the county building made available to the media. However, some Detroit newspaper reporters and television people took that to mean they had exclusive use of those phones for the duration of the trial. They gave local reporters who needed to use these same phones a hard time. Then the out-of-town reporters got into the mix. This case was bigger than the

Washtenaw County Building was designed to handle, and tempers were wearing thin.

When court adjourned for the day, it had been 101 hours and thirty minutes since the case went to the jury. They had deliberated for twenty-seven hours, spent five and a half hours hearing testimony read back to them, and listened to the judge repeat his instructions.

On Wednesday morning, the jurors assembled in the jury room at 8:30 a.m. Fifteen minutes later, the jury foreman knocked from inside the deliberation room for the last time. The foreman told the bailiff they had arrived at a verdict. Calls went out to the county jail for Collins to be brought to the courtroom and for the lawyers, the press, and the Collins family to be notified.

Throughout the trial, Mrs. Collins greeted her son every day with a smile and waved good-bye as bravely as she could when John was taken to the lockup. Whenever possible, she met with her son in the judge's chambers, always in the presence of his lawyers. On this day, she sat in the front row of the gallery as she had for eight weeks of jury selection and trial testimony, merely twenty feet away from her son. Collins entered the courtroom wearing a blue sports coat, dark slacks, a blue shirt, and a blue and white striped tie. His face revealed little emotion as he looked forward with a pale and drawn expression.

The jurors entered the courtroom and filed into their respective seats in the jury box. At 9:33 a.m., court clerk Ruth Welch asked the jury, "Members of the jury, have you reached a verdict? Who speaks for you?"

Jury foreman William G. Billmeier stood up and said, "I speak for the jury. We have reached a verdict."

Collins stared steadily at the jury foreman while the verdict was read.

"We find guilty...We find the defendant guilty as charged."

An audible gasp swept through the courtroom. Collins sat impassively. His mother stared straight ahead benumbed. Defense attorney Neil Fink asked that all the jurors be polled by the court clerk. All twelve were asked by Welch, "Was this, and is this, your verdict?" Each answered yes in turn.

Judge Conlin, his voice tired and strained, noted for the court record that a presentencing report was required. Fink rose and told Conlin, "The defendant is not going to talk to anyone except to give his name and address."

"Of course, that's his privilege," Judge Conlin replied.

After thanking the jurors for their diligent public service, the judge told them they were free to talk to newsmen if they wished, but he recommended they speak with no one. Conlin remanded Collins to the Washtenaw County Jail pending sentencing on August 28. "I declare these proceedings closed," he said as the gavel came down.

As the press scrambled out of the courtroom to report the guilty verdict to their respective news organizations, a young woman who knew John sat with the Collins family and began to cry, then Gail broke into uncontrollable sobbing while her mother tried to comfort her. Mrs. Collins called out to Fink and asked whether she could visit her son. The court officials granted her permission to sit with him at the defense table. Loretta placed her arms around him. One witness reported seeing John shrug her away when she tried to embrace him. She patted and rubbed his back as a mother would a frightened child. The bailiffs locked the courtroom doors and stood outside to keep spectators and the press from looking in the windows while Mrs. Collins spent the final moments with her son comforting him as best she could. Some court personnel said privately that Collins finally wept in his mother's arms.

Loretta broke down as her son was led from the courtroom for the last time. Father Patrick Jackson of Saint Thomas parish—a Roman Catholic priest who served as Collins's spiritual advisor and accompanied the Collins family at many of the court sessions—did his best to console the inconsolable women. As Mrs. Collins and her family left the courthouse, they were rushed by court officials into a waiting car driven by Father Jackson. The family went to the church to regain what composure they could. The doors to Saint Thomas were locked for three hours after the verdict was announced. The Collins family went into seclusion and refused commenting to the press.

———

The jurors were sequestered for four weeks in one of Ann Arbor's nicest hotels—the Campus Inn—but there were only two occasions when they were allowed to see their families. All the newspapers reaching the jurors during the trial had no mention of John Collins or the Charles Manson trial in California. Those news stories were cut out.

The jury was now officially disbanded and free to go about their personal lives. But despite a plea from the judge for the press not to reveal the names of the jurors, there was no legal obligation for them not to. The jurors' names appeared in most of the newspapers by their evening editions. For the record, they were:

- Chair 1: Alice Vining, the mother of two small children and wife of a criminal law professor at the University of Michigan
- Chair 2: Rose Raski, a university researcher whose husband was a zoology professor at the University of Michigan
- Chair 3: Esther Travis, the mother of three small children and a clerk at a home for the aged
- Chair 4: Clifford E. Fishbeck, a retired engineer for Detroit Edison and/or a retired high school principal, depending upon which newspaper one consulted
- Chair 5: Donald Burns, a systems analyst for the Ford Motor Company
- Chair 6: Paul Heuter, a Ford Motor Company engineer (alternate excused)
- Chair 7: Patra Terry, a mother of one and a housewife
- Chair 8: James L. Burns, a father of five, environmental expert, and former military policeman
- Chair 9: William G. Billmeier, an engineer (jury foreman)
- Chair 10: Morton F. Newhouse, a grinder operator in a machine shop
- Chair11: Elizabeth Osborn, a housewife (alternate excused)
- Chair 12: Robert D. Hendricks, an autoworker
- Chair 13: Doris M. Green, a schoolteacher
- Chair 14: Trenna B. Edmonson, wife of a bioengineer at University of Michigan

Karen Sue Beineman's older sister Barbara was seated

with the Leik family in the first row across the aisle from the Collins entourage. Her mother and father declined to attend the trial. It was too painful. When the verdict was read, she wept with Sandra Leik, who openly cried. Barbara Beineman left the courtroom to face a barrage of reporters and simply said she was relieved. When pressed further by reporters, she added, "That's the only comment I want to make." Prosecutors Delhey and Williams then accompanied Sergeant Leik and his wife Sandra, along with Barbara Beineman into Delhey's office. They remained there for almost three hours until the media frenzy died down.

The only trial participant willing to comment openly after the trial was Washtenaw County sheriff Douglas Harvey. He said, "I'm very pleased. The prosecutor's office did a fine job."

Later that morning, Delhey and Williams held a short news conference. In essence, Delhey said Collins was the only suspect in the other six unsolved murders of young women in the area which were still under investigation. There is a distinct possibility there will never be enough evidence to justify charging anyone in the killings."

Moments after she heard the verdict on the radio, a neighbor in Grand Rapids rushed to the Beineman home. "My stomach is in knots," Mrs. Beineman said. "I'm convinced God was on that jury. He was the main member of the jury." A few seconds later, Mrs. Beineman received a call from her daughter Barbara who phoned after leaving the courthouse. Karen's father was contacted at his place of business—Seaway Time Company in Muskegon—but his immediate reaction to the news is unknown. What healing was possible could now begin.

In Lansing, Governor William G. Milliken heard about

the verdict at a daily news briefing. When asked about the extradition of Collins to California as per the request of California Governor Ronald Reagan, all he could say was he had not made any decision about whether Collins would stand trial for the murder of Roxie Ann Phillips in Salinas, California. "That will require more study," the Michigan governor said.

The seventeen-year-old high school senior was murdered 2,200 miles away and less than a month before Collins murdered Beineman in Ypsilanti. The California case hung like a dark cloud over the Collins trial. Great pains were taken to keep any testimony about Collins's California trip with Andrew Manuel out of the record for fear of a mistrial. But now, if Governor Milliken allowed California a writ of extradition, Collins would face another first-degree murder indictment, this time in a death-penalty state. People close to Milliken felt his Catholic faith would make it difficult for him to comply with Governor Reagan's extradition request—a point the governor's handlers were quick to discount.

Karen Beineman's high school friend in Muskegon, Becky Barlow, said when interviewed, "Karen knew the risks associated with going to Eastern Michigan University and said she took precautions. Karen joked about getting a football player for an escort, but said 'then he might be the killer.'"

Barlow continued, "Karen once wanted to be a social worker but gave up the idea when she saw the places she would have to work. She was afraid because she was so little." Karen was a small girl, only five feet one inch tall and weighing only ninety-six pounds. Becky described Karen as "a shrewd thinker and a sensible girl" but added she was "gullible and trusted people."

Arnie Davis heard about the conviction on the radio. Reached by phone, he responded to the guilty verdict his friend received, saying "I'm neither glad nor sad. It wasn't a surprise. But as long as Collins had to be convicted, I'm glad he got life imprisonment in Michigan instead of the gas chamber in California." Arnie Davis continued, "The verdict takes a lot of weight off my mind. It's been an ordeal, and I'm glad it's finally over."

Diane Joan Goshe had a different take on the verdict. "He was the man I saw, and I believe justice was done. Personally, I'm deeply relieved that he'll be behind bars, but my deepest emotion is a feeling of heartfelt sympathy to the girl's parents."

A random sampling of people surveyed outside the courtroom felt Collins got a fair trial and a just verdict. Predictably, many people were disappointed he did not get the death penalty which was not an option in Michigan.

But not everyone agreed. Sharon Riley (25), who lived in Ann Arbor, said she did not "feel it was proven. He got a fair trial but it was all circumstantial evidence." Riley said she met Collins at the Rubaiyat restaurant over a year ago and dated him from time to time. "He was very nice and treated me gently. He appeared very normal." When asked what her reaction to the jury verdict was, she answered, "I feel numb. I heard he showed no emotion when the verdict came in. I'd be concerned about dating him now."

Mrs. John Miskovic walked by the courtroom with her two young children in tow. When asked to give her reaction, she said, "I feel it was a fair trial and he was guilty. With the death penalty, there would be less of this sort of thing. If a murderer knows he'll get out in time, then he is likely to do it again."

Robert Harder, a county employee, also thought the death penalty should be instituted for murder. "We are having too many of these kinds of cases. We're losing too many policemen."

Pearlene Sullivan, a district court employee, said she felt Collins got a fair trial and was guilty. She added that the death penalty ought to be given to persons convicted of more than one murder.

Vicki Smith, an employee in the county building's coffee shop said, "It seems real sad that such a young man should be convicted like this. I feel sorry for him. It seems a shame he has to spend the rest of his life in prison. But he'll have to take his chances."

Patsy Hoobler said, "I wasn't surprised by the verdict because I thought he was guilty last summer. My sorority sisters and I pretty well figured it would have to be someone like Collins—handsome and strong. It wouldn't be so bad if it was someone who looked like a killer."

One young man who asked to remain unidentified said, "The thing I don't understand is why Collins wasn't called to testify. He should have been called to the stand. I feel sorry for his family, but I think we should have the death penalty in Michigan."

Some Center Line residents were reluctant to speak about the case, but others merely wished not to be identified. A student at Saint Clement High School remembers going to mass and the monsignor instructing the assembled student body to pray for guidance and protection for one of their own who was in trouble. The common request of those few people in town who did talk was, "Please don't use my name. After all, this is a small town and everyone knows everyone."

Inquiring reporters looking for a story found the Collins family home on Helen Street with window shades drawn and doors locked. Neighbors on either side refused to comment about John or his family. Several youngsters playing in the street had the good sense not to talk to strangers about it. The principal at Saint Clement High School David Grassi told a reporter for the *Macomb Daily*, "I have no comment to make about the Collins case." The local barber on Van Dyke and Helen streets also had no comment.

Wendell Steinhaus, director of Center Line's recreation department, said, "My wife was surprised by the first-degree guilty verdict; as for me, I really don't know what to say. I understand Collins took the jury's decision rather mildly. If it had been me and I knew I was innocent, I would have shouted my innocence for all to hear." Then he added, "Maybe the long ordeal had broken his spirit. Those of us who knew him find it hard to believe he could have perpetrated such a crime."

A middle-aged housewife interviewed at a local laundromat was one of the few people who would talk openly about the Collins family. "I'll bet his early childhood had something to do with it if he is truly guilty of the crime. You know, his real name is Chapman. He got the Collins name from his stepfather."

She continued, "I've lived around here for forty years and know a lot, and so do others. I'd rather not make it a public matter." The woman paused while she loaded another basket of clothes into the washer, "My daughter's best friend used to date that boy. He never got fresh and respected her. He liked girls and respected girls who had good moral character."

John's former Saint Clement High School football coach

Al Baumgart said he had heard Collins's parents had marital problems. "Maybe that is why he hit people so hard on the football field...to get his venom out."

In California, when Monterey County District Attorney Edward Barnes learned of the jury decision, he reported he would begin extradition proceedings within ten days for Collins to face a grand-jury indictment for the first-degree murder of Roxie Ann Phillips.

———

Judge Conlin called court to order for sentencing at 9:00 a.m. on Friday, August 28. Conlin asked the defendant if he had anything to say on his behalf before the sentencing was imposed. Wearing a green plaid sports coat, a white shirt, and a striped tie, John Norman Collins spoke for the first time in this case in a squeaky voice that wavered from lack of use and the gravity of the prospect before him. He was clearly audible.

"I have two things to say, Your Honor. One, I feel this community tried to give me a fair trial. The jury did not take it too lightly. It did the best it could under the circumstances. Secondly, I never knew a girl named Karen Sue Beineman, I never engaged her in conversation, I never took her on a motorcycle ride, and I never took her to the wig shop. Also, I never took her to my uncle's basement. I did not take the life of Karen Sue Beineman. But in my view of the prevailing mood of the community, I feel that the events presented during the last six or seven weeks have been blown out of proportion. I think my trial was a travesty of justice. I hope that someday this will be corrected."

"Mr. Collins," Judge Conlin began, "if by chance they [the jurors] were wrong, I am sure it will be corrected. A jury of your peers has found you guilty, and under the law of the State of Michigan, I have no other recourse but to impose the mandatory sentence.

"I hereby sentence you to solitary confinement at hard labor for the rest of your life at Southern Michigan State Prison in Jackson. Your attorneys have a right to appeal within sixty days. If you do not have sufficient funds, you should apply to the court for an attorney.

"Although there has been no plea of insanity in the case," Judge Conlin continued, "and although by your courtroom actions there is no evidence of your insanity, I am going to recommend that prison authorities give you a thorough psychiatric examination."

Collins took the sentence stoically while his mother's weeping was heard in the background. As Collins was led out of the courtroom, an unidentified young woman got as close as she could and said smiling, "Don't worry, John. Everything will be all right."

Collins smiled back at her.

Afterward, Loretta Collins was permitted to spend fifteen minutes with her son in the offices of the Washtenaw County Jail. By this time, he was dressed in bluish-green prison denims and white cotton slippers. Mother and son were alone. Before leaving, Mrs. Collins gave her son a long embrace.

After Loretta Collins left, her son's hands were cuffed and shackled to his waist by a chain. John Collins was led to the prison lockup. At ten forty on the same morning of his sentencing, Collins and two other prisoners were led into the jail garage and herded into a jail van. They were driven west on I-94 under heavy police escort to Jackson State Prison thirty-five miles away.

PART THREE

—31—

Prisoner Number 126833

Collins's first full day in Jackson State Prison was Saturday, August 29, 1970. At twenty-three years old, he was the youngest lifer there. Despite the wording of the verdict, "solitary confinement and hard labor," the Michigan Department of Corrections (MDOC) director, Gus Harrison, told reporters those two penalties had not been enforced at Jackson State Prison for about twelve years. "How can you have someone in solitary and also at hard labor? It's pretty difficult."

Collins woke up at 6:00 a.m. and ate breakfast at seven. In addition to testing and interviews, he took a one-hour recreation break in the prison yard like the other five thousand prisoners housed there. At the time, Jackson State Prison was the largest walled correctional facility in the world. Lights-out was at 10:00 p.m. Before long, one day blended into the next.

For his first thirty days, John Collins was in quarantine for testing and an adjustment period. "He'll be in and out of his cell all day long," said Harrison. "New prisoners undergo a complete battery of personality, aptitude, intelligence, and physical tests. They also give interviews to staff members and fill out questionnaires regarding family, possible visitors, and religious preference. Depending on the results, Collins may be allowed to take university classes. The prison classification committee will decide what the best program for Mr. Collins will be."

Judge Conlin recommended Collins be given a complete psychiatric examination. The results of any psychological testing are privileged information and unavailable to the public. Whenever testing is offered to Collins, he consistently remarks on his MDOC paperwork, "Not interested."

———

While Collins was adjusting to his new reality, his lawyers were busy filing a mistrial motion in Washtenaw County Circuit Court. On September 16, 1970, Joseph Louisell cited eight items of "judicial error" in the Collins case and requested a new trial with a different judge. The areas of defense concern were:

1. Judge Conlin "failed to grant repeated motions for a change of venue." Five unsuccessful attempts were made to move the trial to another county.

2. "The court erred in admitting testimony of Diane Goshe and Patricia Spaulding." Their client, they claimed, "was deprived of due process of law which caused a miscarriage of justice." The women were shown a photograph of Collins prior to the police lineup.

3. The court "erred in instructing the jury and was misleading." Judge Conlin did not define *premeditation* in his instructions to the jury.

4. Judge Conlin erred in admitting the testimony of three "so-called experts" in hair analysis.

5. "Improper conduct on the part of the bailiff and improper communications to the jury during the trial and improper reporting of the state of deliberations to the prosecutor and to certain representatives of the media who covered the trial."

6. "Prejudicial misconduct on the part of key prosecution witnesses." Louisell claimed state police sergeant David Leik and his wife, Sandra, did "purposefully and willfully prejudice the jury by attending the proceedings with a man dressed as a priest and did situate themselves where certain members of the jury were sure to see them." (Louisell failed to mention Loretta Collins sat through much of the trial accompanied by Father Patrick Jackson from Saint Thomas parish in Ann Arbor.)

7. Judge Conlin was cited for his failure to grant a mistrial motion on the fourth day of deliberations. The defense motion was made "on the belief that further deliberation amounted to coercion." The defense felt the last remaining jury members favorable to their client were bullied and worn down by the rest of the panel.

8. Louisell claimed "the verdict was void because the jury returned a general verdict of guilty on an open charge." The foreman stumbled when he first gave the verdict. He said, "We find guilty," but he recovered and read the verdict in the proper legal format. "We find the defendant guilty as charged."

Conlin scheduled a 2:00 p.m. hearing for October. It took about an hour. Neil Fink made his case about rumors involving "improper communications with the jury." A television reporter, Fred Stowe of WWJ, channel two, in Detroit, and state police detective Sergeant Max Little were the only witnesses called.

Neil Fink quizzed Stowe about some filming that took place in the lobby of the Washtenaw County Building on the evening of August 15, 1970. "Didn't you make a news film on the ground floor of the county building in which you reported the status of the jury deliberations at the time stood at nine to three for conviction?"

"Yes, Sir, but I would like to explain if I could," Stowe said looking up at the judge. "It was done more or less as a joke. Some of my competitors thought I had an inside edge in Washtenaw County, and they followed me around. While I was waiting to film a story, one of my camera crew told me a competitor was standing in the stairwell eavesdropping. With that in mind, we made a 'dummy' film to hand off some misinformation as a ruse. When my competitor left to file his story, we filmed our original story and sent it to Detroit for showing on the evening newscast."

"And did you discuss this 'dummy film' with *Detroit News* reporter John Peterson?" Fink inquired.

"Yes. We work for the same firm, and we conferred frequently during the trial. When I told John about the film, he said, 'Good. I'll go up and tell him the vote in the jury room is ten to two,'" Stowe testified.

"Did you read Peterson's article after the verdict where he says an unidentified juror claimed the jury count was nine to three for conviction for some time?" Fink asked.

"No, Sir, I have no direct knowledge of that story," the newsman said.

In what can be only explained as a prank by bored newshounds waiting for a jury result to come in, Stowe's testimony stirred passing amusement among reporters covering the hearing. As the television newsman told of his plan to dupe his competitor, Fred Stowe left the stand chastened, making the news that day rather than reporting it.

Fink informed the judge the defense was trying to subpoena John Peterson, but he was out of town on assignment and could not be located. Fink asked Conlin to take judicial notice of a copy of the newspaper story. The judge agreed to do so.

Sergeant Max Little was called to the stand. He was a husky, dark-haired veteran of twenty-four years with the Michigan State Police. He told the court that while acting as a bailiff, he engaged in "general conversation with several people" speculating how the jury deliberation was going.

"I made educated guesses. I had no direct knowledge of what was going on in the jury room. It was just discussion," Little said.

"Did you discuss deliberations with Diane from the sheriff's department?" Fink probed. Diane Davis was a police matron and sheriff's investigator who—at the time of the trial—was stationed at the courtroom door to search the women spectators before they entered.

"Not that I remember."

When Fink was finished, Prosecutor Delhey had no questions for either Stowe or Little.

Judge Conlin said he was satisfied there were no leaks from the bailiff. "It certainly is a serious question, and if you have proof of this, Mr. Fink, I certainly want to be the first to hear it."

To everyone's surprise, Delhey rose and offered to testify his office received no information on the status of jury deliberations.

"I don't think that's necessary, Mr. Delhey. I myself heard all kinds of guesses during deliberations," Conlin said. "I don't see how anyone would know that. I have all the confidence in the world in our bailiffs."

———

On November 12, 1970, Collins made his first court appearance since his imprisonment. He was escorted into the courtroom by sheriff's detectives Roy Couch and Arthur Preston at 2:20 p.m. Collins was dressed in a blue prison jacket, a white shirt open at the collar, and light-green dungaree work pants. His dark hair was trimmed shorter than at the trial, and his sideburns were cut to standard prison length. His face was still pale and wan, but he had gained some weight in prison. Collins was just in time to hear Fink review the eight points of Louisell's petition for a new trial. True to form, Collins did not speak during the thirty-five minutes he was in the courtroom.

Judge Conlin denied all eight defense motions. The judge said there were no grounds for a change of venue though there was substantial publicity about the Collins arrest. Conlin ruled the jury selection was "fair and impartial" and the jurors were not affected adversely by the publicity. The motion regarding the identification of Collins by Goshe and Spaulding was "not tainted." Their identification of Collins in a police lineup was not based on the photograph they were shown days earlier. Both women refused to base their identification on a photograph. The other motions were summarily swept aside. There would be no mistrial ruling or new trial for John Norman Collins that day. Fink vowed to take the case to the Michigan Court of Appeals in Lansing.

At the conclusion of the hearing, there was no rush to the telephones by newsmen. The handful of reporters and spectators quietly filed out of the courtroom in marked contrast to the trial. The only commotion was when Detectives Couch and Preston hustled Collins from the courtroom through the prisoner tunnel leading to the parking lot on the north side of the building. Later, the sheriff's deputies said Collins told them he hoped to get a job as an x-ray technician in the prison hospital.

———

The California extradition sword of Damocles hung over Collins's head. He still faced another murder trial, but this time in a capital punishment state. On August 31, 1970, Monterey County District Attorney Bert M. Young reported that California officials would petition the state of Michigan in a week to ten days for the extradition of Collins in the wrongful death of Roxie Ann Phillips. In his press conference, District Attorney Young said the proceedings usually take thirty to sixty days. Then, he outlined the process:

- First, the Monterey district attorney originates an application to Governor Ronald Reagan.
- Governor Reagan will then sign a requisition form including a warrant issued against Collins and other legal documents.
- The paperwork will be sent to Michigan Attorney General Frank Kelley to examine it for legality.

- At that point, Collins and his attorneys can request a governor's hearing and petition for clemency on the part of Governor William Milliken.
- The governor would then make his decision.

On October 8, 1970, the Monterey County Prosecutors' Office airmailed a request by California Governor Ronald Reagan formally asking Michigan Governor William Milliken to extradite Collins to answer a grand-jury indictment for the first-degree murder of Roxie Ann Phillips.

Certain conditions had to be met before Milliken would release Collins to California. The state of California would have to agree to pay all expenses for transporting Collins and returning him immediately to Jackson State Prison after the California trial to serve out the remainder of his term in Michigan. Collins was ineligible for parole but could be pardoned after twenty years. He had already served two years behind bars in Washtenaw County jail that would be deducted from his sentence if a future Michigan governor should chose to pardon him.

The extradition request in the form of an executive agreement between two states was handed over to Attorney General John Kelley on October 12, 1970. He checked it for legality before handing it off to the governor. In a letter to Milliken on October 19, Attorney General Kelley asked Governor Milliken to make a formal agreement with Governor Reagan under the Uniform Extradition Act to ensure Collins's return to Michigan to serve out his sentence.

Kelley explained there was case law in California that if a convict were extradited, it was considered an act of clemency by the sending state and it precluded any further confinement or punishment. "If this rule were to be followed by the California courts, there is a danger the State of Michigan might never see John Collins again," Kelley warned. "If Collins was found not guilty in California, he would be a free man."

Joseph H. Thibodeau, chief legal advisor to Governor Milliken, announced in a Lansing press conference on November 20, 1970, that the California extradition papers had some faulty provisions and were being returned to Governor Reagan's office for correction. The sticking point was worked out. It was now established on firm legal ground that extradition of Collins to California would not be considered an act of clemency on the part of Michigan. Thibodeau announced further that defense attorney Neil Fink was now Collins's sole attorney and would be notified when the revised documents arrived.

On January 20, 1971, Neil Fink made an unusual request that an extradition hearing be held in Jackson State Prison. Fink asked that the hearing be closed to the press and the public. On February 2, Governor Milliken announced he had scheduled a closed hearing at the Jackson prison for Monday, February 8, at 1:30 p.m. His legal aid Kenneth Frankland would preside.

Frankland said before assembled press reporters in Lansing that the decision to hold the closed hearing in the prison was made for security reasons. "The cost of providing security for Collins in a Jackson County courtroom would be prohibitive."

When Jackson prison warden Perry Johnson was reached for comment, he said, "In my two decades of penal work, I have never before heard of an extradition hearing being held in an institution. The hearing will take place in a conference room used to conduct parole hearings." Warden

Johnson added he would hold a press conference afterward to inform the media of the outcome.

A reporter asked the warden about rumors of Collins being beaten by other prisoners. "There is absolutely no foundation for these stories. There is no record of Collins being treated in the prison hospital and no report of assaults on him. He was brought to my office and asked about his mistreatment. Collins told me he hadn't been assaulted and he had 'no problems.' Presently, he is working in the prison store as a stocker."

When the day for the hearing came, it lasted only ten minutes. At the press conference afterward, Kenneth Frankland said, "The hearing was called to give the defense a chance to present equitable facts which the governor might use in denying the extradition."

Fink insisted he was entitled to subpoena witnesses, confront the governor personally, and obtain a verbatim record of the hearing. He complained Collins was being denied due process. Fink's demands were denied and the hearing was brought to a close. On February 25, 1971, Fink vowed to file a federal suit in Detroit aimed at blocking Collins's extradition.

On March 5, 1971, federal district court Judge Lawrence Gubow denied Fink's defense claim that the Collins extradition raised "substantial constitutional questions." The federal judge disagreed Collins was denied "due process of law" at the hearing because Fink could not call any witnesses, and he could not personally confront Governor Milliken.

Undeterred, Fink said he now planned to appeal the decision to the Sixth Circuit Court of Appeals in Cincinnati. Meanwhile, the extradition process was at a standstill. Milliken announced he wanted to wait until all federal suits were decided before making his decision to extradite Collins.

Four months later, Governor Milliken's legal advisor and spokesperson Kenneth P. Frankland held an unscheduled news conference. "Today, we got word from the Monterey County district attorney that he has a backlog of murder cases from a San Quentin prison riot, and he wants to hold up for a while [on the Collins extradition] until he gets the other cases out of the way." The Monterey County courts had twelve murder cases on their docket, and they were in no hurry to acquire another one.

Two days later, on June 10, 1971, Governor Milliken said in a Lansing, Michigan press conference that he received word from Governor Reagan that the extradition proceeding against John Norman Collins should be halted pending disposition of two appeals now in the courts. New trial motions were filed by Neil Fink: one in the Michigan court of appeals in Lansing, and the other in the United States district court in Detroit. Governor Milliken said Governor Reagan felt it would be inappropriate to remove Collins from Michigan to California until all appeal procedures were exhausted.

Finally, on January 4, 1972, Lansing state capitol sources said the California request to extradite Collins for the murder of Roxie Ann Phillips "is closed and will not be reopened."

The Monterey County district attorney's spokesperson Tom Kennan responded, "This office has elected not to pursue extradition against Collins because this case does not deserve priority attention from local authorities." Other reasons stated by the Monterey County Prosecutors' Office were a huge backlog of murder cases and a lack of scientific evidence. After the trouble the Michigan jury had with conflicting hair evidence experts, their office was reluctant to base their case on similar evidence.

Many observers believed the Phillips case was stronger than the Beineman case. Two years before, two Michigan state policemen traveled to Salinas and helped with the California murder investigation. Washtenaw County prosecutor William Delhey was clearly disappointed in the California decision. "If this was a minor crime, a larceny or something like that, they [California] might be justified. But murder is an entirely different ball game. If nothing else, I think their timing is poor."

An irritated Sheriff Harvey told local reporters, "Apparently they're [Monterey County] balancing a human life against money, and the money wins out. This is the age-old battle of the bookkeeper and those who want justice done. Justice with a dollar sign is what it is." Harvey was responding to a California district attorney's statement that to try Collins for murder and then return him to Michigan to complete his life term would cost upward of $100,000. "They have a strong case against him out there," the sheriff noted. "But I guess that doesn't mean anything if it's going to cost a few dollars."

An even more cynical view may have factored into California's decision not to extradite Collins. Neither Collins nor Phillips was a California resident. The Monterey County prosecutor made a cold-blooded decision that their budget was better spent adjudicating crimes committed by California residents. They decided to spare the expense and let justice take a holiday.

The long-awaited appeal of the Collins verdict and sentence was taken to the Michigan State Appeals Court in Lansing on December 15, 1970. Filing a claim of appeal was the first step in getting the court to hear the case. The claim read, "Defendant-appellant John Norman Collins claims an appeal from the judgment of conviction and sentence of imprisonment pursuant thereto and from the opinion and order denying his motion for a new trial."

Fink told a small group of reporters the substance of the appeal briefs was the same as the motions filed in their Washtenaw County court bid for a mistrial denied on November 12, 1970, by Judge Conlin. In addition, Fink moved that a new judge be assigned to the case, casting aspersions on Conlin.

Fink informed the press that Washtenaw County court reporters must prepare transcripts with briefs and submit them to attorneys for the defendant and the state before a claim of appeal could be heard by a three-judge panel. "I never anticipate failure," Fink said. "I think we have a very meritorious appeal."

On July 9, 1971, Neil Fink announced he had received copies of the trial transcripts earlier in the week and had ninety days by law to file a formal appeal. Then, the attorneys for both sides of the case had sixty days to file briefs.

The defense brief submitted to the appeals court contained the results of an informal but not court-ordered survey by a University of Michigan professor. He concluded before the trial began it was impossible for Collins to get an unbiased trial in Washtenaw County. The survey sampling was limited and the results were never entered into evidence at the two-month-long trial.

Washtenaw County assistant prosecutor John J. Hensel filed papers in Lansing on December 1, 1971, to dismiss the appeal request and strike the part of the appendix that contained material from sources other than the trial transcripts of the court proceedings. On January 20, 1972, the Collins trial court record was returned to the Washtenaw County Courthouse. The Michigan Appeals Court three-judge panel denied the defense suit and struck the public opinion survey from the court record. There was only one more place to go.

On Wednesday, April 3, 1974, Fink filed papers to have the Collins case heard by the United States Supreme Court, but on Friday, April 19, the high court returned the trial transcripts to Washtenaw County and refused to hear the case. There was no evidence any federal constitutional provisions were at issue. Collins and Fink had exhausted every avenue for appeal and finally hit a brick wall.

—32—

The Canadian Gambit

AFTER SEVEN YEARS AT Jackson State Prison, on September 19, 1977, MDOC Deputy Director Brown transferred Collins to Marquette Branch Prison in Michigan's remote Upper Peninsula. Marquette Branch Prison is Michigan's maximum-security facility for the state's most difficult prisoners. Brown advised prison officials to place Collins under close supervision.

> The above resident [John Norman Collins] has been in the SPSM (Jackson Prison) population since 1970. At various times, he has been under investigation for a variety of illegal activities, including drug smuggling, loan sharking, etc. Of recent date, we had an escape attempt from inside the walls in which Mr. Collins, during early investigation, admitted being involved as a co-conspirator. Later in denying his involvement, he admitted being involved with drugs and money. Based on this information, we believe

that maximum supervision is indicated. RISK DES-
IGNATION: VERY HIGH RISK.

Sitting before the Security Classification Committee at
Marquette Branch Prison, Collins admitted to drug traffick-
ing and illicit green money transactions while at Jackson,
but he denied aiding and abetting another prisoner in a successful escape attempt.

Private investigator John Whalen, contracted by MDOC,
discovered Collins was involved in the escape of inmate
Robert Taylor at Jackson and was implicated "in many
nefarious institutional activities." At a security classification hearing held on September 9, 1977, Collins admitted
to Deputy Grant and the Michigan State Police that he conspired with resident Taylor in the escape attempt. During
the interview, Collins said he promised several thousand
dollars to Taylor if he would assist him in escaping from
Jackson. Incredible as it may sound, Taylor was to return to
the prison by helicopter and land in the exercise area where
Collins would be waiting to be airlifted out.

Robert Taylor escaped from Jackson State Prison on
June 5, 1977, and remained at-large. During Collins's interview, he told prison officials he was fearful for his mother's
safety and asked to contact her warning of the possible
danger. Collins asserted Taylor would kill his mother to get
money from her.

In his resident's statement at Marquette Branch Prison,
Collins denied making those statements about Taylor. He
wrote he did not believe he was a threat to the security and
good order of Jackson State Prison, and he did not want the
Marquette Branch Prison transfer. Collins feared a transfer

would interfere with visits from friends and family. The committee was unmoved and recommended the transfer.

Upon his arrival at Marquette Branch Prison on October 25, 1977, Collins was placed in protective custody. He wanted to enter the general population and stated that the threats upon his life were not real and part of a ploy to cancel his transfer to Marquette. Collins was advised to inform staff of any adverse reactions toward him by other prison inmates, and he would be gradually assimilated into the general prison population as space became available. Collins told the classification committee:

They didn't want me down in Jackson. I didn't have nothing [sic] to do with the escape. Mr. Grant told me I was involved. Yes, I received a copy of the report. I didn't do anything to help him [Taylor] escape. If I did, I don't know if I would say so. I've come to accept prisoners threatening me because of my crime. I don't know what the papers said in regard to my life being threatened at Marquette. I didn't say my life would be threatened any more or any less at Marquette than at Jackson. No, I didn't tell my attorney there are people at Marquette who had previously threatened me at Jackson. They said they would fuck me up. Maybe it's all talk. They do things for kicks, you know. I'd like an opportunity to prove myself. It's confusing to me too.

The committee responded:

Resident Collins claims he has been threatened in

Jackson by many residents, some presently at Marquette. He claims he does not know who they are since the threats happened at Jackson and were rather frequent because of the nature of his crime. After portraying himself as an oft-threatened prisoner, although in vague terms and without detail or names, he commences to question the validity of the threats stating some prisoners do these things for kicks. It appears he would want us to believe he feels threatened and also not threatened as he weaves his story in an obvious manipulative fashion. The committee will approach this case with caution and feels protective custody is appropriate at this time.

The classification committee determined Collins should be excluded from the general population and placed in 5-West with a 000 designation—administrative segregation.

———

With all his appeals exhausted, Collins found another promising avenue for an early release from his Michigan life sentence. On June 10, 1980, Governor Milliken signed an agreement with neighboring Canada to exchange prisoners to serve out the completion of their sentences in their home countries—HR4308. The act joined the state of Michigan to the terms of a 1978 treaty between the United States and Canada. Collins was born in Windsor, Ontario, across the Detroit River and became a naturalized American citizen at age five.

On June 18, 1980, the Canadian consulate vice-counsel in Detroit, Douglas Frame, wrote a letter to Al Jandron, supervisor of records for the MDOC, asking for information. "Can you confirm that Mr. Collins is a Canadian citizen, and if so, could you let me know the particulars of his incarceration?" Consul Frame agreed to personally interview Collins on his next trip to Marquette Prison.

A week later, Jandron responded, "We are unable to confirm Mr. Collins is a Canadian citizen since our records only have Mr. Collins's statement that he was born in Windsor, Ontario, on June 17, 1947. We do not even have a detainer filed by the Canadian immigration service. Proof of his Canadian citizenship would have to come from some other jurisdiction rather than ours." A copy of Jandron's letter was sent to the Marquette prison warden.

Seven months later without public notice, John Collins acted as his own attorney and quietly applied for a name change in the Macomb County court on November 10, 1980. Probate Judge James F. Nowicki set January 5, 1981for a hearing on the matter. On that day, deputy registrar of probate court for the county of Macomb Maureen M. Fraser certified a name change for John Norman Collins to John Norman Chapman.

Since he was three years old, John had little or no contact with his Canadian birth father whose last name was Chapman. After John went to prison, his father began to correspond with his son and reconnected John loosely with his Canadian relatives. This was the basis of his transfer claim—he had family in Canada. The change of his last name obscured who he was in the paperwork. Collins had plans for his new identity.

Writing to Jandron on Monday, June 29, 1981, Collins/Chapman asked for paperwork and information about the "Transfer Offenders Act." Chapman also wanted to know if Judge Conlin's letter—dated March 11, 1981—was forwarded to Jandron's office. He wanted credit for his time served in the Washtenaw County jail—one year and twenty-nine days. This credit was significant in John's mind as part of his overall transfer bid took shape.

In a letter dated July 21, 1981, Chapman complained directly to Warden Koehler. "I am a Canadian citizen and wish to transfer to Canada under the 'Prisoner Exchange Treaty' between the U.S. & Canada. The Canadian Consulate, Mr. Douglas Frame and Mr. George Diffenbaucher from the Federal Bureau of Prisons in Wash. D.C. [*sic*] told me I must write to you for the necessary forms. Every state prison has received a copy of the Treaty and all the necessary applications and forms. Jackson State Prison and Ionia Reformatory have the papers, so Marquette should have them too.

"I have been trying to get information about the Treaty, etc. here at Marquette for the last 18 months, and all I get is a big run-around.

"Please send the necessary papers to me right away."

The warden sent the information to Al Jandron, and the next day he and Chapman processed the transfer paperwork and sent it off. The inquiry, signed by Chapman, read, "I hereby indicate an interest in being transferred to continue serving the sentence imposed by United States Judicial Authorities to the country of citizenship indicated above [Canada]. I understand this is just an inquiry to obtain data before the actual request for transfer and is not binding upon either the government or me."

———

On August 7, 1981, Marquette prison warden T. H. Koehler wrote Robert Brown Jr., deputy director of the

MDOC. Koehler had "checked the qualifications for transfer to foreign countries and believe that this resident [John Norman Chapman] meets the necessary qualifications at this time." Certified copies of the record of sentence, parole eligibility report, and basic information were sent in the mailing.

On a Marquette Prison Classification Committee recommendation dated December 27, 1981, Chapman was scheduled for transfer from Marquette Prison on December 29, guarded by prison personnel to the Kinross Correctional Facility. He would then be shuttled immediately into a Riverside Correctional Facility van and taken to Riverside on the same day. From there, he was to be taken to Jackson State Prison to await a hearing in Detroit on January, 11, 1982. These arrangements were made by Mary Benjamin from the Marquette Branch Prison Central Office assisted by Al Jandron on December 28.

When the day of the verification hearing for the transfer came, Ottawa [the Canadian government] had not completed its paperwork for the formal approval of the transfer. The hearing was knocked off the docket and postponed. On the list of possible transferees was John Chapman. He was one signature away from the scheduled transfer on Friday, January 29, 1982.

The first news report of the Collins/Chapman transfer appeared in the *Detroit Free Press* on Friday evening, January 15. Perry Johnson, state corrections director, responded to reporters, saying, "The first I heard of it [the transfer] was the nineteenth of January. I asked deputy director Brown about the news. He told me he hadn't realized that by signing Collins's application he had given the state's approval. He said he was aware who John Chapman was when he signed the application and was opposed to the transfer. I told him to immediately call the United States Justice Department to tell them we made a mistake on this."

The next day, Wednesday, January 20, 1982, Perry Johnson announced in Lansing that the state had officially denied the transfer request of John Chapman because it was "preliminary." On the same day, deputy director of the MDOC Robert Brown shattered the hopes of John Collins/Chapman with this letter:

> Dear Mr. Collins:
>
> As you know, this office had submitted an application to the U.S. Department of Justice for a possible transfer to your country of citizenship. However, I recently learned through diplomatic channels that you would have minimal family contact in Canada since most of your family resides here in the States. Further, you spent the majority of your life here in the States. Since the main purpose of the treaty is to provide re-integration into society and since this re-integration would not be possible in Canada, I am revoking our consideration of your transfer request. I am sorry I could not give you a more favorable reply.

It was clear that Michigan prison officials responded to public outrage and pleas from the family of Karen Sue Beineman.

On January 21, Gail Light, Michigan State corrections spokesperson, put the best spin on the embarrassing situation she could. "State officials had no intention of transferring Collins. Deputy Director Robert Brown signed a form that showed Collins/Chapman met our criteria. Such a transfer between the United States and Canada would be subject to approval of both governments under the terms of the 1978 treaty."

Robert Brown could not be reached for comment.

On January 22, 1982, MDOC's Classification Committee ordered the return of John Norman Chapman to Marquette Branch Prison to serve out the remainder of his life term in Michigan. The next morning, Chapman was in a prison van heading up north, fuming no doubt. He had been so close to repatriation and a better parole deal in Canada.

When Collins returned to Marquette, no cell was available among the general prison population. Prison authorities did not expect him back, and Collins had not expected to be back. Before leaving Marquette, he sold his prison possessions including an eleven-inch, black-and-white television.

As Jim Neubacher wrote in a February 28, 1982, *Detroit Free Press* article, "At the last moment, in a swirl of publicity, political pressure, and bureaucratic back-pedaling, his [Collins] application to serve his time in his native Canada was denied by state officials."

On February 22, 1982, the backstory of a Marquette inmate's prison leak that halted Collins's transfer was reported. It was revealed that a letter landed in the *Free Press* newsroom mail rack on the morning of January 14. It was addressed to the assistant city desk editor William Hart. He often wrote about Michigan prisons and corresponded with this inmate before. Four paragraphs of a multipage, handwritten letter caught the editor's attention.

"Two weeks ago, John Norman Collins was released to Canadian authorities." The letter claimed Collins planned to use a different name (Chapman) once in Canada and he would be eligible for parole in about two years. This was possible, the informant wrote, "with dollars being spread in the right areas." The letter continued, "I would normally not pass information like this out, but if he's guilty of butchering young girls, then he's not the safest kind of dude to be put where he could repeat, and that could be the case in the not too distant future."

Free Press editor Hart had heard nothing public or private about a transfer of John Collins. He was not convinced the information in the letter was true, and much of it turned out to be inaccurate. Hart assigned reporter Marianne Rzepka to investigate the story. She discovered that attorney Miriam Seifer, an undergraduate at University of Michigan when Collins was arrested in 1969, was appointed by the United States district court in Detroit to represent Chapman at a Canadian transfer hearing.

That evening, Rzepka's story "Transfer to Canada for Killer?" was the front page headline. A Detroit Associated Press (AP) employee picked up early copies of the *Free Press* as was his routine. Back at the office, when AP editors saw the headline, they immediately sent the article out on their wire service. Soon, Collins's Canadian transfer story was on its way to thirty-three newspapers and eighty-five radio and television stations across Michigan. Less than a week after Marianne Rzepka's story appeared, Michigan revoked approval of Collins's Canadian transfer.

When the Beineman family heard about the possible transfer of Collins to Canada, they contacted their local prosecutor in Kent County whose father was a United States congressman. By the time the Beineman family contacted Washtenaw County prosecutor William Delhey, he was already in touch with state and federal officials to prevent the transfer. Delhey told Mr. Beineman, "information from Washington D.C. seemed to indicate the transfer had the approval of state corrections officials here." The National Parole Board of Canada was to consider the transfer within the next two weeks, according to Canadian consul Douglas Frame.

The Beineman family was concerned a Canadian transfer might result in an early release from prison for Collins. Barbara Beineman, the now forty-year-old sister of Karen Sue Beineman, broke the family's twelve-year silence and told a reporter, "Whether it's a few months from now or several years from now, he is somebody who should not be released."

The details of the transfer came to light when editorial writer George Hutchinson of the *London (Ontario) Free Press* wrote on January 27, 1982, "If transferred to Canada, Chapman would be eligible for parole in 1985." He wrote that Canadian law allowed a transferred prisoner who is serving time for a first-degree crime to be considered for parole if he is within three years of having completed fifteen years of his sentence from the date of his conviction.

Bruce Mann, director of legal affairs for the Canadian Corrections Ministry, told George Hutchinson that Chapman would be eligible for a "day parole" [known as "work release" in America] exactly twelve years after his conviction date, minus time already served. He could hold a job outside the prison but would have to return to the prison after his shift. "Without the protest from Michigan people, the transfer might have gone through with the signing of one document," the Canadian corrections official told Hutchinson.

All that was required for Canadian authorities to officially close the file on John Norman Chapman was written notification from Michigan that their recommendation for his transfer was withdrawn. In a letter dated January 20, 1982, deputy director Robert Brown notified Collins his approval for transfer to Canada was "revoked." MDOC prison director Perry Johnson rescinded the transfer recommendation and sent word to Ottawa.

On October 20, 1981, John Norman Collins and his mother Loretta had reason to be optimistic about the international prison transfer. Michael Abell, director of international affairs for the United States Justice Department, sent a letter to Canadian authorities in Ottawa.

"This office and the state of Michigan have approved Chapman's transfer application. If it is approved in Canada, he could be included in a group to be exchanged on January 29, 1982."

Canadian Consul Douglas Frame called Loretta Collins with the news, and she cried out with joy. "I was elated," she said.

For over two and a half months after that phone call, people involved in this maneuver had every reason to think John Norman Chapman's transfer was imminent. The Canadian National Parole Board needed to review the case and classify his crime according to Canadian law. Then the board would set a parole eligibility date and send the case to Canadian solicitor general Robert Kaplan for final approval.

When Mrs. Collins heard that her son's transfer had been rescinded, she was outraged. "You can't tell me officials could sign all the papers and move him down to Jackson and then tell him they made a mistake. It's politics, dirty politics. John's hopes were raised; he was moved. Then they slammed the door in his face. It's inhuman," she said.

Chapman's mother and attorney were still hoping to find a way for John to be moved to Canada. They said they might push for a prison hearing or start a civil lawsuit.

"I wouldn't think of helping John if I thought for one minute he was guilty. I will not give up," Loretta Collins said. "If Mrs. Beineman can go to the United States Congress, I can too. I can sit on doorsteps for a long time. It's all political."

When Collins was returned to Marquette to serve out his life sentence, an unidentified prison source close to him said, "You can imagine how disappointed John was. He was shattered, absolutely shattered. He began to talk of suicide."

Then on February 28, 1982, Chapman granted the *Detroit Free Press* a two-and-a-half-hour prison interview—the first in five years. He was friendly and open during the interview but seemed nervous and declined to be photographed. His hair was longer and parted in the middle, and he had grown a moustache.

At one point, he tapped his index finger on a paper outlining MDOC's sixteen-step procedure on prison transfers. "If they'd denied me here at [step] five like it says, I'd have been pissed, but I could have accepted it. I can't accept this. I won't accept this.

"The reason I want to go to Canada is to get away from the hostility I get here. When I first arrived at Jackson in 1970, three thousand people knew I was coming. They had my articles up on the gym wall. People in there were jealous when they saw the amount of publicity I was getting. I hate it!

"If the governor told me I had to go over there [Canada] and start over from Day One, I would go.

"Politics and publicity combined to rob me of my constitutional rights. I don't blame the Beineman family for lobbying against me. I can understand that. They have a right. The thing is, I never killed their daughter in the first place.

"But I can't accept the actions of state prison officials. I'm not going to give up. They're wrong. They're wrong as hell. I think my transfer was denied because of vindictiveness, and that's not what the Treaty is all about.

"I hope to get out someday. If I didn't, I'd go off the gallery [commit suicide]. I know that I can do good. I know that I can become a productive member of society. That's what fucks me up."

John Collins/Chapman wrote MDOC deputy director Robert Brown to reconsider his disapproval of Collins's transfer request. Brown replied on MDOC stationery. "It is the intent of the State of Michigan that you serve your entire sentence under the jurisdiction of the State of Michigan."

———

Five years after Robert Brown withdrew his permission for Chapman's transfer, Chapman filed a civil suit against the now director of MDOC. Chapman and his lawyer, William S. Dobreff of Warren, Michigan, contended Chapman was denied his right to due process and equal protection under the law.

On January 12, 1987, United States District Court Magistrate Thomas Carlson in Detroit heard oral arguments on a motion by Michigan Assistant Attorney General Louis Porter for a summary judgment [dismissal] of the civil suit. Porter, appearing for the state of Michigan, argued the transfer treaty did not have strict guidelines and therefore the reversal of the recommendation for the Canadian transfer was within the warden's discretion.

Federal Magistrate Thomas Carlson had sixty days to respond to the oral arguments. One month later, on February 13, 1987, in a report to United States District Judge Avern Cohn, Carlson ruled that Chapman "failed to establish any violation of his federally secured constitutional rights." Collins's request to return to Canada was summarily denied.

This episode was officially closed on September 23, 1989, when Senior Border Patrol Agent Herbert H. Markle wrote to Cindy Greenleaf, the records supervisor at Marquette Branch Prison, to "remove any hold(s) this Service [US Immigration and Naturalization] has on Mr. Chapman. It has been confirmed he is a naturalized United States citizen."

In addition to the inherent ambiguity over the Collins/Chapman name change, another prisoner by the name of John Chapman became a resident inmate of Marquette Prison. Their jail mail was getting mixed up. MDOC policy now requires that inmates be referred to in prison documents by the same name they were convicted under.

—33—

Doing Time

IN HIS ALMOST FIFTY years in Michigan prisons, John Collins has had over ten major misconduct hearings, according to MDOC documents obtained through the Freedom of Information Act. Misconduct can result in a number of consequences if the resident is found guilty. The penalties range from being classified to a higher level of security, forfeiting five days of disciplinary credits earned for the month in which the misconduct occurred, or losing accumulated good time or disciplinary credits if ordered by the warden. These documents show Collins within the prison environment interacting with other inmates and the prison system.

Collins/Chapman (#126833)—
Major Misconduct Hearings

1. September 5, 1977—Disobedience of Rules. A guard noticed a wire running from inside cell 87-B to the underside of the first gallery four nights in a row. Collins was warned the first three times and on the

fourth the wire was confiscated. Corporal Schultz wrote him up. Found guilty—two days of top lock and privileges suspended for thirty days. (Top lock is a punishment where an inmate must be on his bunk unless at chow.)

2. June 30, 1980—Possession of Gambling Paraphernalia. In a statement taken after being caught, he said, "You busted me with the tickets. What can I say?" Prison guard John C. Clark shook down Collins in the print shop. He had 104 gambling tickets made in the prison with values marked on them from zero to two dollars. Found guilty—two days of top lock.

3. February 19, 1988—Possession of Gambling Paraphernalia (now using the name Chapman). A resident by the name of Hedgar submitted a statement saying the betting slips were his, but Officer DeMerse reported he noticed Chapman, a.k.a. Collins, place two legal-sized sheets of paper into his glove. "During a shakedown, I removed the paper and noticed names of prisoners, money amounts, team names, and behind the names were numbers such as 4, 5, 6, and 6RR. Chapman stated to me, 'That's my store list. I need that,' referring to the two papers removed from his glove." Found guilty—loss of privileges for thirty days.

4. February 21, 1988—Possession of Dangerous Contraband. During a shakedown of Chapman's possessions in the property room, Officer Shane Place dis-

covered a Ray-O-Vac flashlight, two pieces of nylon rope (23'8") tied together, and a drawing of the attic area of Marquette prison. Upon personal inspection of the nylon cord, it was noted it could support a great deal of weight. If the twenty-three-foot section of cord were to be doubled over, it would be more than strong enough to climb with, and it would still be over the critical eight-foot definition of a critical tool. Found guilty—thirty days loss of privileges.

5. February 21, 1989—Possession of Money. Three packs of chewing gum were found in a sealed foot-locker belonging to John Chapman with other items such as clothes, pens, pencils, photos, shaving gear, cosmetics, and candy. The gum did not appear on a packing list. When Officer Michael Wickstrom examined the packs of gum, he noticed the ends had been resealed. He took out the five sticks of gum and bent the first two sticks—the third stick would not bend. He unwrapped the stick of gum and found two bills totaling $150 snuggly fitted into the gum wrapper. He found the same result when he opened the other packs—another had $200 and the third had $100. The center stick in each pack was the best placement for concealing the money. Chapman stated someone must have tampered with his stuff or he was being set up by the prison guards. Found guilty—seven days of top lock and thirty days loss of privileges.

6. March 10, 1989—Creating a Disturbance. Chapman was going to the mini–law library. Officer Dennis

DeRocha's report read. "An inspection of some of the material he [Chapman] was going to bring into the library and found some material not allowed there, according to housing rule number seventeen." When told by Officer Dennis DeRocha he could not bring it in, Chapman started screaming and hollering, "'You can't do that. You'll see.' Then other prisoners in the cell block started hollering and yelling the same thing. Chapman continued to yell for several more minutes." At the hearing, Chapman denied he created a disturbance. Guilty—seven days loss of privileges.

7. November 13, 1989—Insolence. Sergeant Frank Sulskis reported that after denying Chapman a pair of tennis shoes, he called from a distance and said, "Sulskis, you're a motherfucker." Chapman parsed words and claimed he said, "Sulskis, you are acting like a motherfucker." Chapman make the insolent statement to harass the officer and was guilty as charged—four days loss of privileges.

8. December 22, 1990—Possession of Dangerous Contraband (in Riverside Correctional Facility). While conducting a shakedown of Chapman's cell, Officer J. McQuade found one bottle of Wite-Out on Collins's desk, six metal paper clips, and a piece of carbon paper. The Wite-Out brand contained triclorethelyene, a prohibited substance per prison policy PD BCF 30.07. Resident found guilty of possession of dangerous contraband (030). Penalty—time served—six days of detention for six credit days.

9. December 3, 2008—Possession of Dangerous Contraband, Possession of Money, and Contraband. While doing a shakedown of Collins's (Chapman's name reverts back to Collins) property, an officer whose name is illegible on the misconduct report found a number of suspect items. One was an incendiary device—a container of Vaseline with three wicks that at some point had been lit. Collins claimed he got the container from another prisoner and had not examined it. Also found were two pennies, two sharpened items fashioned as a screw driver and a sticker, three needles approximately three inches long, eight boxes of staples, one TV channel changer, three plastic pens with melted tips, one extension cord with one end cut off, fifty-five United States stamps totaling $12.09 hidden inside a typewriter, several screws, and one bag of push pins. Collins was found guilty of all charges—fourteen days loss of privileges.

10. December 23, 2008—Threatening Behavior. An outgoing letter written by Collins was screened which stated in part "I may have to punch Alexander in the nose when I see him though. It would get me out of Marquette." Alexander was the deputy warden. The prisoner's statement claimed he said *may* which does not imply he would do it. Collins believed he could avoid consequences for his writing because of his constitutional freedom of expression, but prison officials were not persuaded. Resident Collins received thirty days detention and thirty days loss of privileges.

11. August 11, 2011—Possession of Dangerous Contraband and Possession of a Dangerous Weapon. While
doing a shakedown of Collins's property, Officer
B. Durano discovered matches and pieces of metal
hidden in his cell that were capable of being made
into weapons. One piece was sharpened to form a
cutting or slashing edge. Also found out of compliance with prison policy were one photo album, one
can of black shoe polish, altered wires, miscellaneous
parts, one green army fatigue jacket, and two pairs
of shower shoes (only one pair is allowed). Collins
received thirty days detention and thirty days loss of
privileges.

***

In addition to his serious misconduct hearings, Collins
has had over fifty administrative hearings covering a wide
range of issues. Notice of package rejection hearings were
often held over disputed material Collins felt he should have
received. On December 11, 1989, two handmade Christmas
cards containing glitter and Elmer's glue made by Collins's
twin grandnieces were deemed a safety and security issue
by prison authorities. On January 12, 2004, a Hallmark
calendar was withheld from Collins because it was not purchased in the prison store. These rejections may seem like
petty tyranny, but the prison has rules that inmates must
obey.

Some package rejections were clearly infractions of
MDOC policy. On August 3, 1995, the relative of another
prison inmate sent Collins a money order for forty dollars
from a fictitious address in Ypsilanti. At the hearing, Inspector Magadanz stated, "A review of a taped telephone con-

versation indicates the funds were sent from another prisoner's family member. In that phone conversation, this prisoner had specifically spelled out John Chapman's name and listed his prison number along with the amount sent, forty dollars."

Collins said, "I don't see the connection between this money order and what another inmate did on the phone. I can't control another prisoner. Other people send me money...What authority do you have to return it to the sender? You can't put it in the Inmate Benefit Fund?"

In the end, the forty dollars was placed in the Inmate Benefit Fund. MDOC policy PD-04.02105 clearly states "funds cannot be sent to a prisoner by unidentified sources or by other prisoners, parolees, or family of same."

Hearing officer Robert J. Wood concluded, "It is clear this is in fact an attempt by one prisoner to send money to another prisoner. By falsifying the name of the sender and because no such address exists in Ypsilanti or Ypsilanti Township, the source of the money order is now unidentifiable and as such cannot be returned to sender."

It is interesting to note how Collins dissociates himself from the money or any attempt to have it sent to him, yet he asserts that prison officials do not have the authority to do that. He wants to control by veto where the money will go.

On March 17, 2008, a Death Index Record was withheld from Collins because it contained a social security number not belonging to him. "It is my grandmother's social security number, and I should be allowed to have it," he demanded. The other contents of the mailing were sent to Collins. The MDOC policy covering this infraction is PD 05.03.118 which states in part, "mail shall be prohibited if it is a threat to the security, good order, or discipline of the facility, may facilitate or encourage criminal activity, or may interfere with the rehabilitation of the prisoner. Legal forms of identification may be used to acquire other identification that can be used in criminal activity." What plans—if any—Collins had for his grandmother's social security number can only be guessed. It is rumored his grandmother and mother set up a bank account contingency fund if John ever made it to Canada, but no proof of that exists.

Other administrative hearing reports deal with more serious matters. For instance, early on in his incarceration, February 1974, Collins got into a fight after being elbowed in the left eye by an inmate named Allen during a rough basketball game. A yard officer yelled at them to stop and blew his whistle before they broke it up the first time. Officer Mahi reported that the two men scuffled again before they stopped. Both men claimed they were just playing around.

In a hearing dated March 1, 1974, resident Allen admitted to accidentally coming down with his elbow striking Collins next to his left eye. They had a shoving match and broke it up after the whistle was blown. Then they started up again. Collins did not remember starting up again. Both men agreed no blows were struck, and they stated they were friends and lock next to each other. The hearing committee believed the dispute went beyond the bounds of a verbal exchange, and both inmates were advised of the seriousness of the situation. Each man received five days detention with suspended sentence and then removed from the honor block.

One of the more interesting asides to Collins's prison tenure happened when he was a kitchen worker at the Park-Davis Clinic. Collins and another resident named Hayton were accused of stealing large amounts of sugar and making spud juice. On April 23, 1976, resident Wright and resident

George got into a fight over gambling debts. Both men had been drinking this spud juice, and prison personnel soon found out where they got it. Despite writing a two-page statement denying any culpability in this incident, Collins was removed from his honor assignment at Park-Davis and was placed on restricted job status.

Almost ten years later during a shakedown, Collins was discovered by prison guards to be running a store out of his cell. Forty-five dollars of expendable store items "were confiscated, placed in a duffle bag, and brought to the Inspector's storage room." Collins's inventory was disposed of per prison policy PD-DWA 53.01.

Excess property and contraband were recurring issues with Collins. On March 1, 1988, a hearing was held regarding an extra footlocker Collins used to store his legal records and pending legal matters. At this hearing, the MDOC granted him the extra footlocker, but during screening, excess property was found.

In addition to a TV and a Walkman with altered numbers, prison staff reported a sewing machine, a typewriter, one piece of pink Plexiglas, three rolls of masking tape, one altered alarm clock, twenty pieces of torn up clothing, two large white cloth bags, one large plastic bag, one metal antenna, one box of staples, two rolls of athletic tape, two rolls of electrical tape, one large bottle of an unknown liquid, six bottles of paint, one small bottle of an unknown substance, one large squeeze bottle of an unknown substance, one broken pair of scissors, one large metal ring, one blue metal box of T-bolts and wire, one large piece of fiber board, and two metal clasps. Clearly, Collins was out of compliance.

Other prohibited contraband also found were five magazines showing explicit sexual acts. At a hearing held a month later, Collins stated he wanted his magazines back and claimed they did not conflict with prison policy. But MDOC policy PD-BCF 63.03 states, "prisoners shall not be allowed to receive the following items or publications as they are considered a threat to the order and the security of the institution or to the rehabilitation of prisoners. Material describing or showing acts of homosexuality, sadism, masochism, bestiality, sexual acts involving children or any other unlawful sexual behavior."

Over and over, Collins is found with contraband or excess property items. Here is a partial list of some of the more interesting finds:

- February 23, 1989. During a general shakedown of his cell, Collins had the following contraband: one paint brush, six road maps, two light adapters, two can openers, thirteen felt-tip pens, two metal cans of shoe polish, three rings, and one roll of Scotch tape. The prisoner was allowed to keep one wedding band and four map books not showing any Michigan roads. Everything else was destroyed.

- June 13, 1989. Contraband found. Collins had one green field jacket confiscated. His resident statement said, "I've had that jacket all this time, and all of the sudden, they say it's contraband. It's not camouflage as PD-BCF-53.01 states. It's a solid color." Section III, paragraph A states, "Clothing traditionally worn by persons in various professions, such as clergy shirts, doctors and nurses uniforms, or military camouflage clothing is prohibited." The coat was a United States

Army fatigue jacket that could blend in with the forested countryside of Michigan's Upper Peninsula. The coat was disposed of.

- March 11, 1990. During a shakedown of Collins's cell, a Miami Dolphins jersey was found with another prisoner's number on it. Collins's cover story was he got the shirt from another prisoner who was leaving and getting rid of some of his clothes. "Prisoner LaFrance was giving his stuff away and selling most of his stuff. He owed a lot out." Prisoner LaFrance reported the Dolphins jersey stolen prior to being transferred. It was returned to him at his new location.

- January 21, 1993. One hundred United States postage stamps and seventy-one dollars' worth of store goods were in excess of prisoner property limits. Fifteen stamps were returned to Collins, and he was allowed to pick out forty-five dollars' worth of store goods. The rest was confiscated as excess.

- January 4, 2001. Excess property. During a routine shakedown of Collins's cell, twenty-two magazines were found. Collins requested they be sent home. The property was held for thirty days and disposed of per prison policy.

- August 12, 2004. During a pack up of Collins's cell, he was found to be seriously out of compliance with excess property and contraband. A partial list of items found in his possession were one altered extension cord, one pair of steel-toed boots, one crucifix necklace, thirty-seven pornographic magazines containing explicit scenes and/or stories on bondage and swinging, numerous pages torn out of adult magazines of a sexual nature, one coiled extension cord with large jacks, one large ACE bandage, two jackets, a broken pair of glasses, one hard plastic brush, one sewing kit and sewing materials, one pair of weight-lifting gloves, one homemade dream catcher, one pair of Koss altered headsets, one plastic bag with shoelaces and Velcro strips, nine TV jacks, one piece of mirror, one AM/FM cassette player, one pair of knee braces, fifty-one assorted magazines, and assorted Hobby Craft art materials. Collins's prisoner's statement said, "Most of the stuff I have collected over time; I can't seem to throw anything away. I have a medical detail for the boots and the knee braces. The cassette player is mine; the other piece of sound equipment is just a radio. I will send some of the items out to a friend with the rejected tapes I got a few weeks ago." The hearing officer's findings indicated that one of the jackets belonged to another inmate named Keubitz and was returned to him. The fifty-one assorted magazines were donated by Collins and sent to the Q unit book rack. The rest of the items were either destroyed or sent out of the facility at the prisoner's expense. Several items of a legal nature were returned to the prisoner—four file folders each thick with materials. One folder contained information on Canadian treaty and transfer issues; another folder contained information on class actions, consent decrees, and more Canadian material; the third file contained information on his case and correspondence with people working on various issues in his criminal case; and the fourth folder file held miscellaneous items.

- December 3, 2008. Collins was found to have
  two duffle bags packed with his property while he
  was in administrative segregation. Prison policy
  PD-04.07.112 states "prisoners in level V shall not
  have property which exceeds that which can be contained in one state issue duffle bag or similarly sized
  container." In addition to an incredible amount of
  excess property, the duffle bags contained the following contraband: twenty-seven nude books with
  penetration, twenty-two pairs of shoelaces, two
  Brother altered typewriter ribbons, two bottles of
  black liquid shoe polish, six toothbrushes, a pair
  of altered ear buds, one packet of string, one large
  mirror, and one homemade filter. A partial list of
  excess items indicated his prison store business was
  thriving: nine packages of Bugler tobacco, one beef
  stick, one box of Little Debbie cookies, one box of
  nutty bars, eleven bags of candy, two bags of chips,
  one bag of protein drink, two jars of honey, two tubs
  of cheese, two packs of Mike & Ike candy, two jars
  of peanut butter, two jars of refried beans, one jar of
  peppers, two Instant Lunches, three monster buns,
  one jar of cocoa, one large candy bar, five Chick-O-
  Sticks, one leather purse, one calendar, one cross, one
  bitewing, one *Michigan Murders* novel, four Alka-
  Seltzer packets, six flour tortillas, three bags of Kar's
  nuts, nine boxes of cookies, three jars of breakfast
  drink, one large bag of M & M's, thirty-nine books
  of matches, two bottles of aspirin, eight AAA batteries, nine nail clippers, six packs of cigarette rolling
  papers, twelve D batteries, four decks of cards, nine
  skin creams, three jars of Vaseline, eleven combs,

eight razors, one musk powder, ninety-three pens, seventeen pencils, thirteen chili packets, four garlic pickles, and six packets of Country Time Lemonade. The disposition was as usual: Collins could have the items sent out at his expense, they could be retained and stored by the facility up to thirty calendar days to be picked up by a person Collins designated, or the contraband would be destroyed.

As evident from his misconduct and administrative hearing reports, Collins often antagonized prison officials, making matters worse rather than better. When found with contraband and stolen property, he rationalized it away and absolved himself of responsibility. Consistently, Collins played the victim card, but prison officials were unimpressed.

34

Now I Lay Me Down to Sleep

On October 13, 1976, William Martin—Hollywood movie producer, director, and writer—reported to the *Ypsilanti Press* he had completed a script dealing with the Washtenaw County murders. He insisted his script was an original work not based on *The Michigan Murders*, a novelization of the Washtenaw County murders released a year earlier.

The movie was slated to be called *Now I Lay Me Down to Sleep* after the children's bedtime prayer. Its words offered a grim irony juxtaposed against the details of these murders. "The filming should start sometime after New Year's," Martin said.

Early in 1977, William Martin began shooting. He made a movie previously in southern Michigan called *Jacktown*, which was coincidentally about an inmate at Jackson State Prison where Collins was imprisoned at the time of the filming of this new project. *Jacktown* was an uneasy mixture of grainy documentary footage from the Jackson State Prison riot of April 1952; location shooting in Royal

Oak, Michigan; and an uninspired script punctuated with wooden, amateur acting.

As with *Jacktown*, Martin hired seasoned actors in the lead roles for *Now I Lay Me Down to Sleep* and used local talent to play the girls. Kathy Pierce, an actress from Chelsea, Michigan, was chosen to play the role of one of the victims. Malibu surf legend and television character actor Robert Purvey, with screen credits for popular 1970s television shows like *Police Story* and *Kojak*, was cast in the role of John Norman Collins. The Collins character would be renamed Brian Caldwell.

Rory Calhoun, best known for his role on the hit TV western, *The Texan* (1958–60), and host of *Death Valley Days*, would play a state police post commander and spokesperson. Because of the complicated police involvement of five different agencies in these cases, a composite role was created to simplify the storyline. For the role of Sandra Leik, Katherine Grayson was chosen. She is best remembered for singing performances in Hollywood musicals like *Anchors Aweigh* and *Kiss Me Kate*.

Psychic Peter Hurkos would play himself in the film. Hurkos was not an actor in the strict sense of the word, but he needed the work and the exposure, so he signed onto the project. Rounding out the cast was local WXYZ anchorman Bill Bonds, who interviewed Hurkos at the time of the Beineman murder. He would reprise himself. Bonds had previously appeared in two of the *Planet of the Apes* movies and *Five Easy Pieces* when he was working as a newscaster in Los Angeles. Appearing in front of a camera was second nature to the popular Detroit television news anchor.

Martin claimed he began writing his script in 1972

when he first learned of the case and insisted his movie was not connected with *The Michigan Murders*, published in 1976. Martin's movie was to be a mood piece about a community in crisis, rather than a laundry list of factual details. "It's not a police story," Martin told reporters. "The whole county was in terror for two years. I'm only doing it from the standpoint of what was running through the minds of the girls, what was happening to the community, and what was happening with the killer at large." Martin stated he was going to portray "the crime through the eyes of the defendant."

Early in 1977, a film crew of thirty-five people from New York City descended upon Ypsilanti and Ann Arbor. The budget for the film ranged from early estimates of one million dollars to a soaring $2.5 million in production costs. Martin announced the film was scheduled by Paramount Pictures for an Ypsilanti premiere around Christmas time in 1978.

Collins was not pleased when he heard the news of the proposed film. In an *Ann Arbor News* article dated January 14, 1977, Collins complained to reporter William Treml that *The Michigan Murders* and the proposed movie *Now I Lay Me Down to Sleep* were both efforts to exploit his situation for profit.

Collins's lawyer tried to get a court injunction to stop production of the movie because it was prejudicial to the appeal process of his client. It was denied. Martin publicly offered to pay for a polygraph test and close down production if Collins could exonerate himself. Neither Collins nor his lawyer took Martin up on the offer.

More serious was an *Ann Arbor News* report from July 30, 1977, about William Martin being approached by "a large man with a beard" at about 10:00 a.m. while he was preparing for the day's shoot. The burly man poked his finger in Martin's chest and told him, "You, you're dead. We'll kill you." After the incident, Martin told of other unspecified threats to him and some of the film's stars. The *Ann Arbor News* article went on to say, "a truckload of roadblocks led some to believe that this film would never be made."

Lead actor Robert Purvey remembers, "There were problems with the screenplay from the beginning. Martin and I spent every night rewriting the script. He had only half a script and asked me to help write the story as we went along. Our days were spent on location and our evenings were spent in his hotel room feverishly preparing for the next day's shoot. Once the film crew returned to New York, additional studio scenes were supposed to be shot but post-production costs soared. We were told the studio shut down the project and the film was shelved."

The director of photography (DP) for the Collins movie—who wished to remain anonymous—recalled that William Martin, known simply as Marty by the crew, hired him to assemble a New York film crew for a four- or five-week shoot in Ann Arbor, Michigan. The DP says he and his crew drove two film trucks to Ann Arbor only to find Marty had no script—just a sketchy outline and nothing else. He had no cast, no locations, and only partial funding for the project. Martin was confident publicity would attract investors and additional funding—the lifeblood of the movie industry. Martin named local attorney Jay Kaufman as producer. It was his job to raise the money. Somehow, Martin was able to land two Hollywood actors in a package deal—Rory Calhoun and Katherine Grayson. Their celebrity would attract investors. The actors' booking agent was thought to owe Marty a favor.

They shot footage for almost five weeks. On a typical day, there would be no casting and no preset location. "Marty rode around in a Cadillac convertible and literally acquired a cast and locations along the way. We were shooting cinema verité style. For example, we went to the Michigan State Police post in Ypsilanti and suddenly real state policemen were playing troopers in the movie, and we were shooting scenes in and around the police post."

"Toward the end of the location shooting, William Martin [a.k.a. Martin Bacow], in response to a federal subpoena, testified in Detroit that he had no knowledge of the murder of teamster president Jimmy Hoffa, nor did he know where his body might be found. Because of the controversy, word came down that the studio had halted the project. That left the crew high and dry," the DP said. "This was the weirdest film shoot any of us had ever been on. We speculated that the film was a scheme to raise money and defraud investors."

When the archivist from Paramount Pictures in Hollywood was contacted about *Now I Lay Me Down to Sleep*, he checked their records and studio film vault. He found no evidence of any film footage rotting in the can or any publicity stills in their files. The studio had no record of any involvement with the film.

If William Martin's earlier film *Jacktown* is any indication, it is better that *Now I Lay Me Down to Sleep* never saw the light of day. The story of the murders of these young women who never had the opportunity for a full life deserves to be told accurately, not cobbled together like some television mystery movie of the week. A sample viewing of *Jacktown* will convince anyone William Martin was no filmmaker.

Further information on William "Marty" Martin (a.k.a. Martin Bacow) can be found in the book *The Last Mogul* by Dennis McDougal, which states, "Martin Bacow, a Hollywood jack of all trades, began his career in Southern California in 1948 as a boxing announcer. He then branched out over the next four decades to become an actor, screenwriter, labor negotiator, and a B movie producer." *The Last Mogul* also notes that Marty Bacow was a close associate of teamster president, Jackie Presser. Bacow was known as the teamster's fix-it man in Hollywood. It was rumored he could start and settle labor disputes in Tinsel Town.

While Marty Bacow was filming in Ann Arbor and Ypsilanti, the DP remembers Marty was always in the presence of two teamster consultants, William "Candy" Davidson and Marvin "The Steel Broker" Mulligan. They acted as Marty's private security force. The movie crew disappeared from the area even faster than it had appeared. People who predicted this film would never be made were correct. Not a single can of footage is known to exist.

35

Manipulating the Media

JOHN NORMAN COLLINS WAS twenty-nine years old when he broke seven years of public silence to give the *Ann Arbor News* reporter William (Bill) Treml a prison interview. The *Ann Arbor News* sought a telephone interview to get Collins's comments about a published book on his case and a proposed movie to be filmed in the spring in Ann Arbor and Ypsilanti. Collins requested an in-person prison interview and said he would permit a photographer to take photos for the exclusive story.

The three-hour interview took place in Jackson State Prison on Thursday, January 13, 1977, and covered a wide range of issues, "everything from high school football to capital punishment." Bill Treml asked Collins why he waited so long to give an interview. "No one really asked," he replied. Later in the interview, Collins admitted he wanted to meet Treml. Bill had covered the Collins case since the Beineman murder, and he wrote the most comprehensive articles of any reporter.

Dressed in institutional blue trousers, heavy work shoes,

and a long-sleeved gray sweatshirt, Collins was led to a vacant prison office where he met Treml and his photographer. The prison officials left the small conference room and shut the door leaving the men free to talk.

During the interview, Treml noted Collins was "articulate, thoughtful, and pondering." Questions about his conviction brought out a number of Collins's key points:

- He proclaimed he was innocent of the murder of Karen Sue Beineman with his mantra, "I never knew her; I never saw her; I never gave her a ride."
- The prosecutors withheld evidence that would have proven him innocent, referring to the running man defense theory at the mannequin stakeout.
- The jury foreman pressured a guilty verdict from the jury through the rationalization "better safe than sorry" and then "hammered" on the undecided jurors.
- Diane Joan Goshe made a false courtroom identification under police pressure and greed for the reward money.
- The jury was bored with the scientific testimony, which he pronounced "scientifically invalid and technically unacceptable."
- *The Michigan Murders* [a novelization of his case] is a crass commercial venture that exploits him and jeopardizes his appeal possibilities.
- Author Edward Keyes "analyzed" him in a totally incorrect and highly fabricated theory although Keyes never spoke with him.
- Collins said the proposed movie *Now I Lay Me Down to Sleep* was even more flagrant than the

Keyes novel because it purported to see through the eyes of the defendant, but no one from the production company came to speak to him about his case.

Regarding the key evidence, Collins broadsided the prosecution. "They withheld information. I don't know what it is, but they do. It was a political game. They had to get someone. Mr. Delhey did his job, but he was overzealous. And look at Booker T. Williams. That's the kind of official that was trying me."

Collins accused the police of threatening J & J Cycle owner Joe Patton with shutting his business down. "They pressured him to say I was there at the time which would fit in with the prosecution's case." Here, Collins failed to cite the four different time frames given by four different motorcycle shop employees, not to mention other serious discrepancies in their testimony.

Collins showed bitterness when he spoke about Diane Joan Goshe: "She was after the reward. She applied for it after the trial." Two other witnesses saw Beineman ride away with Collins also, but he did not mention either of them.

In this interview, Bill Treml allowed Collins to speak freely about anything on his mind. The public had waited a long time to hear Collins speak.

"I never killed anyone. I had no reason to. I was a senior in college. I was going to get my degree in June. I was engaged to be married. I never even slapped a woman in my life. I look down on anyone who does. I never hold a grudge.

"I like girls. I dated often. Of course, I've got a temper. But it's nothing I can't handle…I'm competitive in sports. I play football and basketball here. I play hard. But when it's over, I don't carry it with me."

Regarding *The Michigan Murders* and the proposed movie *Now I Lay Me Down to Sleep*, Collins said, "These people never talked to me. How do they know how I feel? What is in my mind? How can they analyze me? Edward Keyes told millions of readers that I hate my mother and that's why I killed. I didn't kill, and I love my mother. She's been strong; she's been with me.

"How can this movie bunch say they're going to film something through my eyes? They don't know what I see or how I see things. It all comes down to money. To make money off people like myself who are helpless, who have no legal remedy, and no way to protect themselves. It's not right, but they are doing it.

"I was tried and convicted of the Beineman murder. I'm appealing that. But why do the media insist on naming me with other murders? I don't know who did any of them. They say the murders stopped after I was arrested, so that must prove something. I don't think it proves anything. Maybe the person who did the murders died. Maybe he moved away. Maybe he got right. Whoever did something like this has to be sick. There has to be something wrong with him.

"I believe there is a God. There's some Being who got the whole ball rolling. But I don't think you have to go through a priest or minister to have Him hear you. I think you can go directly to Him."

———

On the twentieth anniversary of Karen Sue Beineman's disappearance, forty-two-year-old Collins was reluctant to be interviewed but consented. By this time, he had exhausted all of his appeals, so there was nothing to lose. But there would be no information drop for Jim Mencarelli of the *Ann Arbor News*. Rather than take the opportunity to make a full confession of his crimes and show remorse, Collins waved those questions aside and used the platform to complain about his prison life.

"What good does it do me to talk about it? There is nothing to be gained," said Collins still professing his innocence. He steadfastly maintained he did not receive a fair trial. "I'm still pursuing avenues to reopen my case, although I no longer have an attorney."

Collins told Mencarelli he spends his days in front of a small black-and-white television in a seven-by-twelve foot cell. He leaves the cell for one hour a day, five days a week, for exercise on prison grounds and three times a week for a five-minute shower.

"I sit on my narrow, metal frame bed in F-Block and watch TV, read old newspapers, write letters, and daydream. The mind is a beautiful thing. You can be anywhere you want, anytime you want.

"The fact that you're away from society, that you're locked up, that you're dictated what you can do, when you can do it, and how much you can do is a punishment in itself.

"But telling us we can't talk, can't read books, can't speak to our families and kids is slipping beyond belief. Here they want to destroy everything a person has. They won't give you any incentive to do anything. The prison system picks on me because of my name. I'm being punished for who I am…anytime my name is mentioned, it draws heat. I'm doing hard time because of the sensationalism surrounding my case."

Reporter Mencarelli took the opportunity while at Marquette to interview George Pennell, administrative assistant to the warden. Referring to Collins, Mencarelli said, "He's an average prisoner in that he's not a lot of trouble to us. But overall, he's not an average prisoner because we've never had a prisoner here who's received as much attention or had a book written about him.

"Collins has a quick temper, but he is not classified as an 'assaultive prisoner.' The problems he has in prison were for running a gambling operation, loan sharking, and possessing material considered escape contraband.

"In 1977 while still at Jackson, Collins was accused of plotting a helicopter escape. He admitted [it] to the warden and then denied he conspired with another inmate—Robert Taylor of Port Huron—to escape. Collins injured himself in the exercise yard and was in the prison first aid office when Taylor, dressed as a maintenance man, walked out of Jackson and was never heard from again.

"In 1979 while here at Marquette, Collins was accused of taking part in an attempt to tunnel out of the prison, though the accusation was later dropped."

Collins was implicated with six other inmates in the escape attempt. There are no prison reports other than the initial newspaper articles. It is thought Collins's lawyer successfully challenged the allegation and the charges were dropped. No documentation of the incident exists, nor will Marquette Branch Prison officials discuss the issue. But the five other prisoners accused of being coconspirators in the tunneling attempt were all sent to different Michigan prisons—everyone except Collins.

"And in the mid-eighties," George Pennell continued, "Collins was caught with two hacksaw blades and a drill bit hidden in his cell. Only seventeen months ago, he was found with a length of parachute cord in his cell and was again returned to administrative segregation—a twenty-two-man cell block reserved for our highest risk inmates."

Collins dismissed each prison escape accusation as the prison system's way of warehousing him in administrative segregation—commonly known as solitary confinement or the hole. "You're locked in your cell twenty-three hours a day...Thursday and Friday you don't get out at all...Everything is metal, a metal frame bed, a metal sink and toilet, and a little metal desk for writing letters. You get fed in your cell. They push the food in, you eat it, and you lie down."

Mencarelli asked Collins who he wrote to. Collins replied, "I exchange letters with several people through a prison pen-pal program, and others who have written me over the years." Collins said he receives regular visits from several women.

One woman who visited Collins several times a year in Marquette prison was Marlene Thompson. She ran a small chapel in Warren, near Collins's hometown of Center Line. Reverend Thompson was ordained in a spiritualist church, Sister Dora's National and International Church of Love. She maintained a prison ministry.

Washtenaw County prosecutor William Delhey was asked to comment for the *Ann Arbor News* on Collins's twentieth year behind bars. Delhey said, "When I think back over those times, it brings back a lot of feelings and memories. The case was tried and it's over with as far as I'm concerned. It's in the past. I believe Collins would kill again if he were freed. I think he is a very dangerous individual, and I would oppose any effort to get him released."

As Collins was nearing his third decade in prison, he granted an *Oakland Press* newspaper reporter an interview on September 28, 1988. The media from the beginning of his case was unsympathetic to Collins and gave him no quarter from the start. The defense team harped on Judge Conlin about the amount of sensationalistic and unfavorable press their client was attracting. They believed their client could not get a fair trial in Washtenaw County.

But now, Collins needed the press. They were his only link to the public, so he would take his case to them. All of his appeals for a retrial or a commutation of his sentence were exhausted. Since February 1987, Collins's attempt to transfer to Canada was rescinded. As he was nearing his third decade in prison, he granted an *Oakland Press* staff reporter an interview on September 28, 1988.

John Collins emerged from his isolation cell at Marquette prison and gave the reporter the same statement he made in his closing remarks at the trial, "I never met Karen Sue Beineman, nor did I strangle her."

Collins said he never murdered any of the six other female students in Ypsilanti and Ann Arbor. The dark cloud of the other murders and the indictment of Collins in California for the murder of Roxie Ann Phillips hung heavily over the Beineman trial. Great pains were taken by the prosecution to prevent any testimony regarding the other alleged victims from being entered into the trial testimony.

Neil Fink was quoted in the article as saying, "Unspoken evidence linked Collins with the other six murders in the area because the Beineman slaying was the last of its kind in the area for many years."

Collins disagreed with his former attorney. "The public was led to believe that the murders had stopped after the Beineman killing. I don't think there was anything similar about a lot of the murders. Some were shot. Some were strangled. Some weren't. It's so easy to say, 'Oh, he did it all.'" Collins complained his 1970 trial was marred by circumstantial evidence, police pressure on witnesses, and massive, prejudicial publicity. On the advice of his lawyers, he never testified in his defense but was making up for it now.

The most notable part of the interview was when Collins accused police of scapegoating him into prison. Collins essentially repeated what he told Bill Treml years before: "I honestly believe the police know who did it, and they squashed it one way or another, or they got rid of the person, or they know where he is."

Collins said he hoped to get a new trial to test the hair evidence again using updated analytical techniques. "If they would run them through today, I'd be exonerated. I would have to get a new trial to get the new analysis."

Collins did not mention that prison officials asked inmates to volunteer DNA samples for tests that were in use by 1988 and widely accepted as reliable forensic evidence in American courts. Despite other prison inmates being proven innocent by DNA analysis after they were imprisoned, Collins refused testing. In 2002, all Michigan prison inmates were compelled to give a DNA sample.

———

Three weeks after the *Oakland Press* interview, John Collins signed a media release to appear on a popular Detroit morning talk show—*Kelly & Company*. John Kelly and his wife Marilyn Turner interviewed celebrities and local news makers in front of a live studio audience in Southfield, Michigan, where WXYZ-TV [Channel 7] was located.

The original plan called for a live prison interview with interactive segments between Collins and a panel of key people associated with his case. It was unprecedented. Forty-one-year-old John Collins was scheduled to appear live via satellite from Marquette Branch Prison on Monday morning, October 3, 1988, at 9:00 a.m.

Kelly & Company producer, Chris Sloat, said, "Collins agreed to talk with the media because he never has had a chance to give his side of the story." Of course, Collins could have taken the stand in his own defense against the wishes of his then attorneys. Glossing over that point, the producer and the station manager felt they might have an award-winning show on their hands.

The original concept for the popular audience participation show was a courtroom-type debate. Collins would appear live with Marilyn Turner from Marquette Branch Prison, while her husband, John Kelly, would be in the Channel 7 studios with an audience of about two hundred people. The master plan was to have Collins tell his story, question the panelists live on the air, and between those segments have audience members ask questions of the panel. This was a ready-made public relations forum Collins could not afford to pass up.

Persons scheduled for the panel were Neil Fink for the defense (his partner Joseph Louisell had died in 1974); William Delhey, the lead prosecutor; Douglas Harvey, former Washtenaw County sheriff; Eric Smith, WXYZ reporter; Jackie Calen, a reporter who covered the case for the *Oakland Press*; and Reverend Marlene Thompson, Collins's prison advocate.

Plans began to fall apart the Thursday prior to the show when Prosecutor Delhey balked at appearing. He declined to be a part of a second Collins trial for "television entertainment." He tried the case once and that was enough for him.

Then the producer of the show got more bad news. "The prison authorities reneged on their cooperation," said an associate producer. "They decided not to let Collins appear live with Marilyn. We managed to convince the warden to let us do a taped interview from prison, not exactly what we had in mind."

A last-minute thought by Channel 7 producers was to have Prosecutor Delhey videotape a statement, but he declined. Quoted in an *Ann Arbor News* article Delhey said, "In any statement I would have said exactly what happened and what's been on record for eighteen years: the trial was held, the conviction was affirmed by three courts, and the case is over.

"I was not going to be part of a staged courtroom scene with Collins being given a chance to plead his case and a dozen people off the street shouting out inane questions. I'm a prosecutor, not a question-and-answer man for show business."

Marilyn Turner did the videotaped interview with Collins inside Marquette prison on the Friday before the Monday broadcast. The first segment gave a news summary of the Collins/Beineman case that was essentially accurate until the taped footage showed a shot of the wrong house as the murder site—not the home of David and Sandra Leik on Roosevelt Street in Ypsilanti but the house where Collins's alleged second victim Joan Schell lived.

After a synopsis of the eighteen-year-old case using

vintage video footage, Marilyn Turner did a masterful job of interviewing Collins and making him feel comfortable. If Marilyn's husband John Kelly had gone to the prison instead asking Collins the same questions, the answers would have been the same because they were well-rehearsed, but the tone of the interview would have been different. It seemed Collins had a crush on Marilyn Turner. He played on her sympathies and she let him. Marilyn showed herself to be a real professional.

The videotaped interview was interspersed throughout the live show on Monday morning. *Kelly & Company*'s second segment had John Kelly questioning the trial participants, Neil Fink and Sheriff Harvey. Fink contended it was the "unspoken evidence" of the other area murders that convicted his client and not the circumstantial evidence presented in court. The former sheriff said he believed Collins was guilty of all seven murders and one in California. Nothing had changed in their positions after eighteen years.

The men discussed the mannequin stakeout, which Fink described as "the Keystone Kops." That rankled Sheriff Harvey. Harvey recalled the incident and revealed the mannequin was dusted for prints and none were found. It was reported by a local newspaper that a midnight runner came upon the site and may have stopped and even touched the mannequin. Police on the scene reported this person was a jogger who swept past them so fast they did not have enough time to respond.

In another previously recorded clip from Marquette prison, Marilyn Turner asked Collins about the mannequin incident. The Collins defense team tried their best to use this as proof their client had an alibi for that weekend. Collins said he was in Ortonville sixty miles away with two former fraternity brothers and their wives. One of the wives testified in court to that. The alibi was based on the notion the midnight jogger was the murderer, and the police botched the stakeout. If police had found the runner, they would have captured the murderer, or so the defense theory went

But that reasoning relied on facts not in evidence. With no jogger to question and no reason to suspect he had any interest in the gully where the body was found, there was no basis for a credible alibi. Collins was doing his best to manipulate the audience of the morning show to make his case.

After John Kelly explained to the audience that Prosecutor William Delhey declined to appear on the program because he wanted to put the case behind him, part three of the show ran along the same lines as part two—a question, a brief discussion, and a clip of Collins responding to the same question. This segment was about the county sheriff's alleged offer to buy Collins a steak dinner in exchange for a full confession. In response, the sheriff denied ever making such an offer to Collins while he was detained in the county jail. Somehow, the absurdity of the situation spoke for itself when Collins told Marilyn he almost took the sheriff up on his steak dinner offer.

After another segment of the Collins/Turner taped interview was run, part four of the *Kelly & Company* was reserved for the supporters of John Norman Collins on the panel who gave their assessments of his innocence.

Reverend Marlene Thompson ran a small chapel in Warren, Michigan, near Collins's hometown of Center Line. She was given Collins's name by a prison ministry group in Marquette. Thompson said she visited with Collins "several times a year for the past three and a half years.

John shows great concern for women. He is a caring and intellectual person who couldn't kill anything. If you really take a good look at the evidence, all of it is circumstantial," Thompson said ignoring the scientific hair evidence. "I firmly believe they [the police] needed a scapegoat, so everyone in Michigan could feel more relaxed. There isn't anything in this person that could ever kill anything," she said with conviction. Reverend Thomson spent the rest of her time criticizing the Michigan prison system.

Also included on the panel was Jackie Calen, an *Oakland Press* newswoman who did not cover the case at the time but who had written Collins while he was in prison over the years. She too thought John "may be innocent" and "railroaded" into prison. Calen stated her opinion: "If he did it, he doesn't know he did it. He is open and tells the truth as he perceives it." No mention was made of the word *delusional* or why Collins refused every attempt by prison officials to undergo a psychiatric evaluation and treatment.

The most remarkable and probing part of the show was when Marilyn Turner gently asked John Collins in a calm and soothing voice, "Did you love your mother, John?" With that one well-placed, personal question, Marilyn penetrated Collins's self-protective wall and caught him in an unguarded moment. Until then, he maintained control of the interview; then, he lost his composure and his emotions welled up. Collins was disoriented from that point on. Marilyn Turner did a great job interviewing a difficult subject.

Part five of the show was a question-and-answer segment with the audience. A question was asked about Collins/Chapman's Canadian transfer attempt and why current Michigan Governor Blanchard would not sign it.

There was also a question about the California murder case against Collins that was dropped years before.

The *Kelly & Company* morning show ended with John and Marilyn asking individuals in the audience if they thought Collins was innocent or guilty. Several of Collins's supporters were sprinkled among the audience. Stephanie Smiley, an Eastern Michigan University friend of Collins, was convinced of his innocence. Collins's Theta Chi fraternity brother James Zellen also came to his friend's defense. But still, the votes of the audience ran two to one against Collins. Not the result he hoped for.

—36—

Room for Doubt

AFTER JOHN COLLINS WAS found guilty of Karen Sue Beineman's murder, the six other unsolved murder cases were relegated to cold-case status. But from the start, something was different about Jane Mixer's murder. In 2001, Michigan State Police detective Sergeant Eric Schroeder was placed in charge of cataloging evidence from the other Washtenaw County unsolved murder cases. Schroeder never believed Jane Mixer's murder was related to the others. He sent some evidence from her case to the state police crime lab for DNA testing. Because of the backlog in processing DNA samples, Schroeder waited a year for results. On November 25, 2004—over thirty-five years after Jane was murdered—a sixty-two-year-old retired male nurse named Gary Earl Leiterman was charged with her murder.

Leiterman left three droplets of his perspiration— enough for DNA analysis—on the nylon stocking knotted around Jane Mixer's neck. He was registered in the FBI's National DNA Index System (NDIS)—a supercomputer that networks and cross-references databases nationwide using the Combined DNA Index System (CODIS). Leiterman's DNA was in the CODIS system from an earlier minor drug conviction in 2001 for forging and passing prescriptions for painkillers like Vicodin and Lorcet. The system came up with a solid hit on Leiterman.

Gary Leiterman told authorities he became addicted to painkillers after a painful bout with kidney stones. After a thorough search of his car, investigators found a stack of prescription blanks he had stolen from the Kalamazoo hospital where he worked. Leiterman pleaded guilty and was given probation after agreeing to enter a drug rehab program. As a felon, he was required to give a sample of his DNA under the provisions of a new Michigan state law that went into effect only three days before his drug conviction.

A disturbing wild card in the Leiterman case was someone else's DNA found on Jane's body. A single drop of blood on Jane's hand from John Ruelas, a four-year-old child at the time. How did this cross contamination get there and what impact would it have on the trial?

Leiterman's defense attorney Gary Gabry wanted to exploit this issue as much as he could. "This was proof of cross contamination at the DNA lab." Gabry wanted the judge to remove the DNA evidence from consideration by the jury, thereby expecting a full acquittal of his client.

Closing arguments were made on the morning of July 22. The jury came back with a guilty verdict by 4:15 p.m. after only three hours of deliberation. They found Gary Earl Leiterman guilty of the murder of Jane Mixer. On August 30, 2005, Judge Donald Shelton handed down the mandatory life sentence. Leiterman's family was shocked. The case was appealed but the verdict stood firm. Immediately, they established a foundation to fight for his release. To date they have been unsuccessful.

What makes this case relevant to the other cases is that Collins was proven innocent by default of a murder the general public believed he committed. The shadow of doubt suddenly loomed larger for Collins. After the 2005 Leiterman conviction, some people were willing to consider the possibility that John Norman Collins may not be responsible for the other murders he was thought by the court of public opinion to have committed.

—37—

Final Thoughts

SINCE HIS CONVICTION, JOHN Norman Collins has taken every media opportunity to tell the public the story of his false arrest and unjust imprisonment. Collins alleges he was framed by corrupt law enforcement and railroaded by an overzealous prosecutor. During his murder trial, Collins's attorneys were unable to establish a convincing alibi for their client, nor did they produce any viable evidence to exonerate him. When Collins was given the chance to take the stand in his own defense, his lawyers advised against it fearing he would lose his composure on the stand. Now, he tells anyone who will listen how he was convicted solely on circumstantial evidence, at the same time ignoring eyewitness testimony placing him with the victim and scientific evidence linking the deceased to the murder site, his aunt and uncle's home.

Evidence from the unsolved Washtenaw County murder cases was carefully avoided during courtroom testimony to prevent a mistrial that neither side wanted. But evidence exists linking Collins with the other murdered girls. For instance, when Collins's room was thoroughly searched after his arrest, investigators found a Canadian Expo 67 medallion necklace on top of his dresser that was like the one found missing from Mary Fleszar's belongings two years before. When questioned about it, Collins claimed he never saw the necklace and maintained it was planted by the police to frame him.

———

Acting on a tip two weeks after Joan Schell's body was found, police investigators interviewed two Eastern Michigan University students alleged to have seen John Collins and Joan Schell together the night she disappeared. The couple was on a double date with a Marine Corps friend to pick up his date who was waitressing at Casa Nova on Michigan Avenue. She called at 11:30 p.m. ready to be picked up. This was the marine's last evening before leaving for Camp Pendleton in California and shipping out to Vietnam.

Eastern Michigan University student Edward Lee Knickerbocker told investigators he did not come forward with information earlier because he did not want to get his former Theta Chi fraternity brother in trouble, especially since he claimed he was not positive it was John Collins with the girl he saw crossing the intersection of Emmet and College Place. Knickerbocker falsely estimated the time to be 9:30 p.m.

His girlfriend Doreen Gagnon was interviewed separately. She put the time at just after 11:30 p.m. when her waitress friend called to be picked up from work. But who was correct? The police were left with conflicting reports but discounted the young man's error as a simple mistake.

Knickerbocker said he asked Collins about seeing him with the missing coed, but Collins denied he knew the girl. The Marine Corps witness was on active duty by that time and not available for a police interview.

The same couple was interviewed again a year later after Collins was arrested for the Beineman murder. By this time, Collins was believed to have murdered no fewer than seven young women in Washtenaw County. Doreen Gagnon, who was more truthful than her ex-boyfriend the previous year, said she talked with Knickerbocker two days after Joan Schell's body was found. Knickerbocker told her he did not want to get his fraternity brother in trouble because he knew Collins was stealing motorcycles. On the night in question, Doreen said she recognized Joan Schell and waved to her as she and John Collins crossed the street. She was positive about this.

Knickerbocker had since graduated from Eastern and was now a commissioned army officer at Fort Knox, Kentucky. He was re-interviewed by a different investigator after Collins's arrest. This time Knickerbocker made a positive identification of Collins and placed him and Schell together at the intersection of Emmet and College Place shortly after 11:30 p.m. Knickerbocker added when he asked Collins about that evening, John claimed to be at his mother's home in Center Line that weekend. Then Collins gave his former fraternity brother a cold, withering glare, enough to whip Knickerbocker into line.

After the couple was re-interviewed, the marine was questioned for the first time on November 10, 1969. He had not seen or spoken with the couple since the night Schell went missing. His story matched the couple's including the time frame. The marine remembered driving his car and stopping to allow two people to cross the street. As they crossed in front of his headlights, the couple inside the car waved at them and they waved back. The marine remembered the woman had long brown hair but did not notice anything in particular about the guy who was with her.

———

A female student who worked with Collins in the Alumni Relations Office during the Joan Schell incident remembers John Collins talking incessantly about how mutilated Schell's body was. Collins went into graphic detail describing the corpse, and he enjoyed tormenting her until she complained to her supervisor, who called the Eastern Michigan campus police.

When Collins was questioned, he claimed he got his inside information from his uncle, a well-known Michigan State Police trooper who worked at the Ypsilanti post on Michigan Avenue. When John's uncle Corporal Daniel Leik was asked to corroborate his nephew's statement. Leik said he had not discussed the case with him, and that the state police were not a part of the Schell murder investigation.

The detectives could not help but notice Collins's bogus attempt to establish a reason for his detailed knowledge of Joan Schell's injuries. Perhaps out of professional courtesy for a fellow cop, this thread was never followed up. John was caught in an obvious falsehood. Corporal Leik asked his wife Sandra to call her nephew and ask if he knew the murdered girl. John flatly denied he knew anything about her. One lie compounded another. For the first time, John found himself on the slippery slope of willful deceit, but nothing came of it. Collins's caution might explain why it was eight months before the next slaying.

On August 31, 1970, thirteen months after Collins was jailed, Isabelle Wilson took her children for a Sunday outing along the north side of the Huron River. They were fishing west of the dam and bridge crossing at Superior Road. It was late afternoon when she looked into the water and saw a wallet lying in the mud. She reached in and picked it up. The wallet was still snapped shut. Wilson checked the interior and found a card which read, "In case of emergency, call Mike Millage," with his phone number written down. When Wilson and her children returned home, she called the number. The person on the other end of the line became very excited. Mike Millage took down the woman's contact information and immediately called Sergeant Canada of the Ann Arbor police.

Canada hurried to the Wilson apartment on Huron River Drive. Wilson gave the detective a full account of where she discovered the wallet. He looked inside and found Maralynn Skelton's social security card and numerous photographs. Wilson went on to explain that she and her husband had arrived in this country in February 1970 from Glasgow, Scotland, so neither of them had knowledge of the local murders.

A search was made along the shoreline of the Huron River where the wallet was found. Because the water was shallow and visibility was poor, divers were not called in. Police put on waders and checked the water carefully. Sergeant Janiszewski of the state police located the purse in about three feet of water, twenty feet from shore. When the officer tried to pick the purse up, it broke apart from being in the water under five feet of mud for almost eighteen months. The murderer had weighed it down with rocks before throwing it into the water.

Michael Millage was contacted to confirm this was indeed Maralynn's purse. It contained one change purse, a ballpoint pen, a comb, a nail clipper, one Chapstick, one pink hairbrush, a pair of sunglasses, hand cream, two lipsticks, two keys, and two erasers. The wallet contained numerous photos and Maralynn's identification. Microscopic examination for latent fingerprints was conducted, but nothing of evidentiary value was found, except that Maralynn's murderer passed by the Huron River after he killed her.

Karen Naylor was a part-time Washtenaw Community College student and full-time employee at the old Saint Joseph's Hospital in Ann Arbor. One day, she was riding her Yamaha motorcycle when a handsome college guy pulled up alongside her on a flashy Triumph. The rider asked if she would go riding *with him* rather than asking if he could go riding *with her*. His bold self-confidence attracted her, as did his muscular physique, so she agreed. She dated Collins from March through July of 1969, except for a few weeks in June when he was in California.

In a recent interview, Naylor revealed previously unknown information to the public. On the night of Dawn Basom's disappearance, Naylor said Collins showed up at her doorstep with blood on his T-shirt. Collins told her he accidently ran over a dog with his car and got blood on himself when moving the carcass. Naylor said he appeared quite upset. When she heard about the murder of the girl who lived across the street from her apartment complex, she began to suspect Collins. But like almost everyone, she found it difficult to imagine he could do such a thing. After all, he did not fit the police profile.

When asked if she contacted the police with her suspicions, Naylor said, "Yes, but not until Beineman went missing. You see, I was a tall, lanky blonde in a college town. Guys were always trying to pick me up. It sounds immodest to say, but it's true. I thought it was unusual that John never tried to have sex with me. That seemed odd, but I didn't trust my suspicions. We always had fun riding together in the backcountry."

When police questioned her, she told them she had suspected Collins since April and gave them the details. Investigators took down the information and said they would get back with her. Police were true to their word. Karen Naylor was called to testify for the prosecution against Collins in the Beineman trial, but the Basom evidence was not part of that case.

Naylor revealed in a recent interview that defense attorneys Louisell and Fink were so worried by what she might say on the stand that they sent their legal aid Margo Doble to carry a marriage proposal from Collins in an attempt to prevent her from testifying.

—◆—

Another link ties Collins to Dawn Basom. One of Dawn Basom's cousins, Sherrie Hall Zizmont Benoit, claims her grandmother told her Collins was at her Aunt Cleo's house for the funeral buffet after Dawn's burial. Dawn's grandmother did not recognize the person, so she asked him if he was one of Dawn's friends. He said yes. It was not until Collins's photograph ran in the local papers three months later that she was able to identify him. "Normally, my grand-mother took photos of everything," Benoit said, "but my Aunt Cleo [Dawn's mother] would not allow any picture taking at the buffet."

It seems probable that law enforcement would have positioned investigators outside the Basom house taking photographs of anyone coming or going. When the Michigan State Police were asked if they had any such pho-tographic evidence, the officer in charge of the case would not comment because this cold case was officially open. There is no statute of limitation for murder.

Lieutenant Bundshud explained, "When the evidence chain of custody is broken, it becomes inadmissible in court. Evidence must be preserved in the event these cases are ever brought to trial." It is certain the Michigan State Police have details about these cases locked up in their evidence vault that may never be revealed to the public.

———

In the final analysis, John Norman Collins was indicted by a California grand jury for the murder of Roxie Ann Phillips, and his Michigan conviction for the murder of Karen Sue Beineman brings a tremendous amount of coin-cidence to bear upon one individual. The fact that mutilated bodies stopped turning up after Collins's arrest added to the widespread belief that the State of Michigan convicted the right man.

The secret why Collins derailed is locked in his mind. The combination of factors necessary to unleash Collins's rampages may never be known in the absence of psychiatric documentation or verifiable family history. Since his arrest and through all the decades he has been behind bars, John Norman Collins has never willingly submitted to a single psychological evaluation.

It is clear from reading the newspaper clippings of her son's murder trial that until the time of her death, Loretta Marjorie Collins was John's fiercest defender. Loretta was guilty in the first degree of a mother's blind love for her son. In her last will and testament written in 1979, Loretta left her Marine City clothing store and her Cadillac to her daughter. She left her Buick Skylark to her grandson Dwayne. Loretta's oldest son Jerry was placed in charge of dispensing his mother's jewelry among the women in the family. The rest of Loretta Collins's estate was divided between Jerry and Gail. As for her youngest son, Loretta wrote, "I am not unmindful of my son John Norman Chapman, formerly known as John Norman Collins, but I have intentionally omitted him from my last will and testament for my own personal reasons."

Collins exhausted every legal remedy to obtain an early release from his life sentence. Only a pardon from a sitting Michigan governor can release him. Rather than acknowledge his crimes and show remorse like most imprisoned serial killers do, Collins denies knowledge of the victims and shows no empathy for the suffering of their families. He lives out his remaining days in Marquette prison awaiting death's cold embrace and his final reward.

Appendix 1: Time Line

September 1966 – John Norman Collins transfers from Central Michigan to Eastern Michigan

July 8, 1967 – Mary Fleszar (19) abducted in Ypsilanti

August 7, 1967 – Body found on abandoned farm in Superior Township

June 30, 1968 – Joan Schell (20) last seen hitchhiking to Ann Arbor from Ypsilanti

July 5, 1968 – Body found along roadside in Ann Arbor Township

August 1968-June 1969 – Collins works part-time at Motor Wheel Corporation

September 1968-May 1969 – Andrew Manuel (Collins friend) works full-time at Motor Wheel

March 20, 1969 – Jane Mixer (23) abducted in Ann Arbor with Ride-Share ruse

March 21, 1969 – Body found in Denton Cemetery in Wayne County

March 23, 1969 – Maralynn Skelton (16) hitchhiking into Ypsilanti from U.S. 23

March 25, 1969 – Body found in a back lot of a housing development in Ann Arbor Township

April 13, 1969 – Dawn Basom (13) abducted in Ypsilanti

April 16, 1969 – Body found along roadside in Superior Township

June 7, 1969 – Alice Kalom (21) abducted in Ann Arbor

June 9, 1969 – Body found north of Ann Arbor on North Territorial Road

June 21, 1969 – Collins and Manuel leave Ypsilanti for California in a rented house trailer

June 26 – Collins and Manuel arrive in Salinas, California

June 30, 1969 – Roxie Phillips (17) abducted in Salinas, California

July 3, 1969 – Collins gets his car serviced in Salinas and the trailer hitch removed

July 8, 1969 – Collins and Manuel return to Ypsilanti abandoning house trailer

July 13, 1969 – Roxie Phillips's body found in Pescadero Canyon, Monterey County, California

July 23, 1969 – Karen Sue Beineman (18) abducted in Ypsilanti

July 26, 1969 – Body found in a gully off Riverside Drive in Ann Arbor

July 31, 1969 – John Norman Collins (22) arrested

July 31, 1969 – Ann Arbor attorneys John Toomey and Robert Francis are hired by Collins

August 1, 1969 – Arraignment at Ypsilanti Courthouse

August 7, 1969 – Preliminary hearing held

August 7, 1969 – Toomey and Francis ask to be removed from the case

August 7, 1969 – Loretta Collins pleads poverty and asks for a public defender

August 12, 1969 – Ann Arbor attorney Richard W. Ryan appointed to defend Collins

November 25, 1969 – Joseph Louisell and Neil Fink are hired to defend Collins

December 1, 1969 – Ryan officially removed from case after being fired by Loretta Collins

February 2, 1970 – Louisell suffers heart attack

February 11, 1970 – Announcement made in court—case will be delayed

April 15, 1970 – Collins indicted by California grand jury for murder of Roxie Phillips

April 28, 1970 – Judge Conlin announces trial date—June 2, 1970

June 2, 1970 – Jury selection begins

July 9, 1970 – A jury is seated when defense attorneys are satisfied

July 20, 1970 – Collins trial begins

August 13, 1970 – Lawyers make their final arguments before the jury

August 14, 1970 – Case sent to jury

August 19, 1970 – Collins convicted of Karen Sue Beineman's murder

August 28, 1970 – Collins sentenced to life and sent to Jackson prison

December 19, 1970 – Appeal filed with Michigan State Appeals Court

December 28, 1970 – Appeal denied

January 4, 1972 – The California extradition of Collins for Roxie Phillips's murder is closed

April 3, 1974 – Appeal filed with United States Supreme Court

April 19, 1974 – Appeal denied

October 25, 1977 – Collins transferred to Marquette Prison as a high risk inmate

January 5, 1981 – Collins legally changes his last name to Chapman for Canadian prison transfer

January 20, 1982 – Collins' prisoner transfer denied by Michigan Department of Corrections

July 22, 2005 – Collins exonerated by default of the Jane Mixer murder

Appendix 2: Directory of Places

ANN ARBOR, MICHIGAN—FORTY-NINE MILES west of Detroit

Ann Arbor Inn—where Collins's jury was sequestered

Arborland mall [shopping center]—located between Ypsilanti and Ann Arbor on Washtenaw Avenue

Camelot Room—restaurant adjoining the Inn America motor lodge on Washtenaw Avenue

Center Line, Michigan—where Collins grew up, forty-seven miles northeast of Ypsilanti

Chocolate Shoppe—across the alley from Wigs by Joan on North Washington Street in Ypsilanti

Denton Cemetery—site in Wayne County where Jane Mixer's body was found

Depot House—former Ann Arbor train depot rented out for bands and parties in Ann Arbor

Depot Town—former commercial block of Ypsilanti located next to the railroad tracks

Eastern Michigan University (EMU)—in Ypsilanti, thirty-five miles outside of Detroit

Emmet Street house—Ypsilanti boardinghouse where Collins rented a room

Hendrickson's Trailer Rental—on Ecorse Road in Ypsilanti

Highlands—Ypsilanti apartment complex on LeForge Road across from Dawn Basom's house

Inn America—motor lodge on Washtenaw Avenue where Peter Hurkos stayed while in Ann Arbor

Leik house—Ypsilanti site of Karen Sue Beineman's murder

Jackson State Prison—eighty miles west of Detroit, thirty-six miles west of Ann Arbor

Marquette Branch Prison—Michigan's maximum-security prison in the Upper Peninsula

McKenny Student Union—EMU site where Joan Schell was hitchhiking to Ann Arbor

Motor Wheel Corporation—a division of Goodyear where Collins and Andrew Manuel worked

Plymouth crime lab—Michigan State Police crime center between Detroit and Ann Arbor

Roy's Squeeze Inn—East Michigan Avenue carhop diner in Ypsilanti

Saint Clement High School—Collins's Catholic school in Center Line, Michigan

Task Force Crime Center—former Holy Ghost Fathers' Seminary located between Ypsilanti and Ann Arbor, so known as the Washtenaw County Citizens Service Center

Theta Chi house—EMU fraternity where Collins was a member

University of Michigan—in Ann Arbor, ten miles west of Ypsilanti

Washtenaw County Building—site of the Collins trial in Ann Arbor

Washtenaw County Citizens Service Center—former Holy Ghost Fathers' Seminary

Washtenaw County Jail—across the street from the courthouse

Water Tower—Ypsilanti landmark adjacent to Eastern Michigan University

Wigs by Joan—Ypsilanti shop on North Washington Street in Ypsilanti

Woodland Hills—apartment complex between Ypsilanti and Ann Arbor on Packard Road

Ypsilanti, Michigan—thirty-five miles west of Detroit

Ypsilanti courthouse—site of Collins's arraignment on North Huron Street in historic district

Appendix 3: Directory of People

BARLOW, DR. CRAIG R., Washtenaw County deputy chief medical examiner

Barnes, Dr. Marjorie R., neighbor who lived across the street from the Leik house

Basom, Dawn Louise, thirteen-year-old Ypsilanti resident, fourth victim

Beineman, Karen Sue, EMU coed, seventh victim

Benoit, Sherrie Hall Zizmont, cousin of Dawn Basom

Britton, Harold, attendant at Moore Funeral in Ypsilanti

Brown, Robert, deputy director of Michigan Department of Corrections

Canada, William, Michigan State Police detective

Chapman, John Norman, John Norman Collins after name change

Chapman, John Philip, John Norman Collins's last Canadian blood relative

Chapman, Richard, John Norman Collins's birth father

Christensen, Kennard, chief of the Michigan State Police crime lab in Plymouth, Michigan

Cobb, John, *Ypsilanti Press* reporter

Collins, John Norman, convicted murderer of Karen Sue Beineman

Collins, Loretta Marjorie, John Norman Collins's mother

Collins, William, John Norman Collins's stepfather

Conlin, John, presiding judge at Collins's trial in Ann Arbor

Cygan, Cindy, *Macomb Daily* reporter

Davids, Colonel Frederick, head of the task force crime center, appointed by Governor Millekin

Davis, Arnold, Collins's friend who was given immunity to testify against Collins

Deake, Judge Edward, presiding judge over Collins's arraignment in Ypsilanti

Devine, Michael, Michigan Supreme Court–appointed spokesperson for the trial

Doble, Margo, legal aid for the defense

Fink, Neil, junior defense attorney

Fleszar, Mary Terese, EMU coed, first victim

Fluker, Dr. Curtis, Michigan Department of Health Laboratories

Frame, Douglas, Canadian counsel

Francis, Robert, Collins's first attorney

Golub, Dr. Samuel, defense hair and fiber expert witness

Goshe, Diane Joan, wig-shop owner

Guinn, Dr. Vincent P., prosecution expert hair and fiber witness

Harvey, Douglas, Washtenaw County sheriff

Hendrix, Robert W., Washtenaw County medical examiner

Holtz, Dr. Walter L., chief of the Michigan Health Department of Health Criminalistics Division

Hurkos, Peter, Dutch psychic

Jackson, Father Patrick, Collins family spiritual advisor

Jandron, Al, supervisor of records for the Michigan Department of Corrections

Jervis, Dr. Robert E., defense expert witness and professor of radioactive chemistry

Johnson, Perry, Jackson State Prison warden

Kalom, Alice Elizabeth, University of Michigan coed, fifth victim

Kelley, John, Michigan attorney general

Kelly, Jack, cohost of *Kelly & Company*, a popular Detroit morning show

Krasne, Walter E., Ann Arbor police chief

Leik, David, Michigan state trooper and Collins's uncle-in-law

Leik, Sandra, John Norman Collins's aunt

Leiterman, Gary Earl, convicted of Jane Mixer murder in 2005

Louisell, Joseph W., Collins's lead defense attorney

Lundy, Walker, *Detroit Free Press* reporter

Manuel, Andrew, John Norman Collins's partner-in-crime

Markwell, John E., EMU police sergeant

Martin, William [a.k.a. Marty Bacow], director and writer of the Collins movie never produced

Mathewson, Larry, EMU rookie patrolman

Millage, Michael, Maralynn Skelton's boyfriend/fiancé

Millekin, William, Michigan governor

Mixer, Jane Elizabeth, University of Michigan coed thought to be killed by Collins

Naylor, Karen, Collins's alleged girlfriend

Pasic, Joseph, Brother Bartholomew of an obscure religious sect

Perkons, Dr. Auseklis K., University of Toronto expert defense witness

Phillips, Roxie Ann, seventeen-year-old Californian, sixth victim

Popa, Robert A., *Detroit News* reporter

Reagan, Ronald, California governor

Rzepka, Marianne, *Detroit Free Press* reporter

Santucci, John, Jr., Sharon Santucci's husband

Santucci, Sharon, Maralynn Skelton's Ypsilanti friend

Scannell, Beverly, associate with Wayne County sheriff's narcotics division

Schell, Joan Elspeth, EMU coed, second victim

Schlesinger, Dr. Howard L., prosecution expert witness and forensic chemist

Schoomaker, Ronald, Michigan State Police detective

Sinclair, John, Ann Arbor counterculture figure

Skelton, Archie, Maralynn Skelton's father

Skelton, Helen, Maralynn Skelton's mother

Skelton, Maralynn, sixteen-year-old transient, third victim

Spaulding, Patricia, wig stylist at Wigs by Joan

Tennant, Betty, Washtenaw County court clerk

Treml, William, *Ann Arbor News* reporter

Turner, Maralynn, cohost of *Kelly & Company* who interviewed Collins in Marquette Branch Prison

Welch, Ruth, Washtenaw County court clerk

Wieczerza, Carol, Chocolate Shoppe clerk who identified Collins's motorcycle

Williams, Booker T., chief assistant prosecutor

Index

CPSIA information can be obtained
at www.ICGtesting.com
Printed in the USA
BVHW071141220520
580032BV00001B/12